Romantic Realities

Speculative Realism

Series Editor: Graham Harman

Since its first appearance at a London colloquium in 2007, the Speculative Realism movement has taken continental philosophy by storm. Opposing the formerly ubiquitous modern dogma that philosophy can speak only of the human-world relation rather than the world itself, Speculative Realism defends the autonomy of the world from human access, but in a spirit of imaginative audacity.

Editorial Advisory Board

Jane Bennett
Levi Bryant
Patricia Clough
Mark Fisher
Iain Hamilton Grant
Myra Hird
Adrian Johnston
Eileen A. Joy

Books available

Onto-Cartography: An Ontology of Machines and Media by Levi R. Bryant
Form and Object: A Treatise on Things by Tristan Garcia, translated by Mark Allan Ohm and Jon Cogburn
Adventures in Transcendental Materialism: Dialogues with Contemporary Thinkers by Adrian Johnston
The End of Phenomenology: Metaphysics and the New Realism by Tom Sparrow
Fields of Sense: A New Realist Ontology by Markus Gabriel
Quentin Meillassoux: Philosophy in the Making Second Edition by Graham Harman
Assemblage Theory by Manuel DeLanda
Romantic Realities: Speculative Realism and British Romanticism by Evan Gottlieb

Forthcoming titles

Garcian Meditations: The Dialectics of Persistence in Form and Object by Jon Cogburn
After Quietism: Analytic Philosophies of Immanence and the New Metaphysics by Jon Cogburn
Infrastructure by Graham Harman

Visit the Speculative Realism website at: edinburghuniversitypress.com/series/specr

Romantic Realities

Speculative Realism and British Romanticism

Evan Gottlieb

EDINBURGH
University Press

Edinburgh University Press is one of the leading university presses in the UK. We publish academic books and journals in our selected subject areas across the humanities and social sciences, combining cutting-edge scholarship with high editorial and production values to produce academic works of lasting importance. For more information visit our website: edinburghuniversitypress.com

Edinburgh University Press Ltd
The Tun – Holyrood Road
12(2f) Jackson's Entry
Edinburgh EH8 8PJ

Typeset in 11/13 Adobe Sabon by
Servis Filmsetting Ltd, Stockport, Cheshire,
and printed and bound in Great Britain by
CPI Group (UK) Ltd, Croydon CR0 4YY

A CIP record for this book is available from the British Library

ISBN 978 0 7486 9140 1 (hardback)
ISBN 978 0 7486 9142 5 (webready PDF)
ISBN 978 0 7486 9141 8 (paperback)
ISBN 978 0 7486 9143 2 (epub)

Contents

Acknowledgments   vi
Series Editor's Preface   viii

Introduction   1
1. Wordsworth and Object-Oriented Philosophy   15
2. Coleridge, Nature-Philosophy, and Process Ontology   60
3. Byron, Actor-Network-Theory, and Truth Procedures   99
4. Shelley, Nihilism, and Speculative Materialism   143
5. Keats, Vital Materialism, and Flat Ontology   188
Conclusion   231

Index   236

Acknowledgments

First and foremost, I am grateful to Graham Harman for encouraging me to pursue this project when it was still in its earliest conceptual phases, and to Carol McDonald for shepherding it along the publication process. I would also like to thank several colleagues from both the literary and the philosophical sides of the disciplinary aisle for their advice, help, and support along the way, especially Levi Bryant, Nathan Coombs, Alex Dick, Penny Fielding, Ray Malewitz, Tom Mole, Molly Anne Rothenberg, Chris Washington, Bob Wess, and Nicole Wright. Working drafts of this manuscript were presented at a number of venues; my thanks to organizers, fellow panelists, and audience members at Brigham Young University, the Byron Society, the North American Society for the Study of Romanticism, Syracuse University, the University of Edinburgh, the Wordsworth Trust, and the inaugural World Congress of Scottish Literatures. A fellowship during the summer of 2014 at the Institute for Advanced Studies in the Humanities at the University of Edinburgh provided me with a wonderful environment in which to write Chapter 3; thanks also to Anita Helle, former Director of the School of Writing, Literature, and Film at Oregon State University (my home institution), for funds to make that adventure possible. Also here at Oregon State, I am very appreciative of the many enthusiastic, engaged undergraduate and graduate students who have studied theory and Romanticism with me over the past years. Finally, I am extremely grateful to my family and friends for their encouragement, support, and patience; this book is especially dedicated to my niece, Laine Cocca-Gottlieb, who inherits a planet desperately in need of the kind of paradigm shifts that both Romanticism and Speculative Realism encourage us to explore, adopt, and live.

A version of parts of Chapter 1 was previously published as

"Seeing into the Life of Things: Re-Viewing Early Wordsworth through Object-Oriented Philosophy," in *Beyond Sense and Sensibility: Moral Formation and the Literary Imagination from Johnson to Wordsworth*, ed. Peggy Thompson (Lewisburg, PA: Bucknell University Press, 2015), 145–62, 186–9. Reprinted by permission.

Series Editor's Preface

Perhaps the most favorable omen for the flourishing of Speculative Realist philosophy is its ongoing impact in other disciplines. Such impact for a philosopher is far from automatic. Though analytic philosophy dominates the most prestigious universities in the Anglophone world, it is notably rare that analytic philosophers – with their profusion of dry, often aggressive technical arguments – are read by anyone but philosophy professors. The same holds for mainstream Continental philosophy: while this group has grown impressively large in recent years, its voice has too seldom reached the outside world in any transformative way. Moreover, it often shows contempt even for those of our members who do achieve some sort of impact outside the walls of their home departments. This is somewhat surprising, given that most of the recent heroes of Continental thought first gained prominence in fields outside philosophy proper: Jacques Lacan, Michel Foucault, Jacques Derrida, Gilles Deleuze, and Slavoj Žižek all come readily to mind. By contrast, Speculative Realism has had a large interdisciplinary impact from the start: in architecture, where Object-Oriented Ontology is already a prominent orientation debated in the pages of the professional journal *Log*; in the visual arts, where Speculative Realism and its most visible figures have ranked among the 100 most important influences according to *ArtReview* since 2013; and even in archaeology, where a group of theorists including Bjørnar Olsen and Christopher Witmore has used Speculative Realism to challenge the "postprocessual" trends in archaeology that roughly paralleled postmodernism in the humanities.

In literary studies, we have already seen a certain amount of Speculative Realist criticism, whether in Greg Ellermann's work on Speculative Romanticism, debates in *New Literary History* featuring the likes of Jane Bennett and Timothy Morton, or my own

Weird Realism: Lovecraft and Philosophy. But the present book, authored by the energetic young Canadian-born scholar Evan Gottlieb, is the first known to me to interpret an entire literary school (British Romanticism) with the intellectual tools provided by Speculative Realism. Gottlieb is Professor of English at Oregon State University, where he has taught since shortly after attaining his doctorate in the widely admired department of English in the University of Buffalo. He is a prolific writer, having already published three books before this one: *Feeling British* (2007), *Walter Scott and Contemporary Theory* (2013), and *Romantic Globalism* (2014). Another book, set to appear soon, is entitled *Engagements with Literary and Critical Theory*. As the reader will soon discover, Gottlieb's erudition in literary theory is matched by a more surprising familiarity with key philosophical works: not just those of the Speculative Realists and their contemporaries, but also such earlier figures as Kant and the British empiricists. He engages with all of these schools confidently and accurately. I should add that Gottlieb writes with a wonderful lucidity that makes this book a pleasure to read. Though Gottlieb summarizes his own chapters clearly in the Introduction below, allow me to state what I take to be the key elements of these chapters.

Chapter 1 offers a powerful reading of Wordsworth, including an account of the difference between the early and late phases of the great English poet. While defending Wordsworth's often belittled philosophical acumen, Gottlieb engages with my own work, but also and more importantly with that of Timothy Morton. More than all of the authors of OOP, it is Morton who is at home in literature: a field in which he holds an endowed chair at Rice University, and in which he has developed a full-blown ecological theory with roots in British Romanticism. Working from the aesthetic theory of causation that Morton develops in his book *Realist Magic*, Gottlieb gives a new interpretation of Wordsworth's famous "Lucy poems," which cannot be understood in terms of the old causal model that Morton terms "clunk causality." Nonetheless, the later Wordsworth anticipates and rejects the later Speculative Realist effort to remove humans from the center of the cosmos.

Chapter 2 turns from Wordsworth to the more explicitly philosophical Samuel Taylor Coleridge, who openly expresses his debt to the writings of Immanuel Kant and F. W. J. Schelling. Whereas some ascribe the ambiguities of Coleridge's poetic oeuvre to his own intellectual limitations, and others make a rather formulaic postmodernist appeal to the "undecideability of language," Gottlieb addresses the issue differently. In the highly imaginative new materialism of the Speculative Realist Iain Hamilton Grant and our prominent fellow traveler Manuel DeLanda, Gottlieb finds a conceptual language that should fit quite well with Coleridge's poetic vision. Yet despite the vivid sense of things depicted in Coleridge's great poem "The Rime of the Ancient Mariner," Gottlieb ultimately concludes that Coleridge was insufficiently bold in embracing the autonomy of matter from human designs.

In Chapter 3, we move from the Speculative Realists proper to a pair of older French mentors to the movement: Alain Badiou and Bruno Latour. Their designated parallel in British Romanticism is said to be George Gordon, Lord Byron, the most dashing of the Romantics. While Latour is assigned the early *Childe Harold's Pilgrimage* and the later *Don Juan*, Badiou is paired with a number of Bryon's middle-period works, such as *Manfred*. Gottlieb convincingly reads this latter poem in terms of Badiouian truth-events, and with frequent appeals to Badiou's often-ignored but important *Theory of the Subject*. Latour's first contribution to the chapter is in helping to account for the work of non-human actors in Byron, such as the bull in the famous bullfight scene of *Don Juan*. The prince of networks returns to the stage at chapter's end, through a broader reading of *Don Juan* that draws on Latour's recent masterpiece *An Inquiry Into Modes of Existence*. Gottlieb's reading of key characters in the poem in terms of such Latourian modes as [REL] (Don Juan's mother) may be the first concrete use of Latour's modes in literary criticism. Here as in other chapters, Gottlieb shows himself disarmingly well versed in contemporary philosophy.

In Chapter 4 Gottlieb turns to that young poetic martyr, Percy Bysshe Shelley. While much recent Shelley commentary has been shaped by Paul de Man's interpretation of the poet, Gottlieb reads Shelley through the Speculative Realist positions of Ray Brassier and Quentin Meillassoux. For all the differences between these two authors, Gottlieb is correct to note that both are animated by a spirit of rationalism and materialism, with Brassier partial to the work of the natural sciences, and Meillassoux (like his teacher Badiou) preferring to emphasize mathematics as a privileged form of cognition. Gottlieb reads Shelley as coming down on the French side of this divide, claiming "that Shelley courts but ultimately rejects nihilism in favor of a radically contingent ontology that is strikingly similar to Meillassoux's."

Chapter 5, possibly the most beautiful in the book, considers another poet who died tragically young: John Keats. Gottlieb begins with a fascinating account of how Keats was both utterly emblematic of British Romantic poetry *and* a great source of aesthetic discomfort to the other members of the movement. This lays the table for Gottlieb's link between Keats and the two "New Materialists" most closely linked with Speculative Realism: Jane Bennett, and the recent convert Levi R. Bryant. Gottlieb defends the oft-criticized aestheticism of Keats's verse by appeal to the positive philosophical arguments of Bennett, who asks us to de-emphasize critical thinking in favor of a heightened passionate and ethical engagement with the world. Later in the chapter, Gottlieb extensively deploys the writings of Bryant as a way of understanding Keat's so-called Spring Odes, especially the crucial "Ode on a Grecian Urn," that springboard for the New Criticism of Cleanth Brooks.

Though I have always had a preference for French poetry, Gottlieb's book makes me want to spend months reading nothing but Wordsworth and Coleridge and Keats and the others. His use of Speculative Realism to shed light on British Romanticism has an equally strong counter-effect, since it also teaches the Speculative Realists to view these poets as colleagues and possibly cognitive rivals. Through his productive work of comparison and contrast, Gottlieb has made the Speculative Realist universe much vaster than before. We are fortunate to add this book to the series.

Graham Harman
Ankara
January 2016

Introduction

This book argues that Speculative Realism and British Romantic poetry make a mutually informing pair. In a series of author-centered chapters, I explore how some of the major Romantic poets were interested in themes and questions – including the nature of reality, the status of the "natural" world, and the relationship between humans and the world as a whole – that also animate much Speculative Realist work. Moreover, since British Romanticism developed at a time (the decades around the turn of the nineteenth century) when Kantian philosophy was not yet normative, the Romantics' perspectives on these issues show remarkable affinities with those of many Speculative Realists, who despite their differences are broadly united by their desire to move philosophical thought beyond the limits imposed by Kant and his inheritors.

Accordingly, this book tries to address two different, albeit overlapping, readerships simultaneously. From one angle, the chapters that follow are designed to introduce my colleagues in literary studies (my own academic discipline) to a purposefully wide array of Speculative Realist thinkers, their theories, and their methodologies. At the same time, I hope to show those trained in philosophy and theory, some of whom may already be familiar with Speculative Realism (SR), that British Romantic poetry is an important resource and even a source of new ideas for their work.[1] The inherently interdisciplinary nature of my enterprise, however, means that this book doesn't do everything expected of a more strictly theoretical *or* more traditional literary study. To the extent that it provides an introductory survey of SR, it is neither comprehensive nor especially critical; I make no claims to exhaust the field of SR-related approaches, and I focus on exploring rather than critiquing the foundational methods and concepts of those I discuss.

(Readers looking for more exclusively theoretical introductions to SR already have a number of valuable texts to consult.)[2] This book also differs in several ways from more traditional literary historical studies. For reasons of strategy as well as economy, I do not try to account for the existing bodies of criticism on the Romantic poets whose works I discuss; instead, I generally restrict the critical backgrounds to representative examples of twentieth-century approaches – especially those of New Criticism, deconstruction, and New Historicism – in order to establish the more-or-less traditional readings against which the differences of SR-inflected approaches can best be seen. Furthermore, unlike many literary historical studies, I do not track a developmental narrative (for example, "the rise of the novel") that stretches between chapters; instead, in a kind of historical short circuit, I seek to locate and explore a series of conceptual continuities and mutual illuminations between SR and British Romantic poetry.[3] The results may strike some as quixotic, but I hope readers from a variety of disciplinary backgrounds will find my efforts valuable.[4]

What is Speculative Realism? It is the umbrella term for a loosely affiliated group of philosophers, theorists, and critics who are interested in developing models and methods for thinking about reality – that is, what really exists, regardless of whether we are there to think about it – while attempting to avoid the pitfalls of any naïve realism that believes humans enjoy unmediated access to this reality. The common enemy of SR is what Quentin Meillassoux has influentially termed "correlationism": the belief – enshrined in Kant's *Critique of Pure Reason* (1781, 1787) – that we can only ever talk or think about reality in relation to our human subjectivity. The correlationist circle in which most philosophy and critical theory has operated for roughly the past 200 years holds that we cannot access reality itself, only the correlation between ourselves and the world. It confines us to the realm of epistemology, in other words, whereas practitioners of SR want to return to the realm of ontology, the traditional domain of philosophy as such. In the rest of this introduction, I will lay out some of the basics of SR before outlining what I take to be the main connections, historical as well as theoretical, between it and British Romantic poetry.

As a movement, "Speculative Realism" began as the name chosen for a one-day workshop held in April 2007 at Goldsmiths College, University of London. This event brought together four philosophers who were working, more-or-less independently, on different theoretical frameworks for overcoming, bypassing, or formulating alternatives to correlationism. Graham Harman, the most outspoken and prolific of the participants, had already published several texts setting out what he calls "object-oriented philosophy": an approach to describing reality, initially developed from Heidegger's tool-analysis in *Being and Time* (1927), which focuses on objects as the primary components of mind-independent reality. Ray Brassier, who in fact originated the name "Speculative Realism," had recently written a book defending nihilism as the proper endpoint of the Enlightenment, that is, as the only authentic perspective on a universe that cares nothing for humans, was perfectly operational for billions of years without us, and will presumably go on existing long after we and everything we know have disappeared. In a somewhat similar vein, Iain Hamilton Grant brought to the workshop his particular interest in recovering Friedrich Schelling's vein of German idealism in order to re-establish the bases on which mind-independent reality can be thought. The fourth participant was Meillassoux (already mentioned), whose first book, *Après la Finitude*, was published in French in 2006 and (at the time of the Goldsmith's workshop) was being translated by Brassier for English publication. *After Finitude: An Essay on the Necessity of Contingency* is notable both for defining correlationism as such, and for exploring it with rigorous logic in order to demonstrate that absolute knowledge of reality can be wrung from its self-involutions.

On a personal note, I first heard about SR in late 2009 from a graduate student at a conference – often a good sign that a new intellectual movement is genuinely exciting, innovative, and far from being a top-down affair. Indeed, one of the most interesting aspects of the genesis and relatively rapid diffusion of SR is that it is *not* a product of elite academics imposing their methodological will on others. The four original expositors of SR mostly hailed from relatively marginal institutions, at least from a North American perspective: the American University of Cairo, Middlesex University, the University of the West of England, and (the most prestigious) the Ecole Normale Supérieure in Paris. In other words, the success experienced by SR has been very much of the grassroots, bottom-up variety. Likewise, while SR has become increasingly well-represented in traditional academic formats, much of its initial impetus, for better and occasionally for worse,[5] has come from non-traditional forums: blog posts and online discussion threads, start-up journals, and open-source publications.[6] At the same time, SR has certainly benefitted from some associations with high-profile thinkers, several of whom will be discussed in the chapters that follow, including Alain Badiou (Meillassoux's mentor), Bruno Latour (about whom Harman has written extensively), and Slavoj Žižek (an occasional although not fully sympathetic interlocutor).

Even after accounting for the material factors facilitating the relatively rapid uptake of SR by a variety of humanistic and other fields, we may still productively ask why a return to realism – albeit a modified, self-consciously speculative realism – should prove so attractive and relevant now. One answer lies in the perceived exhaustion of several key trends that informed modern philosophy and literary theory alike, especially the linguistic or semiotic turn. Whether one traces it back to Wittgenstein, Saussure, or Nietzsche, the linguistic turn meant that, for the mainstream of twentieth-century philosophy and theory, epistemology effectively replaced ontology. The roots of this substitution, however, go back at least to Kant's so-called "Copernican revolution," which set strict limits on what humans can and cannot productively think about. Kant was not the first modern thinker to bar intellectual access to "things in themselves" – that distinction may belong to Berkeley, whom Meillassoux has recently denominated the founder of the "era of Correlation."[7] Nevertheless, it wasn't Berkeley's radical "subjectalism" (Meillassoux's term) but David Hume's skepticism to which Kant was directly responding when he deduced his transcendental categories.[8] Henceforth, according to Kant, reason must content itself with interrogating the limits of its own knowledge – limits strictly correlated with human access to what Meillassoux only half-jokingly calls "the *great outdoors*": "the *absolute* outside of pre-critical thinkers."[9]

Kant's insistence that we must restrict ourselves to epistemology suggests a second answer to the question, "Why Speculative Realism now?" If the critical approaches facilitated by Kant and the linguistic turn seem to have "run out of steam," to use Latour's phrase,[10] this is in large part because many of the problems we face today – especially the increasingly likely prospect of worldwide ecological catastrophe due to anthropogenic global warming – have material dimensions that simply exceed the purview of the linguistic, critical, and epistemologically oriented approaches that have directed the humanities for some time now. Put another way, the problem is that, as Levi Bryant points out, "Radical emancipatory political theory has been correlationist and anti-realist through and through."[11] Ontological claims have been critical theory's enemy of choice – with good reason, given their dubious history of being used to naturalize racism, sexism, speciesism, and other discourses of marginalization and oppression – and this has led some critics to worry that SR threatens to undo the progress made on these fronts. An extended examination of these concerns is beyond this book's scope, but it is worth noting that most SR thinkers reject these accusations, and many (as we will see in subsequent chapters) are clear that although they want philosophy to return to its ontological roots, this need not be at the expense of continued critical work in epistemological domains. Harman and Timothy Morton, for example, have each put forward proposals for an "object-oriented literary criticism"; however, whereas Harman calls for texts to be treated like ontological objects on which one can perform thought experiments, my approach in *Romantic Realities* is closer to Morton's when he reads Percy Shelley's extraordinary *A Defence of Poetry* (1821) for the ways it shares the object-oriented tenet that "causality is aesthetics" (a concept I discuss in Chapter 1).[12]

In a simple but important sense, it is the Speculative Realists' desire to explore reality itself that links them most closely in theme and tone with the British Romantics, who frequently display a similar desire to "see into the life of things," in William Wordsworth's famous phrase. Greg Ellermann has recently summed this up nicely with his description of the "romantic coordinates" of SR; especially in Meillassoux's work, says Ellermann, SR "defines itself in relation to the philosophical problems of greatest moment for romanticism . . . the same thematics of mind and world that delineate speculative realism's post-phenomenological and post-deconstructive horizons."[13] I take slight issue with Ellermann's characterization of British Romanticism as both "post-Humean" and "post-Kantian," however, because what makes the British Romantics so interesting from a speculative perspective is their historical positioning at a moment that is *neither* post-Humean, since the force of Humean skepticism was very much alive and well for the Romantics, *nor* post-Kantian, since the latter's ideas were just beginning to be widely disseminated in Britain in the 1790s.[14] But Ellermann is absolutely correct that the relation between SR and Romanticism goes both ways: not only do the Romantics anticipate some of SR's methods and concerns, but SR is also programmatically Romantic in significant ways. To speak broadly, both movements are shaped by their responses to contemporary conditions: the British Romantics to the French Revolution and its aftermath – "the master theme of the epoch in which we live," as Percy Shelley put it[15] – and SR to the abovementioned limitations of critical theory to respond to the ecological crises of the early twenty-first century. In both cases, too, there is a manifesto-like quality to their early work, especially as they set out their ideas against those of their predecessors. Wordsworth's preface to the second edition of *Lyrical Ballads* (1800), for example, uses a sonnet by Thomas Gray to exemplify what is wrong with the poetry of the previous generation. In similar fashion, Harman's first book, *Tool-being: Heidegger and the Metaphysics of Objects* (2002), builds its case for adapting and expanding Heidegger's tool-analysis in large part by critiquing previous interpretations of Heidegger; Brassier's *Nihil Unbound: Enlightenment and Extinction* (2007) also proceeds via critiques of previous thinkers who have misunderstood or misrepresented what, for Brassier, is the basic lesson of the Enlightenment: "Thinking has interests which do not coincide with those of living."[16] Most strident of all may be Meillassoux's *After Finitude*, which – in tones that would not be out of place in the impassioned declarations of William Blake or Percy Shelley – announces its intentions to "wak[e] us from our correlationist slumber, by enjoining us to reconcile thought and absolute."[17]

Above all, it is this yearning for knowledge of the absolute that indicates the Romantic dynamic of the Speculative Realists. For a long time in literary criticism this topic has been largely closed for debate. After the canonizing efforts of influential critics like Northrop Frye, M. H. Abrams, Earl Wasserman, and Harold Bloom, who took the Romantic fascination with the absolute quite seriously, there was an almost inevitable turn away from such questions; the introduction of so-called "French theory," the historicist identification of what Jerome J. McGann called "the Romantic ideology," and the feminist work of critics like Anne K. Mellor and Elizabeth Fay together helped inaugurate a hermeneutics of suspicion toward all Romantic claims to apprehend or articulate anything that lies beyond language, consciousness, embodiment, or the vagaries of history.[18] Furthermore, as Marc Redfield has recently shown, no twentieth-century theoretical movement was more associated with Romanticism – and more skeptical of all metaphysical claims – than deconstruction.[19] On the one hand, then, my pairing of Romantic poets with SR thinkers throughout this book represents a break with deconstruction's previous near-monopoly on Romantic criticism; far from being a purely or even largely rhetorical project, as it frequently appears in deconstructive commentaries, Romantic poetry viewed through the lens of SR reveals itself to be sincerely engaged with ontological questions of the first order. On the other hand, my method of reading literary and philosophical texts as mutually informing rather than as oppositional is itself indebted to deconstruction's repeated destabilization of this supposed opposition.[20] Consequently, although I regularly contrast deconstructive and SR-style readings in the following chapters, I don't want to be misunderstood as advocating for literary critics and theorists to abandon deconstruction or critical theory more generally; likewise, although I sometimes use SR to develop readings of Romantic poetry that diverge significantly from the New Historical accounts that emerged in the last decades of the twentieth century, my obvious commitment to placing the Romantics' ideas in their socio-political contexts is clearly indebted to historicisms both "old" and "new." Ultimately, along the lines of my endorsement of Bryant's position that critical theory and SR need not be oppositional, I strongly believe we need epistemological and ideological critiques as well as ontological descriptions to understand the work of any literary movement or moment, especially British Romanticism.

Of course, as Abrams warned some time ago, "Romanticism is no one thing"[21] – and neither is SR. Indeed, as both its supporters and detractors point out, even the four original participants in the 2007 Goldsmith's workshop agreed on little beyond their shared desire to move thought beyond the correlationist circle and back into some more sustained dialogue with "reality itself." For Brassier, this shared objective is not enough to constitute a viable philosophical movement;[22] for Harman and most of SR's other participants, its variety of approaches is a sign of intellectual vibrancy. In a similar vein, critics and scholars have been arguing about the usefulness of the category "Romantic" to describe the variety of literary productions grouped within it since at least the publication of A.O. Lovejoy's seminal 1924 article on the subject. In both cases, such discussions are most useful when they involve substantive debates over content or methodology, least useful when they devolve into nominalist hair-splitting (to say nothing of name-calling).

There is at least one more thematic area of significant overlap between Romanticism and SR that deserves to be remarked upon: their shared investment in taking *things* – whether "natural" or artificial – seriously.[23] It is a classroom commonplace that the Romantic poets were uniquely interested in the powers of the human imagination. Even to the extent that this is true, however, such interest was frequently directed toward seeing how far the powers of human imagination could carry the mind *out* of itself – a phenomenon whose legitimacy and even normativity both neuroscience and contemporary philosophies of mind increasingly recognize.[24] Yet it is the Romantic interest in attempting to transcend the mind altogether – thus effectively overcoming the subject/object dualism that SR also seeks to think beyond – that is most noteworthy for my purposes. As one among many exemplary passages, consider the last stanza of Book Eight of Wordsworth's *Prelude* (1850 edition):

> Thus from a very early age, O Friend!
> My thoughts by slow gradations had been drawn
> To human kind, and to the good and ill
> Of human life: Nature had led me on;
> And oft amid the "busy hum" I seemed
> To travel independent of her help,
> As if I had forgotten her; but no,
> The world of human-kind outweighed not hers
> In our habitual thoughts; the scale of love,
> Though filling daily, still was light, compared
> With that in which *her* mighty objects lay.[25]

To be sure, Wordsworth's personification of Nature would not sit well with any of SR's proponents, especially Morton, who has decisively argued against the reification of "Nature."[26] As we will also see in Chapter 1, Wordsworth retains a degree of anthropocentrism in most of his poetry that SR-inflected approaches tend to abjure. Nevertheless, there is a great deal of affinity between most SR positions regarding the importance of including non-human actors when composing ontological accounts of the world, and Wordsworth's sense that an investigation of nature's "mighty objects" is the central precept of his life and poetics. Coming into contact with the natural world – literally, the great outdoors – is what initially moved him to care about other people, Wordsworth tells us, and although as an adult he may now act "as if I had for-gotten [Nature]," in fact there is no possibility of such a forgetting, because his love for the world's objects is what makes possible all other kinds of affection. This passage in turn pairs well with Harman's object-oriented battle cry near the start of *Tool-Being* – arguably still the most important single volume in the growing SR canon – that "philosophy must break loose from the textual and linguistic ghetto that it has been constructing for itself, and return to the drama of the things themselves."[27] It is this same drama, I argue throughout this book, that the Romantic poets were engaged in observing and pondering.

In my first chapter, I consider the ways in which Wordsworth's poetry, especially from the early years of his career, anticipates many of the insights generated by the object-oriented philosophy (OOP) developed by Harman and adapted by Morton. Although Wordsworth stops short of being fully non-anthropocentric, the remarkable affinities between his early works and OOP's theoretical commitments strongly bespeak their shared dedication to a non-correlationist vision of the world. Chapter 1 also sets out the philosophical milieu of late eighteenth-century Britain, which formed the Romantics' intellectual inheritance, and the Kantian critical philosophy of which they were just becoming aware. My second chapter turns to Wordsworth's collaborator on *Lyrical Ballads*, Samuel Taylor Coleridge, who has long been regarded as the more rigorously philosophical of the two poets, and who prided himself on introducing German idealism to the British reading public. I compare Coleridge's poetic vision first to the work of Grant, whose re-working of Schelling's nature-philosophy is characterized by an ambivalent relationship to Kantianism, and then to the process ontology of Manuel DeLanda, whose Deleuzian commitment to "the virtual" as what facilitates "the real" finds surprising parallels in Coleridge's most speculative poetic ventures. Chapter 3 pairs the most popular Romantic poet, Lord Byron, with two SR-associated theorists who also happen to have very high profiles: Bruno Latour and Alain Badiou. Here, I argue that Byron's early and later epic poems enact versions of Latour's Actor-Network-Theory and its recent updates, whereas several of Byron's mid-career works illustrate the main concepts of Badiou's eventual philosophy. I then shift to the most radical, politically and perhaps philosophically as well, of the younger generation of Romantic poets in Chapter 4. Juxtaposing Percy Shelley's verse first with

Brassier's exacting nihilism and then with Meillassoux's "speculative materialism," I demonstrate how Shelley moves increasingly close to the latter's positions, especially with regard to the radically contingent nature of reality. Finally, I return to "the drama of things themselves" in my fifth chapter, where I examine how the aesthetic investments of John Keats's poetry take on new meanings when viewed through the prisms of Jane Bennett's "vital materialism" and Bryant's evolving ontological frameworks. Throughout, as mentioned above, I consistently place the Romantic poets' ontological commitments and concerns in the contexts of their own intellectual milieus, as well as in dialogue with contemporary SR perspectives.

Before bringing this introduction to close, a few supplementary comments are in order. Readers may already have noted that the foregoing chapter summaries do not include William Blake, another Romantic poet usually considered canonical. Although it might be possible to argue that his mid-eighteenth-century upbringing prevented him from belonging to the same intellectual moment as the other poets in this book, I will instead plead my relative incapability to account for Blake's unique oeuvre; his absence, in other words, is due to my scholarly limitations and should not be construed as an obstacle to future studies of his work from an SR perspective. Likewise, my focus on canonical, male Romantic poets should not be taken as much more than a mark of convenience; to a greater degree and for longer than their historical peers, they have benefitted from sustained critical and theoretical consideration, and so lend themselves most readily to the kind of work I do in this book. That being said, there is a plethora of other Romantics whose poetry and prose cry out for SR-inflected attention, including at a minimum the poetry of Anna Laetitia Barbauld, Robert Burns, John Clare, Felicia Hemans, Laetitia Elizabeth Landon, and Charlotte Smith; the prose of Thomas DeQuincey, Olaudah Equiano, William Hazlitt, and Charles Lamb; the novels of Jane Austen, Maria Edgeworth, Ann Radcliffe, Walter Scott, and Mary Shelley; and the philosophical treatises of Edmund Burke, William Godwin, and Mary Wollstonecraft. All of these authors have passages and pages that await illumination via SR (and vice versa). Similarly, my decisions regarding which SR thinkers to include should not be misconstrued as definitive; beyond the four participants in the original Goldsmith's workshop in 2007, whose inclusion in a book on

SR is a foregone conclusion, the theorists whom I present reflect above all my own predilections and familiarities.[28]

Will there someday be an anthology, *The Speculative Realists and their Contemporaries*, to match the *Longman Anthology of British Literature: The Romantics and their Contemporaries*? Only time will tell. In the meantime, SR can open up many exciting vistas for those of us in literary studies, especially Romanticism; likewise, Romanticism in particular and literary studies in general have much to contribute to the ongoing explorations that constitute SR. The following chapters, I hope, make productive contributions to both sides of this work.

Notes

1. I am aware that "philosophy" and "theory" are not necessarily or always the same thing; unless otherwise noted, however, I will generally use them interchangeably in this book, as my focus here and throughout will be on so-called Continental philosophy, which enjoys a great deal of overlap with "theory" or "critical theory." See, e.g., David West, *Continental Philosophy: An Introduction* (Cambridge and Malden, MA: Polity, 2010), esp. "Introduction: What is Continental Philosophy?," 1–7.

2. See, e.g., Paul J. Ennis, *Continental Realism* (Winchester and Washington, DC: Zero Books, 2011); Peter Gratton, *Speculative Realism: Problems and Prospects* (London and New York: Bloomsbury, 2014); Steven Shaviro, *The Universe of Things: On Speculative Realism* (Minneapolis: University of Minnesota Press, 2014). There are also several collections of essays by a variety of SR practitioners and critics: see especially Levi Bryant, Nick Srnicek, and Graham Harman, eds., *The Speculative Turn: Continental Materialism and Realism* (Melbourne: re.press, 2011); Richard Grusin, ed., *The Nonhuman Turn* (Minneapolis: University of Minnesota Press, 2015); Roland Faber and Andrew Goffey, eds., *The Allure of Things: Process and Object in Contemporary Philosophy* (London and New York: Bloomsbury, 2015); and Armen Avanessian and Suhail Malik, eds., *Genealogies of Speculation: Materialism and Subjectivity since Structuralism* (London and New York: Bloomsbury, 2016). Jeffrey J. Cohen's edited collection, *Prismatic Ecology: Ecotheory beyond Green* (Minneapolis: University of Minnesota Press, 2013), also boasts a strong SR presence. In addition to many individual interviews with SR thinkers available

online and in scholarly journals, see the following collections: Rick Dolphijn and Iris van der Tuin, *New Materialism: Interviews and Cartographies* (Ann Arbor: Open Humanities Press, 2012); Paul J. Ennis, *Post-Continental Voices: Selected Interviews* (Winchester and Washington, DC: Zero Books, 2010).

3. One of the precedents for the type of study I have tried to write is Ira Livingston's innovative *Arrow of Chaos: Romanticism and Postmodernity* (Minneapolis: University of Minnesota Press, 1997), which investigates convergences of such "postmodern" phenomena as information theory, fractal geometry, and chaos theory with Romantic-era poetry and prose.

4. The fact that several shorter pieces comparing elements of SR and British Romanticism have appeared while this book was in progress suggests that interest in this conjunction is already thriving. See Greg Ellermann, "Speculative Romanticism," *SubStance* 44.1 (2015): 154–74; Chris Washington, "Romanticism and Speculative Realism," *Literature Compass* 12.9 (2015): 448–60. See also Aaron Ottinger, "The Speculative Turn and Studies in Romanticism," blog post on the North American Society for the Study of Romanticism's Graduate Student Caucus website, March 30, 2012, http://www. nassrgrads.com/the-speculative-turn-and-romantic-studies (accessed November 6, 2015). A number of articles or book chapters utilizing SR-related work to shed new light on particular Romantic-era authors have also appeared in recent years; see, e.g., Joshua D. Gonsalves, "The Encrypted Prospect: Existentialist Phenomenology, Deconstruction, and Speculative Realism in 'To Autumn'," *European Romantic Review* 24.3 (2013): 287–95; Chris Washington, "Byron's Speculative Turn: Visions of Posthuman Life in *Cain*," *Essays in Romanticism* 22.1 (2015): 73–95; Roger Whitson, "Digital Blake 2.0," in *Blake 2.0: William Blake in Twentieth-Century Art, Music, and Culture*, ed. Steve Clark, Tristanne Connolly, and Jason Whittaker (Basingstoke: Palgrave Macmillan, 2012), 41–55.

5. For more on SR's early dissemination via non-traditional intellectual outlets and media, especially online, see Adam Kotsko, "A Dangerous Supplement: Speculative Realism, Academic Blogging, and the Future of Philosophy," *Speculations* 4 (2013): 91–8.

6. See, e.g., the journals *Collapse* and *Speculations* and blog sites run by various SR proponents, including *Ecology without Nature* (Timothy Morton), *Larval Subjects* (Levi Bryant), *Object-Oriented Philosophy* (Graham Harman); relatively new publishers with strong

associations with SR include Open Humanities Press, Punctum Books, Urbanomic, and Zero Books.

7. Quentin Meillassoux, "Iteration, Reiteration, Repetition: A Speculative Analysis of the Meaningless Sign," trans. Robin Mackay, 3, https://cdn.shopify.com/s/files/1/0069/6232/files/Meillassoux_Workshop_Berlin.pdf (accessed November 9, 2015).

8. Meillassoux, "Iteration, Reiteration, Repetition," 6, n. 2.

9. Quentin Meillassoux, *After Finitude: An Essay on the Necessity of Contingency*, trans. Ray Brassier (London and New York: Continuum, 2008), 7.

10. See Bruno Latour, "Why has Critique Run out of Steam? From Matters of Fact to Matters of Concern," *Critical Inquiry* 30.2 (2004): 225–48.

11. Levi Bryant, "Politics and Speculative Realism," *Speculations* 4 (2013): 17.

12. See Graham Harman, "The Well-Wrought Broken Hammer: Object-Oriented Literary Criticism," *New Literary History* 43.2 (2012): 183–203; Timothy Morton, "An Object-Oriented Defense of Poetry," *New Literary History* 43.2 (2012): 205–24. See also Jane Bennett, "Systems and Things: A Response to Graham Harman and Timothy Morton," *New Literary History* 43.2 (2012): 225–33.

13. Ellermann, "Speculative Romanticism," 165.

14. See Cairns Craig, *Associationism and the Literary Imagination: From the Phantasmal Chaos* (Edinburgh: Edinburgh University Press, 2007); Monika Class, *Coleridge and Kantian Ideas in England, 1796–1817: Coleridge's Responses to German Philosophy* (London: Bloomsbury, 2012).

15. Percy Shelley, quoted in M. H. Abrams, *Natural Supernaturalism: Tradition and Revolution in Romantic Literature* (New York: Norton, 1971), 328.

16. Ray Brassier, *Nihil Unbound: Enlightenment and Extinction* (Basingstoke: Palgrave Macmillan, 2007), xi.

17. Meillassoux, *After Finitude*, 128.

18. See Jerome J. McGann, *The Romantic Ideology: A Critical Investigation* (Chicago: University of Chicago Press, 1983); Elizabeth Fay, *A Feminist Introduction to Romanticism* (Oxford: Wiley-Blackwell, 1991); Anne K. Mellor, *Romanticism and Gender* (New York and London: Routledge, 1993). Works by the other critics mentioned will be cited as relevant in the following pages.

19. Marc Redfield, *Theory at Yale: The Strange Case of Deconstruction in America* (New York: Fordham University Press, 2016), esp.

Chapter 2, "Theory and Romantic Lyric: The Case of 'A Slumber did my Spirit Seal'," 62–83.

20. See, e.g., Jacques Derrida, "White Mythology: Metaphor in the Text of Philosophy," in *Margins of Philosophy*, trans. Alan Bass (Chicago: University of Chicago Press, 1982), 207–71.

21. M. H. Abrams, "English Romanticism: The Spirit of the Age," in *Romanticism and Consciousness: Essays in Criticism*, ed. Harold Bloom (New York: Norton, 1970), 93.

22. See, e.g., Ray Brassier, "Postscript: Speculative Autopsy," in Peter Wolfendale, *Object-Oriented Philosophy: The Noumenon's New Clothes* (Falmouth: Urbanomic, 2014), 409–21.

23. Although she doesn't engage with SR, a good example of criticism that recognizes this is Mary Jacobus's *Romantic Things: A Tree, a Rock, a Cloud* (Chicago: University of Chicago Press, 2012).

24. On the former, see, e.g., Alva Noë, *Out of our Heads: Why We are Not our Brains, and Other Lessons from the Biology of Consciousness* (New York: Hill and Wang, 2010); on the latter, see Alan Richardson, *The Neural Sublime: Cognitive Theories and Romantic Texts* (Baltimore: Johns Hopkins University Press, 2010).

25. William Wordsworth, *The Prelude: 1799, 1805, 1850*, ed. Jonathan Wordsworth, M. H. Abrams, and Stephen Gill (New York: Norton, 1979), 311, ll. 676–86.

26. See Timothy Morton, *Ecology without Nature: Rethinking Environmental Aesthetics* (Cambridge, MA: Harvard University Press, 2007).

27. Graham Harman, *Tool-Being: Heidegger and the Metaphysics of Things* (Chicago and LaSalle: Open Court Press, 2002), 17.

28. There are a number of theorists working in areas that abut and sometimes overlap with the interests and concerns of SR, whose texts and ideas equally deserve attention: at a minimum, the New Materialism associated with Karen Barad, Rosi Braidotti, William Connolly, and Elizabeth Grosz; the alternative phenomenologies of Sara Ahmed and Tom Sparrow; the animal studies of Mel Chen and Carey Wolfe. Also beyond the scope of this book is the recent work of other writers explicitly influenced by SR, including, e.g., Ian Bogost, Jon Cogburn, Jeffrey J. Cohen, Claire Colebrook, Maurizio Ferraris, Markus Gabriel, Tristan Garcia, Adrian Johnston, and Eileen Joy.

Wordsworth and Object-Oriented Philosophy

Although William Wordsworth wrote the bulk of the poems as well as the prose introductions for every edition of *Lyrical Ballads*, critics and scholars have generally concluded that his friend and collaborator, Samuel Taylor Coleridge, was the philosophical driver of their joint project. The two poets themselves endorsed this view, and it was subsequently institutionalized by prominent men of letters like J. S. Mill and Matthew Arnold, who each considered Wordsworth a great poet but at best an indifferent philosopher.[1] Wordsworth's famous definition of "the Poet" as neither more nor less than "a man speaking to men" appears to confirm his identification as a common-sense, non-metaphysical thinker.[2]

Yet despite Coleridge's more obvious intellectual influences and Wordsworth's frequent self-representations as a naïf, underestimating the latter's philosophical credentials is a mistake. In fact, Wordsworth was well versed in the theories and ideas that saturated the early Enlightenment as well as its later, more sentimental outcroppings. As Stephen Gill has documented, the young Wordsworth closely studied "natural philosophy," especially Newton's *Opticks* (1704), and was later strongly (albeit briefly) influenced by William Godwin's proto-anarchistic writings.[3] More recently, Adam Potkay has argued that Wordsworth deserves recognition for his contributions to our modern understanding of ethical relations, both to each other and to the world at large.[4] Noting that the word "thing" appears in some form a total of 439 times in Wordsworth's corpus, Potkay contends that the poet's sustained interest in things stems from his "receptivity to and delicate evocation of the comprehensive (or perhaps mystical) sense of *thing* that was available at the end of the eighteenth century and that to a lesser degree remains available today."[5] I share Potkay's view that Wordsworth was attuned both to the expansive etymological history of the word "thing," and also to the Stoicist and Spinozist traditions of viewing the universe "as a unity sustained by a rational power or spirit."[6] Whereas Potkay connects this orientation to the "postmodern" ethics of twentieth-century philosophers like Heidegger and Levinas, however, I want to consider how Wordsworth's early poetry and poetics anticipate a related but even more recent philosophical movement: object-oriented philosophy.

Pioneered by Graham Harman in the late 1990s, and more recently taken up by writers and practitioners in a variety of artistic, humanistic, and social-scientific disciplines, object-oriented philosophy argues not only that human existence is necessarily enmeshed with the world of things around us, but also that the extent of these entanglements necessitates questioning our spontaneous anthropocentrism. Wordsworth's seminal contributions to *Lyrical Ballads*, I want to argue, share both the frame and some of the specific qualities of object-oriented philosophy's commitment to taking "things" seriously. In what follows, I initially trace the evolution of Enlightenment theories of subject–object relations, paying close attention to their relevance to Wordsworth's 1800 "Preface to *Lyrical Ballads*," before describing how Harman and others have positioned object-oriented philosophy relative to this tradition. Subsequently, I consider carefully how some of Wordsworth's early poems and supporting prose anticipate these paradigm-shifting developments. Finally, I bring in Timothy Morton's recent work on the aesthetics of object-oriented causation, as well as his provocative concept of "hyperobjects," to test the limits of Wordsworth's commitment to a non-anthropocentric vision of reality.

In his classic essay, "The Eye and the Object in the Poetry of Wordsworth," Frederick A. Pottle notes the tension between two of Wordsworth's central assertions in the 1800 "Preface": "Poetry takes its origin from emotion recollected in tranquility," and "I have at all times endeavoured to look steadily at my subject."[7] How, asks Pottle, can Wordsworth claim to "look steadily" at his subject when his composition method explicitly requires a sufficient period of withdrawn self-reflection before any writing begins? The answer, Pottle argues, is that this claim cannot be taken literally. Comparing Dorothy Wordsworth's expansive journal entry of April 15, 1802, with William's adaptations of her descriptions in his short poem, "I Wandered Lonely as a Cloud," Pottle reconstructs the process whereby Wordsworth chooses which elements to keep (the crowd of daffodils, their rhythmic movements) and which to elide (the keen wind, the rain). He concludes that Wordsworth's idea of "look[ing] steadily at my subject" necessitates a high degree of simplification, "to make the manifold of sensation more meaningful by reducing it to a number of objects that can actually be contemplated." But Pottle is certain that Wordsworth does not finally subscribe to what he calls "a *merely* matter of fact, an *exclusively* positivistic view of nature"; instead, Pottle argues that the "subject" of which Wordsworth speaks in the "Preface" is ultimately an intellectual construct, a "mental image" which the poet first seizes upon, then reduces and infuses with meaning until it becomes "a symbol (to use Hartley's quaint terminology) of sympathy, theopathy, or the moral sense."[8]

Significantly, what Pottle considered "quaint" in the philosophy of David Hartley is once again relevant to contemporary discussions of epistemology and ontology. A brief foray into the intellectual background that informs Wordsworth's "Preface" will help us grasp the stakes of his intervention. For Hartley – whose ideas deeply impressed both Wordsworth and Coleridge in the years leading up to *Lyrical Ballads* – the key to understanding the relationship between the human experience and the natural world lies in the concept of association. In *Observations on Man, His Frame, His Duty, and His Expectations* (1749), Hartley follows John Locke by asserting that all experience is composed at bottom of sensory impressions, which are then transformed into distinct ideas like pleasure and pain. The philosopher's primary task is to chart the myriad paths by which sense impressions and mental ideas interact with each other in more-or-less predictable ways:

> The Pleasures arising from the Contemplation of the Beauties of the natural World seem to admit of the following Analysis. The pleasant Tastes, and Smells, and the fine Colours of Fruits and Flowers, the Melody of Birds, and the grateful Warmth or Coolness of the Air, in the proper Seasons, transfer Miniatures of the Pleasures upon rural Scenes, which start up instantaneously so mixed with each other, and with such as will be immediately enumerated as to be separately indiscernible.[9]

Especially notable here is Hartley's insertion of the pathos-laden adjective "grateful" in front of the spectrum of possible air temperatures – "Warmth or Coolness" – to be experienced outdoors. Unlike David Hume, whose more rigorous *Treatise of Human Nature* (1739–40) had been published almost a decade earlier to far less acclaim, Hartley is so eager to consider the effects of such scenes on the mind that he does not worry overly about violating the causal chain (impressions before ideas) he has just finished establishing.[10]

Despite or perhaps thanks to such suggestive looseness, the influence of Hartleian associationism is apparent throughout Wordsworth's "Preface" to *Lyrical Ballads*, a touchstone of British Romantic poetic theory. As Wordsworth explains, the original collection of poems that he and Coleridge published was "an experiment which, I hoped, might be of some use to ascertain, how far, by fitting to metrical arrangement a selection of the real language of men in a state of vivid sensation, that sort of pleasure and that quantity of pleasure may be imparted, which a Poet may rationally endeavor to impart."[11] Almost every key element of Wordsworth's early poetics is present here. Poetry is a kind of thought experiment; meter is the linguistic feature that most distinguishes poetry from prose; "vivid sensation[s]" represent the truest picture of the human experience; feelings of "pleasure" can be understood both in terms of quantity and quality; the poet's ultimate vocation is to communicate his (or potentially her, although the Preface's language is notoriously gendered) experiences of said pleasure to the reader. All of this is followed by the central assertion, clearly influenced by Hartley, that one of "the primary laws of our nature" which the poems of *Lyrical Ballads* supposedly illustrate is "chiefly as regards the manner in which we *associate* ideas in a state of excitement" (italics added).[12] Less well remarked, however, is the extent to which Wordsworth's Preface mixes additional influences with Hartleian associationism. Noel Jackson argues that by 1800 Wordsworth was likely aware that new medical research, published by influential physicians like William Cullen, was rapidly rendering obsolete Hartley's theory that "nervous vibratiuncles" facilitated the internal communication of ideas and feelings.[13] The young poet had also been reading Erasmus Darwin's *Zoonomia; or, The Laws of Organic Life* (1794) in the spring of 1798, and Jackson speculates that Darwin's ideas regarding organisms' capacities for internal or imaginative sensation are combined with Cullen's neurophysiological theories in the Preface. Recognizing these newer influences helps account for the strange mixture of moralistic and scientific language that Wordsworth uses throughout the Preface.

For my purposes, however, the older influences are of even more interest. Consider Wordsworth's fullest exposition in 1800 of his ideal compositional process:

> For our continued influxes of feeling are modified and directed by our thoughts, which are indeed representatives of all our past feelings; and as by contemplating the relation of these general representatives to each other, we discover what is really important to men, so by the repetition and continuance of this act feelings connected with important subjects will be nourished, till at length, if we be originally possessed of much organic sensibility, such habits of mind will be produced that by obeying blindly and mechanically the impulses of those habits we shall describe objects and utter sentiments of such a nature and in such connection with each other, that the understanding of the being to whom we address ourselves, if he be in a healthful state of association, must necessarily be in some degree enlightened, his taste exalted, and his affections ameliorated.[14]

Much of this statement still echoes Hartley, especially its description of ideas or concepts as mechanically reproduced sensations and its assertion that the poet's sentiments can be transferred to the reader through a secondary process of association. Several new elements are introduced, however, when Wordsworth asserts that a baseline degree of "organic [bodily] sensibility" is necessary for the poet to experience the sensations he will subsequently transfer to the reader. Moreover, he tells us, the would-be poet must also have learned through "repetition" and "continuance" the "*habits* of mind" necessary to convert those sensations into ideas in the first place; only then will he be able to "describe *objects* and utter sentiments . . . in such *connection* with each other" to produce the desired effects of aesthetic and even moral uplift in the reader (my italics).[15]

Habits, objects, connections: I have emphasized these terms to underscore that Hume's ideas still figure largely in Wordsworth's understanding of how people interact with the world around them. Like Hartley, Hume believed that all ideas begin as sensations; unlike his successor, the Scottish philosopher was convinced that human cognition is essentially a matter of habit or custom rather than logic or scientific certainty. He argues this position at many points in his *Treatise*, but nowhere more definitively than in Section One of Part IV, "Of skepticism with regard to reason," where he concludes that *"all our reasonings concerning causes and effects are deriv'd from nothing but custom . . ."*[16] Hume's famous thought experiment of the man observing "the communication of motion" between two billiard balls arrives later, in the *Enquiry Concerning Human Understanding* (1772), but it establishes the same principle, albeit on more restricted grounds: we move from an observation of two events being "conjoined" to their being causally "connected" primarily on the basis of observed repetition.[17] In fact, this principle is laid down quite early in the *Treatise*, when Hume states that "Our judgments concerning cause and effect are deriv'd from habit and experience: and when we have been accustomed to see one object united to another, our imagination passes from the first to the second, by a natural transition, which precedes reflection, and which cannot be prevented by it."[18] Hartley, committed to a more materialist view of the communication of sensations and ideas, jettisons much of Hume's vocabulary of the imagination in his own accounts of associationism; Wordsworth, as we have seen, retains it for his poetic purposes.

Where Wordsworth deviates most from Hume turns on his commitment to the object form itself, which both separates him from the English empiricist tradition and unexpectedly aligns him with today's object-oriented philosophy. If Hume stands behind Hartley, however, then before moving forward we need to say more about another philosopher clearly standing behind Hume: Locke, whose *Essay Concerning Human Understanding* (1689; 4th ed. 1700) inaugurates or at least anticipates key aspects of the linguistic turn that SR seeks definitively to move beyond.[19] In Book I of his *Essay*, Locke famously stipulates that since our ideas must be generated from experiences, Aristotle's classic distinction between "Substance" and "Accident" – that is, between a perceived thing's essential qualities and its superficial ones – is practically null; we can have no definite knowledge of what Locke calls the "real essence" of a material thing, only knowledge of its characteristics or qualities. As Jonathan Kramnick observes, Locke thereby opposes the materialism of earlier philosophers like Democritus, arguing instead that "the identity of a living thing cannot be reduced to the parts from which a thing is composed."[20] Yet naming a thing does not get at its essence either, but merely moots the problem by transferring the thing in question into consciousness: "The Essence of any thing, in respect of us, is the whole complex *Idea*, comprehended and marked by that Name; and in Substances, besides the several distinct simple Ideas that make them up, the confused one of Substance, or of an unknown Support or Cause of their Union, is always a part."[21] In subsequent books of Locke's *Essay*, epistemological questions replace ontological ones almost entirely.

A generation later, Hume retains Locke's notion of objects' core unknowability but adds a characteristic gloss worth quoting at length:

> 'Tis confest by the most judicious philosophers, that our ideas of bodies are nothing but collections form'd by the mind of the ideas of the several sensible qualities, of which objects are compos'd, and which we find to have a constant union with each other. . . . This easy transition is the effect, or rather the essence of relation; and as the imagination readily takes one idea for another, where their influence on the mind is similar; hence it proceeds, that any such succession of related qualities is readily consider'd as one continu'd object, existing without any variation. The smooth and uninterrupted progress of the thought, being alike in both cases, readily deceives the mind, and makes us ascribe an identity to the changeable succession of connected qualities.[22]

Hume clearly ascribes our sense of a thing's essential coherence not to our powers of reason but to those of our imagination. In even stronger language than Locke, he condemns this activity as self-deception: we fool ourselves into thinking we perceive unified objects, whereas in reality – or at least in the only reality we can perceive – we are merely experiencing groups or bundles of "*successive* qualities," not "the same unchangeable object." For Hume, *habit* becomes the only reliable explanation for how we create unities and project causalities that exist nowhere but in our own minds.

If, as I have been suggesting, Wordsworth's Preface reflects an intellectual movement from empiricism to early psychologism adumbrated by the figures of Locke, Hume, and Hartley, then we also need to move beyond this tradition to appreciate how the poems of *Lyrical Ballads* frequently surpass this horizon. To do this, however, we must first look at the philosophical revolution instantiated by Hume's great challenger and successor. By his own account, Immanuel Kant succeeds Hume in the same manner Hume succeeded Locke: by first adopting and then altering his key assumptions. Famously awakened from his self-described "dogmatic slumber" by Hume's writings,[23] Kant responded to Humean skepticism by positing the existence of two related but separate realms of reality: the noumenal – roughly speaking, things as they truly are – and the phenomenal, or things as we perceive them. The mind, Kant makes very clear, has access only to the latter. Having thus sidestepped the question of what things "really" are, Kant also answers Hume's questioning of empiricism with his Transcendental Analytic: the deduction of shared, *a priori* apprehensions of the categories of time and space by and through which humans perceive the phenomenal world. As Kant explains in the preface to the second edition of *Critique of Pure Reason* (1787),

> Until now it was assumed that all our knowledge must conform or be adjusted toward objects. But upon this assumption all attempts to figure out *a priori* by concepts anything regarding such objects . . . were failures. Therefore let us try to see whether we can get ahead better with the tasks of metaphysics, if we assume that the objects should conform or be adjusted to our knowledge. This would harmonize better with the desired possibility of *a priori* knowledge of objects. . . . It is like the first thought of Copernicus who, when he could not get ahead with explaining the motions of the heavenly bodies as long as he assumed that the stars revolved around the observer, tried whether he might not be more successful if he let the observer revolve and allowed the stars to remain stationary.[24]

Kant knows full well that previous attempts to understand things as they are failed to provide stable, objective knowledge of reality "in itself." His ingenious solution is to determine that the problem lies not with reality but with the methodological approach traditionally used to try to apprehend it. By essentially mandating that the noumenal sphere is unknowable, Kant effectively requires that philosophers shift from investigating objects of knowledge to investigating knowledge itself. After Kant, in other words, Western philosophy will no longer ask "What are objects?" but rather "What can we say that we know about objects?"

This epistemological and therefore necessarily anthropocentric turn in philosophy has borne many varieties of intellectual fruit, from the anti-realisms of Hegel, Schopenhauer, and

Heidegger to Sartrean existentialism, Derridean deconstruction, and Foucaultian historicism.[25] Even more recently, Kant's misnamed "Copernican Revolution" has come under increased scrutiny for cordoning off all reality outside consciousness from absolute human knowledge. As I mentioned in my introduction, Meillassoux calls this philosophical mindset "correlationism": the conviction that one cannot speak or think directly about reality, only about reality *for* humans. Kant's taboo on noumenal thinking not only greatly restricted the domain of philosophy, Meillassoux argues, but also left too much room for various fundamentalisms to fill the void left by philosophy's retreat from reality; in Meillassoux's words, "by forbidding reason any claim to the absolute, the end of metaphysics has taken the form of an exacerbated return of the religious."[26]

The further ramifications of Meillassoux's critique of Kant, as well as his proofs against correlationism, will be discussed at more length in Chapter 4.[27] For now, we know enough to appreciate what Harman – the founder and chief practitioner of object-oriented philosophy – means when he declares that Western philosophy has traditionally lacked the conceptual resources to do justice to objects. Indeed, says Harman, even those "realist" philosophers who have wanted to talk about material entities have generally avoided objects themselves. On one side, ranging from ancient philosophers like Empedocles and Democritus to contemporary thinkers like Gilles Deleuze and Manuel DeLanda, realist philosophers have tended to undermine objects by treating them as illusory or temporary manifestations of some underlying and therefore more real level of existence, be it atoms or a "'heterogeneous yet continuous' plane of virtuality."[28] On the other side, philosophers have regularly dismissed objects by "reduc[ing] them upward rather than downward"; this group includes not only critical theorists like Foucault, who for all his interest in material history tends to absorb individual entities into larger schemas or forces with names like "power" and "knowledge," but also "relational" theorists like Alfred North Whitehead and Bruno Latour, for whom objects are merely the sums of their relations with other objects, and therefore have no distinct identities or even qualities in and of themselves.[29]

Objects themselves have thus traditionally been underserved by philosophy. Because the question of what constitutes an object in Harman's philosophy frequently comes up, it is worth noting from the outset his definition: "To be an object does not mean to be physical material without dignity, but simply to be a unified entity irreducible to its component pieces or to its effects on the surrounding environment."[30] Whereas Meillassoux effectively argues *through* the human–world correlate in order to arrive at a set of conditions whereby humans can think the non-human (as we will see in Chapter 4), correlationism itself holds little power for Harman. Instead, drawing extensively although not exclusively on his novel interpretations of Heidegger,[31] Harman argues that objects have at least two essential qualities, that is, two features that exist regardless of whether they are interacted with or even perceived: their "autonomous reality" can be understood "in two separate directions: emerging as something over and above their pieces, while also partly withholding themselves from relations with other entities."[32]

The ramifications of these simple-sounding characteristics are worth unpacking. First, Harman clearly rejects both the classical and empirical traditions of distinguishing between living and non-living things, since an "object" for him is anything that exists and functions as a unit. As a result, object-oriented philosophy clearly opposes Hume's insistence that objects are mere bundles of qualities. After all, an apple – one of Harman's favorite examples – can be sweet, juicy, cold, etc., while nevertheless clearly also existing as something more than simply the accumulation of its inherent (primary) or perceived (secondary) qualities. This rift between an object and its qualities, which exists at the ontological level, is a central insight of OOP. Yet Harman's approach also rejects the overmining of a thinker like Latour, whose Actor-Network-Theory tends to treat individual objects as neither more nor less than the sum of their relations, and therefore fully exhausted, qualitatively speaking, by any given interaction or situation in which they find themselves.[33] By contrast, Harman extends the implications of Heidegger's tool-analysis, in which objects are not fully present to consciousness until they stop working in their usual ways,[34] to argue that the qualities of objects are never fully deployed, much less exhausted, in the relations, transactions, or networks in which they happen to be engaged. In fact – and this point will be key to my consideration, in the following section, of the place of objects in Wordsworth's poetry – for Harman, unlike for Heidegger, objects are not only never fully exhausted in use, but also never fully apprehended in thought:

For the tool-analysis teaches us something much deeper than the emergence of conscious awareness from the prior unconscious use of things. . . . To oppose the arrogant pretensions of theory, the tool-analysis shows us that the being of an apple, hammer, dog, or star is not exhausted by its presence in consciousness. No sensual profile of these things will ever exhaust its full reality, which withdraws into the dusk of a shadowy underworld. But if something hides behind the many profiles of an apple, what hides from view is not our *use* of the apple, but rather the apple itself. After all, using a thing distorts its reality no less than making theories about it does.[35]

By "sensual," Harman means what Edmund Husserl calls the "intentional" qualities of an object: those qualities we perceive when we intentionally focus our thoughts on the object in question. Neither theory nor practice, it turns out, is sufficient to exhaust fully an object's always-multiple qualities, any more than the object in question can be reduced to the sum of its parts. "No sensual profile of these things will ever exhaust its full reality" can thus stand, for our purposes, as the motto of object-oriented philosophy – a philosophy, I will now argue, which Wordsworth's early poetry pointedly anticipates.

In his review of the first edition of *Lyrical Ballads*, Robert Southey praises what he considers its few "serious pieces" – Coleridge's "The Foster-Mother's Tale" and "The Dungeon," Wordsworth's "Lines Left Upon a Seat in a Yew-Tree" and "Lines Written a Few Miles above Tintern Abbey" – before stating that the volume as a whole is a failure, "not because the language of conversation is little adapted to 'the purposes of poetic pleasure,' but because it has been tried upon uninteresting subjects."[36] Based on his examples, Southey's disappointment seems directed primarily at Wordsworth's unconventional choice of socially marginal protagonists. The anonymous critic of the *New London Review* agreed, asserting that "Our poet seems to want nothing, but more fortunate topics than those he has, at times, unhappily selected."[37] But Wordsworth's powers of description were generally not impugned when they were applied to more conventional poetic subjects like landscapes and natural objects; the *Antijacobin Review*, for example, declared that *Lyrical Ballads* "has genius, taste, elegance, wit, and imagery of the most beautiful kind," and other publications frequently reached similar judgments.[38] If critics were more apt to praise Wordsworth's descriptions of natural objects over his choice of human subjects, this may be because they generally missed the radical implications of the former.[39] When we change our optic for viewing these poems from the social or epistemological to the ontological, however, what becomes visible is Wordsworth's commitment to representing objects – primarily naturally occurring ones – as characterized by absence and withholding at least as much as by presence and plenitude. The fit between object-oriented philosophy and Wordsworth's poetics is by no means perfect, however, and by drawing out differences between them even while focusing on the points of commonality, I hope also to demonstrate the historical and philosophical specificity of Wordsworth's Romantic vision.

The first poem by Wordsworth in *Lyrical Ballads*, "Lines Left Upon a Seat in a Yew-Tree," was written in 1795, several years before the collection came together. The poem's description of its natural setting is immediately characterized by several absences: "here/ No sparking rivulet spread the verdant herb;/ What if these barren boughs the bee not loves"?[40] Later, Wordsworth suggests that although the yew tree inscription's author may have erred by allowing "visionary views" (l. 41) to seduce him into morbid quietism, the one "whose heart the holy forms/ Of young imagination have kept pure" (ll. 44–5) will nevertheless achieve a truer sense of "the great outdoors," to use Meillassoux's phrase in its most literal sense, than "he, who feels contempt/ For any living thing" (ll. 48–9). Yet the poem offers no guarantee that reality can be accessed in an unmediated or complete way, nor does it really seek to dispel Wordsworth's suspicion that even the most ardent openness to "living things" eventually leads back to "the silent hour of inward thought" (l. 58). The poet's vocation, as Wordsworth will say explicitly in his 1800 Preface, instead requires seeking "what is really important to men,"[41] rather than displacing a human-centered perspective altogether.

Elements of a recognizably object-oriented approach are foregrounded in the series of Wordsworth poems dating from 1798 that appear next in *Lyrical Ballads*: "Lines written at a small distance from my house," "Lines written in early spring," "Expostulation and Reply," and "The Tables Turned." Whether regarded as announcements of Bloom's "visionary company," articulations of Abrams's "Romantic creed," or instantiations of what McGann labeled "the Romantic ideology," these poems (together with "Lines Written a Few Miles above Tintern Abbey," which I discuss below) have traditionally been understood to set out Wordsworth's belief in the supreme importance of establishing and maintaining harmonious relations between man and nature. More recently, however, they have been critiqued from deconstructive and New Historicist perspectives for failing to deliver or guarantee the insights and certainties they seem to promise, at least without recourse to more or less veiled acts of erasure or silencing.[42]

Like these latter critiques, an object-oriented approach finds that "nature" in these poems consistently evades the speaker's attempts to know or experience it in a full or unmediated fashion. Whereas from a post-structuralist perspective such absences or aporias have generally been read as signs of Wordsworth's failure to achieve coherence or authenticity, from an object-oriented perspective these poems become visible as evidence of the world's resistance to being fully exhausted by human (or other) agency. In "Lines written at a small distance from my house," for example, the speaker intuits a vital presence in nature – "the blessed power that rolls/ About, below, above" (ll. 33–4) – which anticipates the more extensive articulation of this quasi-pantheism in "Tintern Abbey." Earlier in "Lines," however, when he tries to describe this power in more concrete terms, Wordsworth can only assert that "There is a blessing in the air,/ Which seems a sense of joy to yield" (ll. 4–5). The speculative quality of this assertion should not be overlooked, especially as it reappears in similar statements later in the collection. Of the birds to whose songs he listens in "Lines written in early spring," for example, Wordsworth admits that "Their thoughts I cannot measure," and when they hop about, he can only speculate that "the least motion which they made/ ... seem'd a thrill of pleasure" to them (ll. 13–16). The same attitude informs his halting understanding of the mysterious relations between the "budding twigs" and the "breezy air": "And I must think, do all I can,/ That there was pleasure there" (ll. 19–20).

Such conditional or conjectural statements need not be read as fatal admissions of doubt regarding Wordsworth's Romantic creed, as post-structuralist critics have generally concluded.[43] Instead, from an object-oriented perspective, they indicate Wordsworth's recognition that the world's depths can never be entirely sounded. Indeed, not only do humans never exhaust the other entities with which we engage, but also objects themselves consistently fail to exhaust each other's reserves. When the twigs of "Lines written in early spring" "spread out their fan/ To catch the breezy air" (ll. 17–18), for instance, they "touch" some of the breeze's qualities – its velocity, temperature, and of course its carbon dioxide content – but not, presumably, other qualities like its scent. By contrast, Wordsworth himself seems aware of this last quality, as suggested by the previous stanza's description of "that sweet bower" (l. 9); but since the breeze seems weak at best, it is unlikely that the speaker is literally moved by it. "Lines written in early spring" not only represents the way all objects withdraw from human knowledge, but also captures the way objects withdraw from each other too.[44]

Similar veins run through both "Expostulation and Reply" and "The Tables Turned." In the former, Wordsworth is chastised by a friend for wasting time sitting outside rather than studying. In solemn yet dynamic lines, the poet justifies his (in)action:

Nor less I deem that there are powers,
Which of themselves our minds impress,
That we can feed this mind of ours,
In a wise passiveness.
Think you, mid all this mighty sum
Of things for ever speaking,
That nothing of itself will come,
But we must still be seeking? (ll. 21–8)

This passage does not move strictly along the lines Harman wants philosophy to follow – toward "pursu[ing] a model of . . . things as autonomous objects, not just as humanly accessible objects"[45] – since Wordsworth frankly views the natural world's "powers" as meaningful primarily insofar as they "feed" human minds. Nevertheless, the agency attributed here to things in themselves is remarkable: *they* approach and communicate with humans, whose primary role is to be open and receptive to them. As Wordsworth famously concludes in "The Tables Turned," neither human science nor art is needed to receive such natural transmissions: "Close up these barren leaves;/ Come forth, and bring with you a heart/ That watches and receives" (ll. 29–32). This "reception model" of human agency – also explored by Coleridge in poems like "The Eolian Harp" and "This Lime-Tree Bower my Prison" from the mid-1790s, albeit with less happy results for the poet, as

I will discuss in the next chapter – is remarkably congruent with object-oriented philosophy's basic project of displacing human activity from the center of our accounts of the world.

This inclination reaches its pinnacle in the poem Wordsworth appended at the last minute to the end of *Lyrical Ballads*: "Lines Written a Few Miles above Tintern Abbey." This poem has long been recognized as the zenith of Wordsworth's early poetic efforts in terms of both form and content; Abrams finds it the most successful example of what he influentially terms "the greater Romantic lyric," arguing that it anticipates Wordsworth's auto-biographical masterpiece, *The Prelude*, "both in overall design and local tactics."[46] From its loco-descriptive beginning through its doubled-consciousness structure, in which the poet meditates on the gap between his memories of the landscape around the River Wye from five years earlier and his current relationship with it, and into its concluding statements, the poem achieves a sense of completion unmatched by Wordsworth's other *Lyrical Ballads* pieces. As Frances Ferguson suggests, even those New Historical readings of the poem that purport to demystify its transcendent musings and expose its reactionary politics ultimately confirm the poem's power insofar as they testify to "the poet's molding of the scene."[47]

What is truly remarkable about "Tintern Abbey," moreover, is that instead of trying to cover up his active shaping of the landscape, Wordsworth regularly draws attention to it. Although the poem initially subscribes to an associationist logic in which "these steep and lofty cliffs . . . impress/ Thoughts of a more deep seclusion" (ll. 10–12), it rapidly accumulates statements that openly admit the limits of human comprehension, associationist or otherwise. With phrases like "If this be but a vain belief" (ll. 50–1), "With many recognitions dim and faint,/ And somewhat of a sad perplexity" (ll. 61–2), and "other gifts/ Have followed, for such loss, I would believe/ Abundant recompense" (ll. 87–9), Wordsworth explicitly allows that his Romantic ability to "see into the life of things" (l. 50) is at best sporadic and partial, at worst entirely illusory. Even when "the weary weight/ Of all this unintelligible world" is momentarily lifted (ll. 40–1), Wordsworth recognizes the fleetingness of these epiphanic visions by repeatedly calling them "mood[s]" (ll. 38, 42), that is, momentary states of mind that by definition do not last.[48]

A second attempt to articulate such a mood yields what is

probably the poem's most famous passage, in which Wordsworth registers and records

> A presence that disturbs me with the joy
> Of elevated thoughts; a sense sublime
> Of something far more deeply interfused . . .
> A motion and a spirit, that impels
> All thinking things, all objects of all thoughts,
> And rolls through all things. (ll. 95–7, 101–2)

Here, the hesitations and qualifications of earlier passages drop away and we are presented with a sublime vision of holistic illumination. Even as these lines movingly express Wordsworth's sense of the interconnectedness of everything, however, they notably display both of the philosophical bad habits identified by Harman: they overmine objects by sublating them into "a sense sublime" that rises above earthly phenomena, and – thanks to the language of eighteenth-century vitalism – they undermine the autonomy of objects by reducing everything to a basic common substance.[49] Although the above passage is clearly the poem's philosophical climax, then, Wordsworth more closely approaches an object-oriented perspective elsewhere. In the poem's middle stanzas of boyhood recollection that lead up to the above passage, for example, we are treated to a litany of natural objects which Wordsworth remembers interacting freely with and immersing himself in at that time: "The sounding cataract . . ./ . . . the tall rock,/ The mountain, and the deep and gloomy wood" (ll. 77–9). But just as he admits that his boyish immersion in nature did not entirely engage with all of its qualities (since his intellectual and spiritual appreciations were not yet fully developed), so he admits that his new, more mature relationship to nature involves the necessary "loss" (l. 88) of that earlier, animal-like relation. The poem thus bears witness to the truth of Harman's insight that neither practice (i.e., youthful Wordsworth) nor theory (i.e., mature Wordsworth) exhausts an object.

If an object-oriented perspective helps clarify the stakes of Wordsworth's hesitations and qualifications in "Tintern Abbey," by allowing us to see them as admissions of the world's unknowable plenitude rather than of the mind's inherent limitations, then it can also help us re-read the poem's ending. The final stanza of "Tintern Abbey," in which Wordsworth addresses his sister

Dorothy, has long disappointed critics. In Tillotama Rajan's influential deconstructive reading, the turn to Dorothy – whose presence has gone unmentioned up to this point – represents a tacit admission of failure or at least insecurity on Wordsworth's part regarding his ability to incarnate his Romantic convictions through language alone. Although he addresses and then blesses her, Rajan argues that Dorothy actually undermines the poet's claim to see into the life of things, since her supplementary presence disrupts his attempt to bring word, image, and thing into alignment: "There is a recognition . . . that Dorothy is not really a naïve being, and that for her too the physical presence of the landscape will be displaced by its imaginary representation, as the past which has been recovered in the future is again lost in the past."[50] Likewise, although Ferguson finds the turn to Dorothy less artificial than Rajan, she is equally concerned that it indexes the poem's failure, understood by Ferguson as an inability to force nature to confirm the poet's self-sufficient subjectivity without the supplement of Dorothy's presence.[51]

But what if this failure is not in fact supplementary to the poem's project? From an object-oriented perspective, the apparent necessity of Dorothy's sudden, clinching appearance in the poem is not a sign of fatal doubt, but rather a final recognition that no amount of description can ever do full justice to an object's necessarily hidden or withdrawn depths. In this way, the turn to Dorothy simply confirms that no object can ever be fully represented in, much less assimilated to, a human-centered perspective because, as Harman pithily puts it, *"reality itself is not a content."*[52] Necessarily unable to plumb nature's depths as thoroughly as he would like, Wordsworth essentially has little choice but to turn to another person – here, the sister whom he positions as a younger version of himself – to seek confirmation of his vision of "the life of things." What Mary Jacobus calls the "doubled ending" of "Tintern Abbey" thus represents neither the failure of Wordsworth's creed nor the dogmatism of so-called Romantic ideology, but rather an acknowledgment of the more general predicament that Harman calls the *"untranslatability"* of being: the fact that "reality is too real to be translated without remainder into any sentence, perception, practical action, or anything else."[53] Dorothy, for better or worse, is that remainder in the poem's logic.[54]

By arguing that "Tintern Abbey," along with several of

Wordsworth's other contributions to the original edition of *Lyrical Ballads*, anticipates a number of object-oriented philosophy's basic principles and insights, I do not mean to claim for it some sort of prophetic power. Margaret Koehler has recently pointed out, for example, that versions of the poem's famous image of being "laid asleep/ In body, and become a living soul" (ll. 46–7) already appear in a number of Restoration and early eighteenth-century "odes of absorption."[55] Furthermore, as I discussed earlier, Wordsworth's early views on epistemology and ontology are deeply enmeshed in the developing philosophical trajectory that saw Lockean empiricism engender Humean skepticism, Hartleian associationism, and Kantianism. If, as Harman argues, the Kantian (counter-)revolution has run its course, then Wordsworth's early poetry and prose become newly visible as precursors to object-oriented philosophy, not because they are untimely, but precisely because of their historical situatedness just prior to the hegemony of Kantian dualism.

After his contributions to the first edition of *Lyrical Ballads*, Wordsworth began a slow but steady turn toward more traditionally anthropocentric negotiations with things and objects. Many of the poems added to the expanded, 1800 edition already display a Kantian-style turn toward nature as significant primarily insofar as humans have access to it. (Harman's term for philosophical methodologies that rely on versions of the human–world correlate is, precisely, "philosophies of access.") How much of this turn can be ascribed to Wordsworth's explicit desire to make the second edition of *Lyrical Ballads* more accessible to general readers and less vulnerable to critical censure, and how much to conscious philosophical decision-making, is of course a matter of speculation (pun intended).[56]

Consider "Nutting," one of the most haunting and powerfully compressed poems of the second volume of the expanded *Lyrical Ballads*. In it, Wordsworth remembers a boyhood ramble in the countryside, in the course of which he discovers a seemingly untouched glade:

> Among the woods,
> And o'er the pathless rocks, I forc'd my way
> Until, at length, I came to one dear nook
> Unvisited, where not a broken bough
> Droop'd with its wither'd leaves, ungracious sign

Of devastation, but the hazels rose
Tall and erect, with milk-white clusters hung,
A virgin scene! (ll. 12–19)

Given the highly sexualized tone of its evocative descriptions, modern interpretations of this poem generally veer toward the psychoanalytic. Although the plant life is granted a certain amount of agency – the hazels "rose," the clusters "hung" – it is rendered for the most part as passive; hence, its feminine vulnerability to defilement. Slightly later, Wordsworth remembers that his boyhood self eventually became impatient with the locale's passivity. The only warning we get before he seemingly spontaneously ruins the scene by destroying the vegetation all around him is the oddly pejorative terms (recognizable as such only in retrospect, after the damage has literally been done) of his last description of its peacefulness: the "dear nook" put him

In that sweet mood when pleasure loves to pay
Tribute to ease, and, of its joy secure
The heart luxuriates with indifferent things,
Wasting its kindliness on stocks and stones,
And on the vacant air. (ll. 37–41)

Here, things – the objects of the world, outside the chains of human significance – are characterized as "indifferent," or unfeeling and insensible. As a result, it is a "waste" to direct emotional energy toward them, and Meillassoux's great outdoors seems merely "vacant," composed of lack or absence. Typically, literary critics have interpreted this as a kind of tragic foreshadowing of the bower's subsequent desecration. But upon re-reading the first passage cited above, we can see that even in its "virginal" state the bower is described as merely awaiting human presence. Even as Wordsworth seems to intend to celebrate its freedom from human interference, his negative constructions – the nook was "unvisited," its boughs were "not ... broken" – suggest a fatal complicity between nature (understood in its colloquial sense as the "opposite" of culture) and humanity. Viewed through an object-oriented lens, Wordsworth's choice of terms suggests a shift from ontology to epistemology, in which "the great outdoors" only or least primarily has meaning and importance insofar as it means something to humans.

The more objects in Wordsworth's poems are treated metaphor-ically, the more they fall prey to what the Victorian critic John Ruskin famously called "the pathetic fallacy," in which objects are anthropomorphized and especially granted emotional states and intentions that in fact reflect the speaker's ideas rather than their own. Of course, this has long been a staple of poetic diction; con-trary to popular belief, Ruskin did not condemn it universally,[57] nor did T. S. Eliot when he coined a similar phrase, "objective cor-relative," to describe the roles objects and things often play in lit-erature as reflections of the speaker's cast of mind. From an OOP perspective, however, such frameworks are problematic when they come to seem naturalized, that is, when the meaningfulness of objects or things *for humans* becomes the primary or even sole way to understand or value them. This certainly appears as the pre-dominant mode of Wordsworth's contributions to the expanded, 1800 edition of *Lyrical Ballads*, which contains a second volume of poems written entirely by Wordsworth. Of the new additions beyond "Nutting," "The Waterfall and the Eglantine" and "The Oak and the Broom, A Pastoral" anthropomorphize their titular natural objects to such a degree that they address each other in didactic, rhymed verse. Even many of the more subtle poems of the second volume, like "There was a Boy," decline to unsettle anthro-pocentrism. Although most of this short poem carefully describes Lake Windermere and its environs, its concluding revelation that the title character "died when he was ten years old" retroactively recodes the preceding natural descriptions as primarily objective correlatives for the pathos of human mortality (l. 32). As Timothy Morton – whose contributions to OOP will be introduced later in this chapter – puts it, with reference to the title character's fond-ness for making bird calls resound across the lake: "The whole poem becomes an 'echo' of the boy."[58]

To be fair, Wordsworth makes some similar gestures in his original *Lyrical Ballads* poems; in particular, one of the hall-marks of the first edition, "The Thorn," repeatedly uses its titular plant as both burial marker and symbol ("not higher than a two years' child" [l. 5]) of the dead infant whose mother's suffering forms the ballad's burden. But what is frequently missing from the second edition's new poems is the profound sense, present in many of Wordsworth's original *Lyrical Ballads* entries, that some "essence" of the world's things necessarily withdraws and remains veiled, hidden, or inaccessible to interaction, human or otherwise.

What is mostly lost in these later poems, one might say, is what Harman (adapting Žižek's phrase) calls "the inherent stupidity of all content": the OOP sense that, no matter how hard one tries, one can never entirely "translate" reality into meaningful content.[59] Ironically, if Wordsworth's contributions to the later editions of *Lyrical Ballads* have generally proven less memorable than their earlier counterparts, this may be because in trying to become a better poet, Wordsworth tries to make everything in nature meaningful – at the cost of obscuring its real strangeness. Occasionally, Wordsworth himself seems aware of this problem. "The Brothers," one of the most substantial additions to the collection's second edition, describes the experience of Leonard, a shepherd who has returned home after many years at sea, as he gazes around the scenery of his native Lake District for the first time in decades:

> he lifted up his eyes,
> And looking round he thought that he perceiv'd
> Strange alteration wrought on every side
> Among the woods and fields, and that the rocks,
> And the eternal hills, themselves were chang'd. (ll. 92–6)

In these lines, Wordsworth draws attention to the subject-centered nature of the account he is giving; if the woods and hills appear differently to Leonard now than when he last viewed them, years ago, this "strange alteration" is clearly due to Leonard's changed mental state, not to any changes in the "eternal" features of the landscape itself. This kind of insight, it's fair to say, anticipates not OOP but rather one of its partial forerunners, phenomenology. It fits nicely, for example, with Merleau-Ponty's definition of objects as "complexes": "The things of the world are not simply neutral *objects* which stand before us for our contemplation. Each one of them symbolises or recalls a particular way of behaving, provoking in us reactions which are either favourable or unfavourable."[60] But if we are looking to Wordsworth for his poetic affiliations with OOP's sense of the unaccountable, literally inhuman "strangeness" of the world's objects – a world in which, as Harman puts it, "objects themselves . . . are already aflame with ambiguity, torn by vibrations and insurgencies equaling those found in the most tortured human moods"[61] – then we will not find it here, nor in much of his poetry after the 1798 *Lyrical Ballads*.

Instead, Wordsworth's tendency to correlate things to their human significances generally increases in his later poems. Let us consider for a moment one of his most iconic sonnets, written in 1802–4 and published in his 1807 *Poems in Two Volumes*. In "The world is too much with us," Wordsworth condemns the increasing commercialization of human society and with it the loss of our sympathetic connection to the natural world:

> The world is too much with us; late and soon,
> Getting and spending, we lay waste our powers:
> Little we see in Nature that is ours;
> We have given away our hearts, a sordid boon!
> This Sea that bares her bosom to the moon;
> The winds that will be howling at all hours,
> And are up-gathered now like sleeping flowers;
> For this, for everything, we are out of tune;
> It moves us not. – Great God! I'd rather be
> A Pagan suckled in a creed outworn;
> So might I, standing on this pleasant lea,
> Have glimpses that would make me less forlorn;
> Have sight of Proteus rising from the sea;
> Or hear old Triton blow his wreathèd horn. (ll. 1–14)

The poem begins with an implicit dichotomy that is central to Wordsworth's Romantic creed: the identification of a gap between "the world," which is "too much with us," and "Nature," with which we have lost contact as a result. According to the terms of this distinction, "world" corresponds to commercial society, the realm of "late and soon, / Getting and spending"; nature, by contrast, is the non-human space outside or beyond society. We once had access to this "outside" realm, but we have "given away our hearts" to commercial modernity, and thus "waste[d] our powers" of perception and sensation. Lines 5–7 describe this realm in more detail, and here for a moment at least we seem to enter Harman's world of objects engaged in multifarious, mind-independent relations with one another. They are necessarily "translated" into human terms as Wordsworth represents them, of course: the sea "bares" herself to the moon in terms that both personify and eroticize it, the sound of the wind is represented as a mournful or angry "howling," and so on. (The explicit simile "like sleeping flowers" draws attention to the poetic valence of these lines.) Near the octave's end, however, Wordsworth essentially makes the same move that occurs near the end of "There was a boy," as he suddenly reveals that the preceding descriptions of so-called "Nature" are in fact directed almost entirely toward a human audience, however imperceptive we have become: "For this, for everything, we are out of tune;/ It moves us not." This is not totally dogmatic correlationism, since Wordsworth does not claim that if were we to lose entirely our powers of perceiving or appreciating the natural world, it would effectively cease to exist; but he comes uncomfortably close.

This closeness is confirmed in the poem's adapted sestet, which begins after the caesura in line 9 with the sudden epithet "Great God!" Wordsworth's subsequent use of classical allusions signals his abandonment of the possibility of recovering something like "the great outdoors" in any form untouched by human culture and commerce; the closest he can get is to fantasize about a return to a vital, pagan, but still recognizably *human* version of nature, its forces anthropomorphized into classical gods of the ocean. (Some seventy years later, Nietzsche would fantasize about a similar liberation from modernity's constraints in the form of the Greek mythical imagination.)[62] In fact, the language of commerce has threatened to corrupt this fantasy from the sonnet's start, since the diction of Wordsworth's early assertion, "Little we see in Nature that is ours," embraces both possessive and identificatory connotations. The poem assumes from its inception, in other words, that we should be able to find in the natural world something "that is ours," that belongs to us, if not as our actual property then as a reflection of our supposed human qualities.

Interestingly, although nothing could appear farther from the intent of Harman's OOP, this position echoes a claim made by some of OOP's critics. They assert that in purporting to identify the characteristics all objects share in common – and here I should note that I have restricted my discussion primarily to their tendency toward "withdrawal," whereas in fact Harman identifies a fourfold set of shared characteristics[63] – OOP makes the mistake of projecting human qualities onto the rest of the world's entities, thus participating in an extreme version of the anthropocentrism it claims to resist. What these critics misunderstand, however, is that OOP does not extend the "humanness" of humans to objects; rather, it expands the "objectness" of objects to include humans as well. OOP is thus guilty at most of "panpsychism" – a charge the force of which Harman has acknowledged, and which not coincidentally dogged Wordsworth too – to the extent that it redefines perception simply as the ability to engage in relations with other things, and as something all objects possess to a greater or lesser degree.[64] To quote Morton's succinct synopsis of this important perspectival adjustment, "What we call subjectivity is just a causal event that 'happens to us' ... Consciousness just is what I shall shortly describe as *interobjectivity*, the configuration space of relatedness."[65] What some of OOP's critics have called epistemological hubris is, from Harman's and Morton's perspective, simply ontological humility.

By contrast, Wordsworth's poetry grants an increasingly privileged place to specifically human consciousness. This is not to condemn Wordsworth for trying and failing to anticipate OOP, but to recognize how difficult it is even for a genuinely committed "worshipper of Nature" (as Wordsworth calls himself in "Tintern Abbey," [line 153]) like Wordsworth to think "the great outdoors" without eventually inevitably thinking the great outdoors *for us*. To see how the consequences of this slippage bear ethical and ecocritical as well as philosophical weight, I want now to consider some of Wordsworth's post-1798 poetry while extending the discussion of OOP to include Timothy Morton's specific contributions. Prior to the emergence of Harman's philosophy, Morton had already established himself as an influential scholar of British Romanticism, publishing on a wide variety of subjects including the roles and representations of taste, food, medicine, and spices in the period's literature and culture.[66] When he turned his attention fully to ecological questions, Romanticism continued to play a large role in Morton's thinking. In fact, critics have been tracking what Lawrence Buell calls "the environmental imagination" back to the Romantic era for some time now.[67] Morton's most important contribution to this critical tradition, however, has been to indicate the ways in which environmental writing, including that of the Romantics, has been all-too-frequently caught in a double-bind of its own making. The first of Morton's two ecologically minded studies of the later 2000s, *Ecology without Nature: Rethinking Environmental Aesthetics* (2007), investigates how environmental writers and ecocritics from the Romantic era forward have tried to create a sense of aesthetic immediacy in their nature writings only to end up routinely positing "nature" as something "over there," separate from the daily business of human life. Environmental thinking, in other words, has too frequently been guilty of precisely the kind of anthropocentrism it supposedly seeks to remedy. His follow-up, *The Ecological Thought* (2010), continued to lay the groundwork for a radically different kind of ecological thinking, one that decenters humans and human consciousness from our picture of "the worldness of the world."[68]

Clearly, Morton's work overlapped with some of the key interests and concerns of OOP even before he began to take up Harman's specific ideas. Subsequently, OOP has provided Morton with a language and a philosophical framework to continue his investigations into ecology, aesthetics, and causality. In order to appreciate what Morton has in turn brought to OOP in his most recent publications, however, we need first to return to Harman, and specifically the development of his theories regarding how objects interact with each other. As I discussed earlier, for Harman an object is always minimally different from its qualities; otherwise, we would not be able to perceive a unified object that exists in excess of its superficial (and always potentially changing) attributes and appearances. But what happens when two objects come into contact with each other? Early in his theorization of OOP, Harman formulated the concept of "vicarious causation," his term for the idea that two "real" objects – that is, objects that have physical existence and endure for a time, regardless of the degree to which they are being perceived or interacted with at any given moment – only ever meet through the mediation of a third. (This was in contrast to how "sensual" objects – his adaptation of the "intentional" objects of perception theorized by Husserl – are always interacting, since they "exist side by side in the same perceptual space from the outset . . .")[69] More recently, Harman has nuanced this position, explaining that since every relation involves a translation of qualities (with some aspect or element of the "real" objects necessarily "withdrawing" from full view or engagement), a real object only ever encounters a sensual object, which is to say that version or profile of the other object with which it is interacting. (Harman calls this relation "involvement.")[70] When I encounter a tree, for example, the "sensual" tree that I am interacting with has certain sensual qualities to me and certain real qualities independent of my consciousness; I am not encountering the "real" tree *tout court*. At the same time, the tree encounters a version of me based on what it can perceive of my sensual qualities – but as Harman notes, "this must occur as part of a different relation, not as the reverse side of the same one."[71]

With this deeper (although by no means complete) description of OOP's model of objects, their qualities, and their relations, we can get closer to seeing how such relations lend themselves to a renovated understanding of aesthetics. There is, however, one more important element to add. Since Kant, the realm of aesthetics – like everything else – has been limited to the study of how humans perceive the world; aesthetic judgment, for Kant, "denotes nothing in the object, but is a feeling which the subject has by itself and in the manner in which it is affected by the image."[72] But from an OOP perspective, the subject–object divide itself is a false representation of the world; what we (following Kant) privilege as "thinking" or more generally as "consciousness" is just another way of interacting with other objects in the world – an important difference of degree, to be sure, but not of kind altogether. As Harman put it plainly in a recent talk, OOP reconceives the world as "a flat or democratic ontology in which the human–world relation exists on the same plane as the relations between thing and thing."[73] Thus OOP effectively tears down the calcified divide between subject and object, and once it is gone there is no longer any reason to restrict aesthetics to merely human interactions. Instead, as Morton observes in his first explicitly OOP study, *Realist Magic: Objects, Ontology, Causality* (2013), it becomes possible to say that "*the aesthetic dimension is the causal dimension.*"[74] Every time one object interacts with another, their interaction takes place in the "zone" that Morton encourages us to understand as aesthetic: "If things are intrinsically withdrawn, irreducible to their perception or relation or uses, they can only affect each other in a strange region out in front of them, a region of traces and footprints: the aesthetic dimension."[75] Aesthetics, Morton concludes, *is* causality – not the Humean model of causality in which billiard balls strike each other unproblematically, but a "weirder" model in which "an object affects another object by translating it, as best it can, into its own terms. A plane gouges a plane-shaped hole in a skyscraper."[76]

Let us consider how some of these ideas play out in one of Wordsworth's most compelling poetic series, which (perhaps not coincidentally) represents something of an exception to the increasing correlationism of his post-1798 work: the so-called "Lucy poems." Critics have long been fascinated by this group of short lyric poems, some of which were included in the 1800 edition of *Lyrical Ballads*, which describe the speaker's relation to a mysterious young woman. In the first poem, "Strange fits of passion I have known," the speaker travels toward Lucy's cottage and worries that he may find her dead; in subsequent poems – "Song" ("She dwelt among th'untrodden ways"), "A slumber did my spirit seal," "Lucy Gray," and "Three years she grew in sun and shower' – he mourns her untimely passing. By and large, critics have focused on the seemingly autobiographical questions raised by these poems. Was there a real Lucy Gray, and if so were she and Wordsworth lovers? Is Lucy a stand-in for Wordsworth's beloved sister, Dorothy? Or is she entirely imaginary? Such conjecture has been largely fruitless.[77] Nevertheless, some years ago Frances Ferguson observed that the Lucy poems demonstrate an almost palpable anxiety regarding whether language can ever adequately signify what it points toward: "heaping poem after poem on one mysterious object . . . the Lucy poems make quiet mockery of ideas of poetic representation which involve an imitation of reality . . . a radical ambiguity of the status of the object of poetic representation underlies these lyrics on the most basic level."[78] As Ferguson and other critics frequently note, Lucy herself – the object of the speaker's affections and interest – is absent from every poem nominally about her; at best, she exists only in the past, as a series of memories that the speaker struggles to reassemble into a coherent whole. Instead of only seeing the fact of Lucy's absence as evidence of the elusive and anti-representational nature of language, however, OOP helps us read it also as a commentary on the elusive nature of reality itself. The fact that Lucy never appears directly in any of the poems about her corroborates Harman's insight that if language fails to capture the "essence" of reality, this is not (only) because language is imperfect, but also because reality is not a content, that is, not something that can ever be perfectly captured or exhausted. In this case, neither thinking about Lucy nor attempting to interact with her "exhausts" her as an autonomous entity.[79]

The Lucy poems do more, however, than merely reiterate the recognition in "Tintern Abbey" of the withdrawal of objects; they also ponder the ramifications of overcoming the subject–object divide on which conventional, Kantian-style philosophies of access depend. "Strange fits of passion" establishes a conventional ontology in which perceiving consciousnesses – the speaker's and Lucy's

– are prioritized: references to the speaker appear in three out of the first four lines, and the poem reinforces this anthropocentrism by highlighting Lucy's vitality in the second quatrain:

When she I lov'd, was strong and gay
And like a rose in June,
I to her cottage bent my way,
Beneath the evening moon. (ll. 5–8)

As both the set-up for a successful courtship and as the basis for a traditionally human-centered lyric sequence, this is a highly traditional opening; the speaker's initial comparison of a woman to a natural object ("like a rose in June") is a particularly well-worn poetic convention. But as the poem unfolds, the second appearance of a "natural" entity – the "evening moon" that lights the speaker's way – takes on unexpected importance. The speaker observes it again immediately at the start of the third stanza – "Upon the moon I fix'd my eye" (l. 9) – after which it appears, seemingly inevitably, in each subsequent stanza. Indeed, the moon soon exerts a nearly supernatural "pull" on the speaker's attention:

. . . as we climbed the hill,
Towards the roof of Lucy's cot
The moon descended still.

. . . And all the while, my eyes I kept
On the descending moon.

. . . When down behind the cottage roof
At once the planet dropp'd. (ll. 14–16, 19–20, 23–4)

This is immediately followed by a final stanza of morbid intensity:

What fond and wayward thoughts will slide
Into a Lover's head –
"O mercy!" to myself I cried,
"If Lucy should be dead!" (ll. 25–8)

The apparent *non sequitur* of the last two lines has long been noted by critics; although the mood of the previous stanzas becomes increasingly melancholy and even foreboding, thanks in part to the atmospheric effects of the moonlight, there is still no explicit causal link between the moon disappearing behind the roof of Lucy's cottage and the speaker's sudden, prophetic worry that she is no longer alive. It is clearly *not* an example of what Morton caricatures as "clunk causality": the overly simplistic, linear model of causality, predicated on Hume's billiard balls, which passes for common sense. From an OOP perspective, however, the relation between the moon's apparent "descent" and the speaker's premonition of Lucy's death can be viewed as causal precisely to the degree that it is aesthetic. As Morton explains, because OOP comprehends that objects never fully touch each other, except perhaps in cases of the destruction of one object by another, it becomes possible to appreciate how "action at a distance happens all the time if causation is aesthetic."[80] The gap or silence between the penultimate and final stanzas of "Strange fits of passion" thus implicitly represents the ever-present, minimal gap or space between objects in which causality resides.

In the subsequent "Song," the speaker's description of "A Maid whom there were none to praise" – later identified as Lucy – turns entirely on natural analogies. In the second stanza, for example, the speaker explains that she was like

A Violet by a mossy stone
Half-hidden from the Eye!
– Fair, as a star when only one
Is shining in the sky! (ll. 5–8)

Having underscored that the only fit comparisons for Lucy are to natural phenomena, this short poem suddenly ends:

She *liv'd* unknown, and few could know
   When Lucy ceas'd to be;
But she is in her Grave, and Oh!
   The difference to me. (ll. 9–12)

Critics have understandably focused on the final line, often reading it as symptomatic of Wordsworth's egotism and self-absorption: Lucy is dead, but the speaker only feels sorry for himself. But this misses the crucial point that Lucy is not in fact dead, at least not in the conventional sense. Like an object that has been thoroughly "touched" by another, she has simply "ceas'd to be" what she once was. From an anthropocentric, correlationist perspective, Lucy is of course dead; she is, after all, "in her Grave." But as the next poem in the sequence makes clear, being in the grave extinguishes only one's human consciousness, not one's earthly existence.

To indicate the difference in perspective between these alternatives, here is the entirety of "A slumber did my spirit seal":

A slumber did my spirit seal,
   I had no human fears:
She seem'd a thing that could not feel
   The touch of earthly years.

No motion has she now, no force
   She neither hears nor sees
Roll'd round in earth's diurnal course
   With rocks and stones and trees!

As Marc Redfield has demonstrated, this poem has held a special fascination for critics and theorists, making it "an iconic display text for twentieth-century literary-theoretical debates" from E. D. Hirsch's "Objective Interpretation" through Steve Knapp and Walter Benn Michaels' polemical "Against Theory."[81] One reason for this is that, thanks to its tightly packed rhyme scheme, the poem embodies formally what it also represents rhetorically: the speaker's sudden realization of Lucy's mortality. To the speaker, Lucy's existence originally appeared ("seem'd") immortal or unearthly, but as her passing shows, she was always mortal and it was simply the speaker's naivety or perhaps infatuation that prevented him from recognizing this. But Wordsworth's peculiarly plangent wording at the poem's end suggests that the speaker's traumatic admission of Lucy's mortality coincides with a strange recognition that her newfound earthliness is so literal that she has become effectively immortal. Focusing on Wordsworth's unusual adjective "diurnal" in the poem's penultimate line, Mary Jacobus observes that "The ancientness of the earth and the still, sad music of humanity come together in the word 'duration,' which means not only 'lasting' but 'hardening': Latin *durare* (to endure, to last) and *indurare* (to harden), from *durus* (hard)."[82] What Jacobus calls the "[i]deas of nonhuman time and endurance" implied by "earth's diurnal course" apply to Lucy when she becomes purely object-like in death, and thereby – ironically – of much greater endurance than she ever was in life.[83] Here we might also note that the speaker's "sealed spirit" in the poem's first stanza anticipates Lucy's corpse "roll'd round" in the second stanza: their mirroring becomes yet another way in which the poem, like OOP, challenges our assumptions about the primacy of consciousness to existence, and thus undercuts the hegemony of correlationism.

Whereas our usual anthropocentrism would dictate that the speaker mourn for Lucy's death, it may be his buried (pun intended) recognition that Lucy can only truly endure in death that explains the second stanza's oddly enthusiastic tone. After all, although Lucy now "neither sees nor hears," she clearly still exists and has effects, both on the soil around her and on the speaker's memories and emotions – and, by extension, on the reader's as well. In this weirdly happy mourning for Lucy's death and subsequent "rebirth" in the earth itself, I want to suggest that we find a version of what Morton calls "dark ecology." Where a conventional lyric would mourn the death of the speaker's loved one and perhaps imagine her spiritual transcendence in some neo-Platonic afterlife, the speaker in "Strange fits of passion" seems to celebrate Lucy's absorption or encryption into a planetary crust that simultaneously removes her from human access and delivers her to a more-than-human state of earthly suspension. Likewise, Morton encourages conceptual and behavioral movement beyond conventional forms of environmental thought and action, which typically endorse a positive vision of human–nature alliances while leaving intact the implicitly anthropocentric and ultimately destructive division between nature/objects "over there" and humans/subjects "over here." Morton's "dark ecology" thinks interconnectedness differently: "Dark ecology undermines the naturalness of the stories we tell about how we are involved in nature. It preserves the dark, depressive quality of life in the shadow of ecological catastrophe."[84] Lucy's transformation/return to the earth in "Strange fits of passion" thereby not only undermines or throws into doubt our inherited subject–object and human–nature oppositions, in the process disclosing OOP's insights regarding the shared qualities of all things, but also anticipates Morton's understanding of "dark ecology" as melancholic and uncomfortable. As Wordsworth imaginatively, speculatively enters into Lucy's literally post-human existence – an existence that is no less real for no longer possessing consciousness, at least as understood anthropocentrically – he arguably realizes the truth of Morton's insight that, to embrace a properly melancholic vision of the interconnectedness of things, we must recognize that "The ecological thought is intimacy with the strangeness of the stranger."[85]

Morton, of course, is no stranger to Wordsworth's poetry; references to Wordsworth pop up throughout his ecocritical and OOP-related texts, and the poet plays an especially important role in *Ecology without Nature*, where his writings are frequently used to illustrate what Morton calls the "overdetermined" quality of the Romantic legacy with regard to environmentalism: the Romantics in general, and Wordsworth in particular, have been marshaled to support eco-movements ranging from the holistic to the pragmatic, the spiritual to the instrumental. Morton identifies this as "a sure sign that we are in the warped space of ideology,"[86] and he is surely right. At the same time, a certain degree of ambivalence is undeniably embedded in much of Wordsworth's most powerful poetry. We have seen this already in "Tintern Abbey," which falls back into correlationism after moving extraordinarily close to an OOP-like position in its middle stanzas; we see it again in the final two "Lucy" poems, "Lucy Gray," and "Three years she grew in sun and shower," which repeat many of the same images and analogies of the poems discussed above, but in a more openly anthropomorphic mode. (Thus, for example, "Nature" itself narrates its decision to "take" Lucy and "make/ A Lady of my own" in the latter.)[87] When Morton observes that "At his most visionary, William Wordsworth loses his vision," he is thinking in particular of some of the famous "spots of time" in Wordsworth's autobiographical epic, *The Prelude*, in which the poet literally loses awareness of his surroundings. In what remains of this chapter, however, I want to suggest that Morton's observation functions on the figurative level as well: at key moments of *The Prelude*, Wordsworth's vision fails him insofar as his latent anthropocentrism mitigates against his OOP-like ability to "see into the life of things." This is especially true, moreover, when the "things" in question are what Morton importantly identifies as "hyperobjects."

What are hyperobjects? According to Morton in his book *Hyperobjects: Philosophy and Ecology after the End of the World* (2013), this "refer[s] to things that are massively distributed in time and space relative to humans."[88] Building on Harman's conceptualization of objects, Morton proposes that hyperobjects exhibit properties that make them unusually difficult to apprehend, at least from a human perspective: viscosity (hyperobjects like radiation tend to "stick" to humans and other objects), non-locality (hyper-objects like global warming do not manifest themselves entirely in any one space or point), and phasing (hyperobjects like evolution exist on timescales "that [make] them impossible to see as a whole on a regular three-dimensional human-scale basis").[89] Morton's point, however, is that despite our human inability to grasp or apprehend hyperobjects in their totality – which, of course, makes it easy to deny their existence on purely evidentiary or common-sensical grounds, as continues to bedevil those who proclaim the dangers of global warming in particular – the very viability of the planet may increasingly depend on our ability to recognize them. That many of the hyperobjects Morton identifies (the biosphere, evolution, global warming, microwaves) do not simply coexist with humans but at least partially *contain* us only increases the urgency of coming to terms with them.

Can the concept of hyperobjects help us see anew certain aspects of Wordsworth's autobiographical epic, *The Prelude*? As Morton indicates, the Romantic period's ramping up of indus-trialization marks "the very advent of the Anthropocene,"[90] the proposed name for our current geological era in which human effects on the planet have become both global and irreversible. But as Wordsworth makes clear in *The Prelude*'s very subtitle – "Growth of a Poet's Mind" – his *magnum opus* is unabashedly anthropocentric and correlationist.[91] In the poem's second book, he specifies that tracing the growth of his imaginative powers will mean above all tracking the "enlarge[ment]" of his sympathies as "the common range of *visible* things/ Grew dear to me" (2.175–7; my italics). Hyperobjects, by contrast, are never fully visible. Granted, the above quotation is from *The Prelude*'s description of Wordsworth's earliest awakening to the beauty and power of the natural world, and as in "Tintern Abbey," such descriptions grow increasingly sophisticated as the poem unfolds; later in the same book, he even echoes that earlier poem quite closely when describing how, thanks to benign maternal influences, the child can become aware of how "there exists/ A virtue which irradiates and exalts/ All objects through all intercourse of sense" (2.238–40). But this impression of the possibility of apprehending wholes where there are only sensible parts to be experienced remains unrealized throughout much of *The Prelude*; instead, Wordsworth repeatedly "blanks out" when confronted with objects or processes that are larger or more intense than he can apprehend all at once.

The "spot of time" in *The Prelude* that Morton mentions explicitly is the episode in Book One in which a young Wordsworth rows a temporarily stolen boat on a midnight lake. He is thoroughly enjoying himself until the sight of a looming cliff brings him to his senses and he returns the skiff to its dock. Morton convincingly describes this as an example of the viscosity of hyperobjects: "it is as if the mountain is stuck to Wordsworth, as if it won't let him go."[92] Yet the larger point of the anecdote – and, moreover, of almost every "spot of time" Wordsworth remembers and relates in *The Prelude* – is to underscore the way in which the natural world consistently speaks *to* Wordsworth, informing and shaping his morality. Even as the looming cliff momentarily takes on some of the properties of a hyperobject, in other words, it remains embedded within a profoundly anthropocentric worldview. This is surely the most productive way to understand the gorgeous passage of reflection that follows the boat-stealing spot of time:

> Wisdom and spirit of the universe,
> Thou soul that art the eternity of thought,
> Thou giv'st to forms and images a breath
> And everlasting motion – not in vain,
> By day or star-light, thus from my first dawn
> Of childhood didst thou intertwine for me
> The passions that build up our human soul,
> [. . .] with high objects, with enduring things,
> With life and Nature, purifying thus
> The elements of feeling and of thought,
> And sanctifying by such discipline
> Both pain and fear, until we recognize
> A grandeur in the beatings of the heart. (1.401–7, 409–14)

As in "Tintern Abbey," Wordsworth's remarkable ability to "see into the life of things" is fully on display here. At the same time, however, a passage like this not only reinforces his fundamental anthropocentrism but also confirms that Wordsworth's life-long interest in "high objects" and "enduring things" is profoundly correlationist, since the powerful neo-vitalism that subtends much of his early poetry is dependent on a human consciousness – "elements of feeling and of thought" – to be recognized as such. The problem with this approach from the perspective of Morton's hyperobjects, of course, is that such objects challenge us to apprehend their existence and negotiate their effects *despite* the fact that we cannot ever fully recognize them in the human-centered, even physically embodied (in the heart) mode of recognition promoted by Wordsworth as most authentic. The hypberobject we call "global warming," for example, will never be felt as "a grandeur in the beatings of the heart" – yet if we fail to act because we can neither fully feel nor know its existence, we are abetting its destructive power.[93]

This tendency recurs in several of *The Prelude*'s other key episodes. Slightly later in Book One, for example, Wordsworth remembers skating in wintertime on the frozen lakes near his childhood home and often enjoying the vertiginous feeling of skating in circles, stopping suddenly, and experiencing the whirling continue in his head: "yet still the solitary cliffs/ Wheeled by me, even as if the earth had rolled/ With visible motion her diurnal round" (1.458–60). The final adjective here directly echoes the language of "A slumber did my spirit seal," yet with a notable difference: whereas in that poem Lucy becomes absorbed into the earth, here Wordsworth makes himself the still center of an apparently spinning planet. The anthropocentric, correlationist dynamics of this gesture are hard to miss. As Saree Makdisi has noted (albeit in a different interpretive context, that of reading Wordsworth's resistance to modernity), in *The Prelude* "the threat to subjectivity, the threat to the lonely bourgeois self" is repeatedly identified as the greatest threat to the poet's visionary powers.[94] In Makdisi's argument, this leads Wordsworth to construct "Nature" as a space that exists outside the dynamics of modernity; from an OOP perspective, however, "Nature" itself can sufficiently threaten to overtake the poet's subjectivity, such that it too must be contained and brought back into a proper correlation with consciousness.

This is made explicit in the famous "Simplon Pass" episode of Book Six, in which Wordsworth relates his ascent over the Alps in a such a way that his crossing of the peak itself is obscured; since it happens without the poet realizing it, the experience becomes as much a celebration of the powers of the human imagination as of the sublimity of nature itself. In the 1805 *Prelude*, the recognition that "we had crossed the Alps" is followed by a new stanza which begins thus:

Imagination! – lifting up itself
Before the eye and progress of my song

> Like an unfathered vapour, here that power,
> In all the might of its endowments, came
> Athwart me. I was lost as in a cloud,
> Halted without a struggle to break through,
> And now, recovering, to my soul I say
> 'I recognize thy glory.' (6.525–32)

Geoffrey H. Hartman noted several decades ago that the episode represents in miniature one of the great thematic patterns of the work as a whole: a moment of literal blindness (the poet does not realize he has climbed the mountain until he is already on the other side) is more than compensated for by a subsequent moment of visionary empowerment.[95] Wordsworth's ability to recuperate the anti-climax of the unperceived summit into an opportunity to celebrate the world-making power of "Imagination" confirms what we have suspected all along: even in his more radical, early-career poetry, Wordsworth is highly ambivalent regarding the implications of an OOP-style repudiation of correlationism and anthropocentrism.

That this ambivalence became outright rejection later in his career can be verified by comparing different versions of the epic poem. It is well known that the version of *The Prelude* that Wordsworth directed to be published, and which appeared (with further changes not authorized by the poet) posthumously in 1850, contains numerous changes to the 1805 manuscript edition (itself not published until 1926), most notably the division of Book Ten in the early version into two separate books. But for our purposes, we can let Hartman direct us to a single, smaller revision that helps tell the tale of Wordsworth's increasing orthodoxy. In the 1850 *Prelude* (completed around 1839), the passage quoted above has been revised to read as follows:

> Imagination – here the Power so called
> Through sad incompetence of human speech,
> That awful Power rose from the mind's abyss
> Like an unfathered vapour that enwraps,
> At once, some lonely traveller. I was lost;
> Halted without an effort to break through;
> But to my conscious soul I now can say –
> 'I recognize thy glory.'[96]

In his commentary on these changes, Hartman notes that the 1850 version allows Wordsworth the mountaineer to experience immediately the insight of Wordsworth the poet – a moment of illumination that the 1805 version, likely with more veracity, makes clear does not transpire until many years later, as part of the "progress" of writing the poem itself. This alone, I think, speaks to the poet's increasing insistence on placing himself – and, by extension, humanity in general – at the center of his vision of the natural world; both correlationism and anthropocentrism are subtly but unmistakably supported by Wordsworth's increasing certainty that nature only "means" anything insofar as it is "translated" by the Imagination into moral and spiritual uplift. Equally important for my purposes is the way the 1850 passage above makes sure to specify that the "Power" which rises "like an unfathered vapour" – a phrase referring to inspiration's uncertain origin – now issues not only in the moment of crossing the pass but also quite clearly "from the mind's abyss," which is to say from human consciousness rather than from any external source or force. Here, even the vital pantheism of "Tintern Abbey" has clearly and finally been abandoned.

As we will see in the next chapter, Wordsworth's early friend and collaborator on *Lyrical Ballads*, Samuel Taylor Coleridge, was also initially attracted to ideas – especially those coming from Europe – that led him to adopt SR-like positions. Coleridge may have outdone Wordsworth, however, in his ambivalence to these positions – an ambivalence, moreover, that will allow us opportunities to investigate Coleridge's connections to Kant, Schelling, and contemporary philosophers and theorists too.

Notes

1. See David Simpson, "Transcendental Philosophy and Romantic Criticism," in *The Cambridge History of Literary Criticism, Volume 5: Romanticism*, ed. Marshall Brown (Cambridge: Cambridge University Press, 2000), 72.
2. William Wordsworth, "Preface to *Lyrical Ballads, with Pastoral and Other Poems* (1802)," in *Literary Criticism of William Wordsworth*, ed. Paul M. Zall (Lincoln: University of Nebraska Press, 1966), 48.
3. Stephen Gill, *William Wordsworth: A Life* (Oxford: Oxford University Press, 1989), 27–8, 85.
4. For another recent but differently oriented reading of Wordsworth

as an important critic of commercial modernity, see David Simpson, *Wordsworth, Commodification, and Social Concern: The Poetics of Modernity* (Cambridge: Cambridge University Press, 2009).

5. Adam Potkay, "Wordsworth and the Ethics of Things," *PMLA* 123.2 (2008): 391.

6. Potkay, "Wordsworth and the Ethics of Things," 395.

7. Quoted in Frederick A. Pottle, "The Eye and the Object in the Poetry of Wordsworth," in *Romanticism and Consciousness: Essays in Criticism*, ed. Harold Bloom (New York: Norton, 1970), 274.

8. Pottle, "The Eye and the Object," 280–1. See also M. H. Abrams's similar assertion, made at an even more general level, that "to the Romantic poet, all depends on his [*sic*] mind as it engaged with the world in the act of perceiving. Hence the extraordinary emphasis throughout this era on the eye and the object and the relation between them": *Natural Supernaturalism: Tradition and Revolution in Romantic Literature* (New York: Norton, 1971), 375.

9. David Hartley, *Observations on Man, His Frame, His Duty, and His Expectations* (1749), in *Romanticism: A Sourcebook*, ed. Simon Bainbridge (Basingstoke: Palgrave Macmillan, 2008), 153.

10. In fact, Hume commits a similar logical error in his account of sympathy, when he decides that emotional states are shared between people on the basis of ideas that are then converted back into impressions; but he does so with far greater care than Hartley. See David Hume, *A Treatise of Human Nature*, 2nd ed., ed. L.A. Selby-Bigge and P. H. Nidditch (Oxford: Oxford University Press, 1978), 319–20.

11. Wordsworth, "Preface" to *Lyrical Ballads, with Other Poems. In Two Volumes*, in *Lyrical Ballads: 1798 and 1800*, ed. Michael Gamer and Dahlia Porter (Peterborough, Ont., and Buffalo, NY: Broadview Press, 2008), 171.

12. Ibid., 174. Gamer and Porter note Wordsworth's recent reading of Erasmus Darwin on p. 174, n. 1.

13. Noel Jackson, *Science and Sensation in Romantic Poetry* (Cambridge: Cambridge University Press, 2008), 76–8.

14. Wordsworth, "Preface" to *Lyrical Ballads*, ed. Gamer and Porter, 175.

15. On the poets' self-conscious characterization of *Lyrical Ballads* as experimental, and on the fascinating relationship between that characterization and the scientific culture of late eighteenth-century Britain, see Robert Mitchell, *Experimental Life: Vitalism in Romantic Science and Literature* (Baltimore: Johns Hopkins University Press, 2013), 26–36.

16. Hume, *Treatise of Human Nature*, 183.

17. David Hume, *An Enquiry Concerning Human Understanding*, in *Enquiries Concerning Human Understanding and Concerning the Principles of Morals*, 3rd ed., ed. L.A. Selby-Bigge and P. H. Nidditch (Oxford: Oxford University Press, 1975), 75–6.

18. Hume, *Treatise of Human Nature*, 147. See also Jonathan Kramnick's discussion of causation in Hume in *Actions and Objects from Hobbes to Richardson* (Stanford: Stanford University Press, 2010), 50–7.

19. William Hatherell, "'Words and Things': Locke, Hartley and the Associationist Context for the Preface to Lyrical Ballads," *Romanticism: The Journal of Romantic Culture and Criticism* 12.3 (2006): 224.

20. Kramnick, *Actions and Objects*, 88.

21. John Locke, *An Essay Concerning Human Understanding*, ed. Peter H. Nidditch (Oxford: Oxford University Press, 1979), 450. Locke's distinction between "Real" and "Nominal" essence occurs first on p. 417. See also the helpful discussion of this distinction and its ramifications by Jan-Erik Jones, "Locke on Real Essence," *The Stanford Encyclopedia of Philosophy*, Spring 2013 ed., ed. Edward N. Zalt, http://plato.stanford.edu/archives/spr2013/entries/real-essence/ (accessed May 3, 2013).

22. Hume, *Treatise of Human Nature*, 220.

23. Immanuel Kant, *Prolegomena to Any Future Metaphysics*, ed. and trans. Paul Carus (Chicago and La Salle: Open Court Press, 1961), 7.

24. Kant, Preface to *Critique of Pure Reason*, 2nd ed., trans. J. M. W. Meiklejohn (Electronic Classics Series Edition), 13, http://www.metaphysicspirit.com/books/The%20Critique%20of%20Pure%20Reason.pdf (accessed March 21, 2016); quoted (in a different translation) in Carl J. Friedrich, Introduction to *The Philosophy of Kant: Immanuel Kant's Moral and Political Writings*, ed. Carl J. Friedrich (New York: Modern Library, 1993), xxxiv–xxxv.

25. For a history of these developments, see Lee Braver, *A Thing of This World: A History of Continental Anti-Realism* (Evanston: Northwestern University Press, 2007). For a divergent view of the roots of contemporary theory, see Andrew Cole, *The Birth of Theory* (Chicago: University of Chicago Press, 2014).

26. Quentin Meillassoux, *After Finitude: An Essay on the Necessity of Contingency*, trans. Ray Brassier (London and New York: Continuum, 2008), 45 (italics removed).

27. See, e.g., "Interview with Quentin Meillassoux," trans. Marie-Pier

Boucher, in *New Materialism: Interviews and Cartographies*, ed. Rick Dolphijn and Iris van der Tuin (Ann Arbor: Open Humanities Press, 2012), 71–81.

28. Graham Harman, *The Quadruple Object* (Winchester and Washington, DC: Zero Books, 2011), 9. The internal quotation is from Manuel DeLanda's *Intensive Science and Virtual Philosophy*, where it reads "continuous, yet heterogeneous" (London and New York: Continuum, 2002), 27.

29. Harman, *Quadruple Object*, 10, 12.

30. Graham Harman, "The Four Most Typical Objections to OOP," in *Bells and Whistles: More Speculative Realism* (Winchester and Washington, DC: Zero Books, 2013), 39.

31. See especially Graham Harman, *Tool-Being: Heidegger and the Metaphysics of Objects* (Chicago and La Salle: Open Court Press, 2002).

32. Harman, *Quadruple Object*, 19.

33. See, e.g., Bruno Latour, *Reassembling the Social: An Introduction to Actor-Network-Theory* (Oxford: Oxford University Press, 2005).

34. Heidegger's original "tool-analysis" can be found in his *Being and Time*, trans. Joan Stambaugh, rev. Dennis. J. Schmidt (Albany: State University of New York Press, 2010), 66–75.

35. Harman, *Quadruple Object*, 42.

36. Robert Southey, unsigned review of *Lyrical Ballads*, *Critical Review* 24 (October 1798): 197–204, in *Lyrical Ballads*, ed. Gamer and Porter, 149–50.

37. Anonymous review of *Lyrical Ballads*, *New London Review* 1 (January 1799): 33–5, in *Lyrical Ballads*, ed. Gamer and Porter, 155.

38. Anonymous review of *Lyrical Ballads*, *Antijacobin Review* 5 (April 1800): 434, in *Lyrical Ballads*, ed. Gamer and Porter, 165.

39. By contrast, some critics were clearly concerned by the collection's "experimental" implications; Jeffrey in particular was unhappy with this characterization, which seemed to threaten the boundaries between art and science; see Mitchell, *Experimental Life*, 36–8.

40. "Lines Left Upon a Seat in a Yew-Tree Which Stands near the Lake of Esthwaite, on a Desolate Part of the Shore, yet Commanding a Beautiful Prospect," in *Lyrical Ballads*, ed. Gamer and Porter, ll. 2–4. Subsequent citations of this and other poems from the 1798 and 1800 *Lyrical Ballads* refer to this edition and are given parenthetically in the text by line number.

41. Wordsworth, "Preface" to *Lyrical Ballads*, ed. Gamer and Porter, 175.

42. See, e.g., Paul de Man, *The Rhetoric of Romanticism* (New York: Columbia University Press, 1984); Marjorie Levinson, *Wordsworth's Great Period Poems* (Cambridge: Cambridge University Press, 1986); Alan Liu, *Wordsworth: The Sense of History* (Stanford: Stanford University Press, 1991).

43. Cf. Tillotama Rajan, *Dark Interpreter: The Discourse of Romanticism* (Ithaca: Cornell University Press, 1980).

44. Harman's most extensive examples of this phenomenon may be found in his collection of philosophical parables, *Circus Philosophicus* (Winchester and Washington, DC: Zero Books, 2010).

45. Graham Harman, *Guerrilla Metaphysics: Phenomenology and the Carpentry of Things* (Chicago and La Salle: Open Court Press, 2005), 17.

46. M. H. Abrams, "Structure and Style in the Greater Romantic Lyrics," in *Romanticism and Consciousness: Essays in Criticism*, ed. Harold Bloom (New York: Norton, 1970), 202.

47. Frances Ferguson, *Solitude and the Sublime: Romanticism and the Aesthetics of Individuation* (New York and London: Routledge, 1992), 126. The best-known of the New Historicist readings of "Tintern Abbey" is Marjorie Levinson's "Insight and Oversight: Reading 'Tintern Abbey'," in her *Wordsworth's Great Period Poems: Four Essays* (Cambridge: Cambridge University Press, 1986), 14–57.

48. For a thorough account of Romantic states of mind, see Thomas Pfau, *Romantic Moods: Paranoia, Trauma, and Melancholy, 1790–1840* (Baltimore: Johns Hopkins University Press, 2005).

49. See, e.g., Catherine Packham, *Eighteenth-Century Vitalism: Bodies, Culture, Nature* (Basingstoke: Palgrave Macmillan, 2012); Mitchell, *Experimental Life.*

50. Rajan, *Dark Interpreter*, 220.

51. See Ferguson, *Solitude and the Sublime*, 126–7.

52. Graham Harman, *Weird Realism: Lovecraft and Philosophy* (Winchester and Washington, DC: Zero Books, 2013), 12.

53. Mary Jacobus, *Romantic Things: A Tree, a Rock, a Cloud* (Chicago: University of Chicago Press, 2012), 73; Harman, *Weird Realism*, 16.

54. This is not to deny the feminist reading of Dorothy as "a silenced auditor" (Anne K. Mellor, *Romanticism and Gender* [London and New York: Routledge, 1991], 19), but rather to confirm the overdetermined quality of her role in the poem.

55. Margaret Koehler, *Poetry of Attention in the Eighteenth Century* (New York and Basingstoke: Palgrave Macmillan, 2012), 99–100.

56. For the conditions and practical motivations surrounding the second

edition of *Lyrical Ballads*, see Gamer and Porter's "Introduction" to *Lyrical Ballads 1798 and 1800*, esp. 27–31; for an in-depth account of the publishing history of all editions of *Lyrical Ballads*, see Bruce Graver's "Editor's Preface" to the scholarly electronic edition of *Lyrical Ballads* at the *Romantic Circles* website, http://www.rc.umd.edu/editions/LB/ (accessed December 11, 2013).

57. For a helpful exposition of Ruskin's concept, see George P. Landow, "Ruskin's Discussion of the Pathetic Fallacy," *The Victorian Web: Literature, History, and Culture in the Age of Victoria*, www.victorianweb.org/technique/pathfall.html (accessed November 19, 2015).

58. Timothy Morton, *Ecology without Nature: Rethinking Environmental Aesthetics* (Cambridge, MA: Harvard University Press, 2007), 75.

59. Harman, *Weird Realism*, 12.

60. Maurice Merleau-Ponty, *The World of Perception*, trans. Oliver Davis (London and New York: Routledge, 2008), 48. For a much fuller, more technical account of his theories, see Merleau-Ponty, *Phenomenology of Perception*, trans. Colin Smith (London and New York: Routledge, 1962).

61. Harman, *Tool-Being: Heidegger and the Metaphysics of Objects*, 19.

62. "[T]he waking life of a mythically inspired people—the ancient Greeks, for instance—more closely resembles a dream than it does the waking world of a scientifically disenchanted thinker. When every tree can suddenly speak as a nymph, when a god in the shape of a bull can drag away maidens, when even the goddess Athena herself is suddenly seen in the company of Peisastratus driving through the market place of Athens with a beautiful team of horses—and this is what the honest Athenian believed—then, as in a dream, anything is possible at each moment, and all of nature swarms around man as if it were nothing but a masquerade of the gods, who were merely amusing themselves by deceiving men in all these shapes." Friedrich Nietzsche, "On Truth and Lies in an Extra-Moral Sense," http://oregonstate.edu/instruct/phl201/modules/Philosophers/Nietzsche/Truth_and_Lie_in_an_Extra-Moral_Sense.htm (accessed November 20, 2015).

63. Most succinctly but thoroughly in Harman, *Quadruple Object*.

64. See Harman, *Quadruple Object*, 122.

65. Timothy Morton, *Realist Magic: Objects, Ontology, Causality* (Ann Arbor: Open Humanities Press, 2012), 63–4.

66. See, e.g., Timothy Morton, *Shelley and the Revolution in Taste: The Body and the Natural World* (Cambridge: Cambridge University Press, 1995); Morton, *The Poetics of Spice: Romantic Consumerism and the Exotic* (Cambridge: Cambridge University Press, 2000).

67. See, e.g., Jonathan Bate, *The Song of the Earth* (Cambridge, MA: Harvard University Press, 2002); James McKusick, *Green Writing: Romanticism and Ecology*, new ed. (Basingstoke: Palgrave Macmillan, 2010); and, more recently, Scott Hess, *William Wordsworth and the Ecology of Authorship: The Roots of Environmentalism in Nineteenth-Century Culture* (Charlottesville: University of Virginia Press, 2012). For a now-classic study of the roots of specifically American environmentalism, see Lawrence Buell, *The Environmental Imagination: Thoreau, Nature Writing, and the Formation of American Culture* (Cambridge, MA: Belknap Press of Harvard University Press, 1996).

68. Timothy Morton, *The Ecological Thought* (Cambridge, MA: Harvard University Press, 2010), 132; see also Morton, *Ecology without Nature*.

69. Graham Harman, "On Vicarious Causation," *Collapse* 2 (2007): 179.

70. Graham Harman, "Seventy-Six Theses on Object-Oriented Philosophy (2011)," in *Bells and Whistles: More Speculative Realism* (Winchester and Washington, DC: Zero Books, 2013), 67.

71. See, e.g., Graham Harman, "Asymmetrical Causation: Influence without Recompense," *Parallax* 16.1 (2010): 96–109; Harman, *Quadruple Object*, esp. 73–8.

72. Immanuel Kant, *Critique of Judgment*, trans. James C. Meredith, in *The Philosophy of Kant*, ed. Carl J. Friedrich (New York: Modern Library, 1993), 313.

73. Graham Harman, "Response to Louis Morelle (2012)," in *Bells and Whistles: More Speculative Realism* (Winchester and Washington, DC: Zero Books, 2013), 76.

74. Morton, *Realist Magic*, 20.

75. Ibid., 17–18.

76. Ibid., 199.

77. See Nicholas Halmi's note to "Strange fits of passion I have known," in *Wordsworth's Poetry and Prose*, ed. Nicholas Halmi (New York: Norton, 2014), 113–14. Subsequent citations of the "Lucy poems" refer by line number to this edition.

78. Frances Ferguson, *Wordsworth: Language as Counter-Spirit* (New Haven, CT: Yale University Press, 1977), 172–4.

79. Significantly, the manuscript version of "Strange fits of passion" contains an extra stanza in which the speaker recalls Lucy's laughter when he tells her of his fears; Wordsworth removed this stanza before publication, effectively recognizing that the poem works better *without* Lucy's direct appearance. See Halmi, notes to "Strange fits of passion" and "Song," in *Wordsworth's Poetry and Prose*, 114–15.

80. Morton, *Realist Magic*, 21. For the argument that total touching is physically as well as philosophically impossible, see 72–3.

81. See Marc Redfield, *Theory at Yale: The Strange Case of Deconstruction in America* (New York: Fordham University Press, 2016), 62–83.

82. Jacobus, *Romantic Things*, 171.

83. For a fascinating recent study of the life of geological phenomena that owes much to object-oriented ways of thinking, see Jeffrey J. Cohen, *Stone: An Ecology of the Inhuman* (Minneapolis: University of Minnesota Press, 2015).

84. Morton, *Ecology without Nature*, 187.

85. Ibid., 94.

86. Ibid., 82.

87. Wordsworth, "Three years she grew in sun and shower," in *Wordsworth's Poetry and Prose*, ed. Halmi, 131–2, ll. 4–6.

88. Timothy Morton, *Hyperobjects: Philosophy and Ecology after the End of the World* (Minneapolis: University of Minnesota Press, 2013), 1. The term is first introduced in his *Ecological Thought*, 130–5.

89. Morton, *Hyperobjects*, 70. See also 27–54, 69–80.

90. Morton, *Hyperobjects*, 164.

91. William Wordsworth, *The Prelude of 1805, in Thirteen Books*, in Wordsworth, *The Prelude, 1799, 1805, 1850*, ed. Jonathan Wordsworth, M. H. Abrams, and Stephen Gill (New York: Norton, 1979). Subsequent citations of this edition are given parenthetically in the text by book and line number. Although the 1850 edition of *The Prelude* was the first to be printed (posthumously), scholars have subsequently identified two earlier, distinct versions.

92. Morton, *Hyperobjects*, 51.

93. This is one facet of what Morton identifies as the inherently hypocrisy-inducing quality of hyperobjects; see *Hyperobjects*, 134–58.

94. Saree Makdisi, *Romantic Imperialism: Universal Empire and the Culture of Modernity* (Cambridge: Cambridge University Press, 1998), 36.

95. Geoffrey H. Hartman, "A Poet's Progress: Wordsworth and the

Via Naturaliter Negativa," *Modern Philology* 59 (1962): 214–24; reprinted in *The Prelude, 1799, 1805, 1850,* ed. Wordsworth, Abrams, and Gill, 598–613.

96. Wordsworth, *Prelude of 1850,* 6.592–8.

2

Coleridge, Nature-Philosophy, and Process Ontology

Samuel Taylor Coleridge cultivated the image of himself as a highly philosophical poet. In the ninth chapter of his *Biographia Literaria* (1817), he extravagantly lays out his intellectual debts to Kant:

> The writings of the illustrious sage of Konigsberg, the founder of the Critical Philosophy, more than any other work, at once invigorated and disciplined my understanding. The originality, the depth, and the compression of his thoughts; the novelty, and subtlety, yet solidity and importance, of the distinctions; the adamantine chain of the logic ... took possession of me as with a giant's hand. After fifteen years familiarity with them, I still read these and all his other productions with undiminished delight and increasing admiration.[1]

To most Britons in the early nineteenth century, Kant was still known best (when he was known at all) as a supporter of the French Revolution – an unpopular position, to say the least, in a country that would remain almost continuously at war with France until 1815. Of course, both Coleridge and his on-again, off-again friend Wordsworth had been youthful enthusiasts of the Revolution in its early days. Accordingly, the passage above does double duty as it seeks to establish Coleridge's philosophical *bona fides* and to make Kant and the German idealists who succeeded him seem more respectable in British eyes. (This is what Nigel Leask refers to as the "'exculpatory' project" of the *Biographia Literaria*.)[2] As David Simpson has shown in his foundational study, *Romanticism, Nationalism, and the Revolt against Theory* (1993), Anglo-American hostility toward Continental thought – some versions of which survive today, both within and outside academia – coalesced in the 1790s in a highly overdetermined fashion: rationalism, invested in the power of "method" going back at least to Descartes, fused with the conservatism of texts like Edmund Burke's *Reflections on the Revolution in France* (1790) to help make Continental philosophy become "regarded as wild and visionary delusion – a delusion of 'theory.'"[3]

To counter such views, Coleridge positions his admiration of Kant as primarily aesthetic, and therefore politically harmless, in the *Biographia*. He also works hard throughout his famously opaque, fragmented memoir to reconcile his philosophical passions with his long-held Christian beliefs. The best-known example of this occurs in Chapter 13, where he presents a theory of imagination that is simultaneously an onto-theological vision of the highest order:

> The IMAGINATION, then, I consider either as primary, or secondary. The primary IMAGINATION I hold to be the living power and prime Agent of all human Perception, and as a repetition in the finite mind of the eternal act of creation in the infinite I AM. The secondary I consider as an echo of the former, co-existing with the conscious will, yet still as identical with the primary in the *kind* of its agency, and differing only in *degree*, and in the *mode* of its operation.[4]

Coleridge adds that the secondary imagination consistently tries "to idealize and to unify. It is essentially *vital*, even as all objects (*as* objects) are essentially fixed and dead." There could be no stronger statement, it would seem, of idealist anthropocentrism. He follows these definitions, furthermore, by providing a third term – "the fancy" – that counterbalances the first two even as it throws their awesome power into relief: lacking creative power, the fancy can only rearrange memories and impressions already present in the mind, "receiv[ing] all its materials ready made from the law of association." As this last reference makes clear, Coleridge here incorporates his earlier interest (shared with Wordsworth, as we saw in the previous chapter) in David Hartley's proto-psychological theories of association with his devotion to Kant's critique of knowledge – both of which, in turn, are clearly subjugated to the onto-theological principle of "the infinite I AM."

As many critics have noted, Coleridge's theory of the imagination is neither as original nor as coherent as he claims. It is offered to readers as a substitute or placeholder for a future, fuller theoretical exposition of the imagination – but Coleridge never published this promised longer version. Furthermore, the poet-philosopher admits that he added his theory to the chapter only at the request of an anonymous manuscript reader who, in a letter reprinted in full, encourages Coleridge to forego the lengthy exposition of idealism with which the chapter begins in favor of something more easily understandable. Given that the preceding paragraphs are nearly unreadable, this is not a bad suggestion; as Coleridge later revealed, however, the anonymous letter writer was invented by Coleridge himself.[5] And there is yet more evidence that the poet was less than convinced by his own ideas: according to Sara Coleridge, his wife, in at least one first edition of the *Biographia* Coleridge crossed out the final clause specifying the primary imagination as a finite echo of "the infinite I AM," seemingly indicating dissatisfaction with his subordination of the human mind to onto-theology.[6] Last but not least, it is hard not to wonder why Coleridge feels compelled to specify that for the secondary imagination "all objects (*as objects*) are essentially fixed and dead." His recourse here to redundancy (objects *as objects*) as well as oversimplification (the vital human mind versus dead, inert reality) suggests stridency at best and repressed doubt at worst.

Over the years, literary critics have treated Coleridge's philosophical pretensions with a variety of critical responses ranging from respect to puzzlement to skepticism. For Abrams, Coleridge is clearly a "philosophical monist" who desires to return to the unbroken mesh of mind and matter. Accordingly, Abrams is able to make sense of the apparent contradictions in *Biographia Literaria*'s Chapter 13 by positing that "For Coleridge, as for many German contemporaries, to take thought [in the abstract] is inescapably to separate that which is one in primal consciousness . . . For Coleridge a cardinal value of the arts was that they humanized nature and so helped repossess it for the mind from which it had been alienated."[7] In this light, Coleridge's poetic output can be read as a generally successful attempt to put into practice the idealist philosophy outlined in his prose. With the rise of deconstruction and New Historicism, however, literary critics became less eager to fill the gaps and patch the contradictions of Coleridge's thought and work; this trend reached one of its peaks in the nuanced readings of critics like Tilottama Rajan, who finds Coleridge's lyrical poems to be replete with lacunae and antinomies only artificially resolved via various acts of discursive and narrative legerdemain, and Jerome McGann, whose reading of Coleridge's "Kubla Khan" plays a central role in his exposure of "the Romantic ideology."[8]

Rajan's deconstructive method posits Coleridge caught within the limitations of language; McGann's historicism makes him exemplary of the Romantics' tendency to substitute symbols for historical facts (about which I have more to say later in this chapter); more recently, Paul Hamilton has gone a step further and argued that the trajectory of Coleridge's poetic career represents one long retreat into obfuscation: "Coleridge's development as a poet appears necessarily bound up with a triumphant progress from Unitarian poems full of political, philosophical, and theological debate to mystery poems whose rhetoric characteristically contrives an adequate reticence on these subjects."[9] Bridging these critical approaches is Seamus Perry, who praises Coleridge for his willingness to remain "muddled" – but at the cost of leaving his oeuvre verging on incoherence and self-cancellation.[10]

Is there a way to identify some coherence in Coleridge's output while acknowledging his career-long penchant for ambiguity and ambivalence? With the help of some non-object-oriented Speculative Realist positions, I argue in this chapter that the internal conflicts that animate much of Coleridge's best poetry can be ascribed to something other than language's constitutive undecidability or the poet's failure of imagination. Instead, I locate in these poems a sincere but troubled attraction to an imaginative materialism that bears no small resemblance to the varieties of SR found in the works of Iain Hamilton Grant and Manuel DeLanda. The former's interest in resuscitating post-Kantian German idealism, specifically the nature-philosophy of F. W. J. Schelling, can help delineate the philosophical stakes of Coleridge's "conversation poems," especially his various revisions of "The Eolian Harp," which show him grappling with many of the ontological questions that occupy Schelling. The tension in these poems between transcendence and immanence, I then argue, is temporarily relieved in the "mystery poems," which I re-read as triumphantly speculative visions of the virtual underpinnings of all material phenomena. Far from representing a mealy-mouthed "adequate reticence," as Paul Hamilton claims, I find these poems to be the most forthright, probing, and provocative of Coleridge's poetic oeuvre. Their unfettered representations of nature's inherent excessiveness, moreover, makes them especially relatable to DeLanda's Deleuzian "process ontology." Ultimately, I find that Coleridge, like Wordsworth, was not prepared to accept fully the radical implications of a reality that exists autonomously from humanity's thoughts and needs.

Coleridge's interest in Kant and German idealism was preceded by an infatuation with the writings of Friedrich Schiller. An English translation of Schiller's classic *Sturm und Drang* play, *The Robbers* (1781), which Coleridge read in November 1794 when he was 22 years old, provoked a strong reaction, as he wrote to his friend and fellow poet Robert Southey:

> 'Tis past one o clock in the morning—I sate down at twelve o'clock to read the 'Robbers' of Schiller—I had read chill and trembling until I came to the part where Moor [*sic*] fires a pistol over the Robbers who are asleep—I could read no more—My God! Southey! Who is this Schiller? This Convulser of the Heart? Did he write his Tragedy among the yelling of Fiends?[11]

As a youthful political radical and religious dissenter, Schiller's *Robbers* helped Coleridge discover the power of Gothic imagery and extreme flights of imagination.[12] Although he would not immerse himself in the writings of Kant and the German idealists until after 1798, Coleridge clearly already sensed that German writers and thinkers had access to philosophical and poetic ideas unknown to the British.

This intuition was correct. Just starting to cross the Channel in the 1790s, idealism offered a seductive set of alternatives to the empirical tradition, represented most prominently by Bacon and Locke, which had dominated English thought previously. With the notable exception of the radical ideas of George Berkeley, more recent Anglo-Scottish philosophical developments – Humean skepticism, Hartleian associationism, and Thomas Reid's Common Sense philosophy – were still primarily responses to or variations on the empirical tradition, rather than entirely new philosophies; they did not deny the existence of a mind-independent reality, but variously nuanced or problematized the "natural" fit between mind and matter assumed by the scientific method. Far from rejecting empiricism, as critics used to believe, the majority of Romantic-era Britons – including a good number of writers and thinkers – accepted it, while remaining highly skeptical of Cartesian rationalism.[13] Accordingly, first Kant and then the German idealists seem to have offered Coleridge (who, despite his claims, was not the first British intellectual to take up the new ideas coming from the Continent)[14] a philosophical worldview that was novel, inspiring, and – importantly – compatible with his Christian beliefs. As

Lee Braver has shown in detail, Kantian philosophy represented a unique synthesis of empiricism and rationalism thanks to its "epoch-making claim that the mind actively processes or organizes experience in constructing knowledge, rather than passively reflecting an independent reality."[15] Braver's description should be recognizable to Romanticists familiar with M. H. Abrams's reconstruction of this formulation in his classic study of theory and practice in the Romantic era, *The Mirror and The Lamp* (1953), whose title alone sums up the distinction between an earlier, merely reflective version of the human mind's relationship to the external world, and a Romantic-era understanding of "the mind in perception as active rather than inertly receptive, and as contributing to the world in the very process of perceiving the world."[16]

In fact, even before Coleridge's exposure to Kant and then to German idealism – or perhaps as a result of contact with earlier British readers of Kant[17] – he had begun to articulate this lamp-like view in his poetry. Around the same time, however, Coleridge became enamored with a plan that would have taken him quite literally in the opposite direction from Germany: in 1795, he and Southey had concocted a scheme to move to Pennsylvania. Inspired by William Godwin's proto-anarchist *Enquiry Concerning Political Justice* (1793), the two young men sketched an elaborate scheme to start a utopian colony on the banks of the Susquehanna River, far away from the increasingly oppressive atmosphere of wartime Britain. Southey had even chosen suitable partners for their endeavor: the Fricker sisters, one of whom was already engaged to Southey. Coleridge obligingly became engaged to Sara Fricker, the eldest sister, and attempted to raise his share of the funds to underwrite their voyage. When their idealistic, dubiously financed plan inevitably fell apart,[18] Coleridge was left with an engagement to a woman he barely knew, a great deal of bitterness, and few good prospects.

Nevertheless, the combination of exposure to German Romanticism and radical politics seems to have fired Coleridge's imagination. Previously, most of his poetry had been relatively conventional; now he produced one of his most innovative early poems. Originally entitled "Effusion XXXV," but better known by its later title "The Eolian Harp," it begins as an address to his fiancée on the occasion of renting a cottage where they would begin their married life:

My pensive Sara! Thy soft cheek reclined
Thus on mine arm, most soothing sweet it is
To sit beside our Cot, our Cot o'ergrown
With white-flowered Jasmine, and the broad-leav'd Myrtle,
(Meet emblems they of Innocence and Love!)
And watch the clouds, that late were rich with light,
Slow saddening round, and mark the star of eve
Serenely brilliant (such should Wisdom be)
Shine opposite![19]

In these opening lines, natural phenomena are observed chiefly to be translated into conventionally symbolic terms: white jasmine for innocence, myrtle for love, a star for wisdom. The poem thus begins in a clearly anthropocentric mode, in which the correlation between mind and nature is presumed and the latter matters primarily insofar as it can be seen or made to reflect the values or virtues of the former.

In the second stanza, however, Coleridge begins to problematize such correlationism as he introduces the poem's titular image:

And that simplest Lute
Placed length-ways in the clasping casement, hark!
How by the desultory breeze caress'd,
Like some coy maid half yielding to her lover,
It pours such sweet upbraiding, as must needs
Tempt to repeat the wrong! (ll. 12–17)

Beyond its conventional sexism, what stands out about this passage is not its anthropomorphism but the unusual adjective "desultory" which Coleridge uses to describe the wind that activates the wind-harp's strings. According to the *Oxford English Dictionary*, the most common usage in Coleridge's era – as evidenced by the *OED*'s citation of his friend William Hazlitt – is "Coming disconnectedly; random." In the lines that follow, however, the harp is described as emitting "long sequacious notes" (l. 18), another curious description which suggests that, however random the breezes, their effect – the notes they create via the wind-harp – is sequential or patterned. The wind-harp and its music thus exemplify the volatile mix of order and randomness, autonomy and contingency – or, to put this into more ontological terms, subjectivity and objectivity – with which the poem is ultimately concerned.

At this point, the poem's tortuous publication history begins to reflect Coleridge's changing philosophical views. In the original "Effusion," the subsequent lines spin an extended quasi-anthropomorphic simile, in which the "soft floating witchery of sound" created by the harp is likened to the noises made by "twilight Elfins" as they ride "gentle gales from Fairy-Land" (ll. 20–2). Perhaps on account of his increasing philosophical seriousness – Monika Class argues that Coleridge began reading Kant's *Critique of Pure Reason* directly in winter 1800–1[20] – most of these lines were removed in 1803, and Coleridge instead ends the stanza by asserting that in such an environment of wondrous sounds

> Methinks, it should have been impossible
> Not to love all things in a World like this,
> Where e'en the Breezes of the simple Air,
> Possess the power and Spirit of Melody! (ll. 21–4)

For the 1817 republication of the poem in *Sibylline Leaves*, the fairy images were restored. But in a compensatory move, "simple Air" becomes "common Air" and "Melody" becomes "Harmony," thus infusing the stanza's conclusion with an even greater sense of Coleridge's wonder at the meshwork of natural things.[21]

1817 also marks the first appearance – initially just in the "errata," but later as an integral part of the second stanza – of what became "The Eolian Harp"'s most famous lines:

> O! the one Life within us and abroad,
> Which meets all motion and becomes its soul,
> A light in sound, a sound-like power in light,
> Rhythm in all thought, and joyance every where – (ll. 26–9)

Brilliantly utilizing synaesthesia to convey the integrative power of a unified vital force or inspiring spirit, Coleridge creates what Abrams praises as "the lines that best epitomize the Romantic constellation of joy, love, and the shared life."[22] Here, Coleridge's verse draws closest to the ideas of Schelling, the Romantic-era philosopher whom Iain Hamilton Grant has definitively identified as an important precursor to Speculative Realism. Coleridge did not directly mention Schelling in his writings until late 1813; over the next two years, however, he studied Schelling relatively intensively, paying special attention to his early works.[23] In Chapter 9 of *Biographia Literaria*, the poet praises Schelling as the greatest of Kant's "followers" and initially presents himself as a mere translator: "With the exception of one or two fundamental ideas, which cannot be with-held from FICHTE, to SCHELLING we owe the completion, and the most important victories, of this revolution in philosophy. To me it will be happiness and honor enough, should I succeed in rendering the system itself intelligible to my countrymen . . ."[24]

In fact, Schelling was no mere follower of Kant. Although he still does not enjoy the reputation of the "Sage of Konigsberg" or his best-known successor, G. W. F. Hegel, Schelling has attracted plenty of scholarly interest in recent years, thanks in part to Slavoj Žižek's promotion of him as a quasi-Lacanian thinker. For Žižek, Schelling's primary significance resides in his insights regarding the impossibility of locating an origin for any particular "ground" of thought; this means, for Žižek, that he can be regarded as "first and foremost a philosopher of freedom" whose notion of the pre-original abyss anticipates Lacan's seminal distinction between the Real and the Symbolic.[25] Grant's interest in Schelling also takes off from the latter's characteristic "ungrounding" move, but whereas Žižek reads Schelling as establishing thought's freedom in an implicitly anthropocentric context, Grant sees the Schellingian abyss as evidence of thought's necessary enmeshment in the material world. As Grant explained in his talk at the 2007 conference that gave Speculative Realism its name,

> I think that, unless you're some kind of convinced dualist, it's absolutely necessary that we accept that there's something prior to thinking, and that there are several layers of dependency amongst what is prior to thinking. . . . So if we accept that there are naturalistic grounds for the production of thought, then we have to accept that the naturalistic grounds for the production of thought are not themselves evident in thought except in so far as thought is regarded as part of nature.[26]

This is Schelling's "central contribution to philosophy" and the foundation of his "speculative physics." In Schelling's own words, humanity and nature are sundered only artificially:

> As soon as man sets himself in opposition to the external world . . . he takes the first step towards philosophy. For with this separation reflection first begins. Henceforth he separates what nature had forever

united: object from intuition, concept from image, and finally, by becoming his own *object*, he separates himself from himself.[27]

This separation in the form of self-reflection is welcome, Schelling asserts in the introduction to his *Ideas on a Philosophy of Nature* (1797; rev. 1803), but only as a means to an end: the restoration of a lost wholeness between the human and natural worlds.

Here we can productively distinguish Schelling's thought from both Kant's and Fichte's. Whereas Kant invokes his well-known categories to explain the forms that human consciousness of the world can take, and Fichte sees consciousness arising solely from its ability to reflect upon its own operations, Schelling understands individual thought as distinguishing itself by degree from the material background of life that necessarily precedes it.[28] In his "Treatise Explicatory of the Idealism in the *Science of Knowledge*" (1797), Schelling begins with an explanation of Kantianism that rapidly opens onto to his own, more speculative approach:

> If Kant spoke of a synthesis by the imagination in intuition, then surely this synthesis was an *activity* of our subjectivity [*des Gemüths*] and, consequently, space and time as forms of this synthesis [are] *modes of activity* of our subject. [. . .] To be sure, Kant proclaimed the laws of nature to be our spirit's modes of activity, that is, to provide the conditions under which alone our intuition would become possible; yet he added that nature is nothing different from these laws, that nature itself is but a continuous activity of the infinite spirit, that the latter will attain self-consciousness in nature alone, and that through nature the spirit would bestow extension, duration, continuity, and necessity on this self-consciousness.[29]

The initial conditional statement ("If Kant spoke . . . consequently") of the above passage is separated from the second assertion ("To be sure") by several pages in the original, but putting them side-by-side allows us to perceive clearly the core of Schelling's deviation from Kant (even as he continues to attribute these ideas to him). In granting that our intuitions of time and space are produced by the subject's imagination, Schelling clearly accepts the basic hypothesis of Kant's transcendental schemata. Yet by stressing the continuity between the mind and the nature it supposedly produces – "nature is nothing different from these laws" – he moves distinctly away from Kant's "two-worlds" schema of accessible phenomena and inaccessible noumena. Furthermore, if "the infinite spirit . . . will attain self-consciousness in nature alone," then human imagination and the material world are not only mutually entangled but also potentially equally active. Even as he claims to be clarifying Kantian idealism, in other words, Schelling is already embarking on his career-long project of (in Grant's potent formulation) "rend[ing] Kant to shreds."[30]

To make good on this reading of Schelling, in *Philosophies of Nature after Schelling* Grant tracks the evolution of the German philosopher's ideas in near-exhaustive detail, weaving together the varied threads of Schelling's career to show how the latter "arrives at a conception of *'nature as subject'* . . . [that] affirms the *autonomy* of nature; nature, then, not as it appears to Mind, but *nature itself*."[31] What emerges is a portrait of Schelling as a speculative realist *avant la lettre* who consistently asserts the literal priority of nature over the human in order to deconstruct the supposed difference between them; as Grant puts it, for Schelling "natural history exceeds and grounds the possibility of history insofar as the deposition of a ground over time is necessary to any later prosecution of events upon it."[32] Evidence of this unexpected realism appears throughout Schelling's "Ideas on a Philosophy of Nature," including this characteristic passage:

> For we presuppose as an undeniable fact that the representation of a succession of causes and effects outside ourselves is as necessary for our spirit as if it belonged to our spirit's being and essence. . . . That our representations follow each other in this determined order, that, for instance, lightning precedes thunder and does not follow it, of such things we do not seek the ground *in ourselves*.[33]

Contrary to Kant's assertion of a rift between human consciousness and the world, Schelling locates them on a sensual and intellectual continuum. Furthermore, this relation is uni-directional: since consciousness emerges from nature, and not vice versa, the ontological basis of the former resides in the latter. This is what Grant identifies as "the constitutive asymmetry of consciousness with regard to nature" in Schelling's thought.[34] As Schelling explains later in "Ideas on a Philosophy of Nature" while recapitulating the necessity of moving beyond Humean skepticism, "We have no choice but to attempt to derive the necessity of a succession of representations from the *nature* of our spirit . . .

and to let things themselves arise in the spirit simultaneously with the succession, so that this succession is truly *objective*."[35] This is not empirical objectivity; rather, it is an assertion (in Grant's apt words) of the "necessary conjunction of matter and intuition without which experience is inconceivable."[36] This, we can now say, is precisely what is described by "the one Life within us and abroad" passage added to "The Eolian Harp" in 1817. This was the same year, moreover, that Coleridge published his *Biographia Literaria*, in which he tried to head off accusations of plagiarism by asserting that he had developed his ideas independently:

> For readers in general, let whatever shall be found in this or any future work of mine, that resembles, or coincides with, the doctrines of my German predecessor, though contemporary, be wholly attributed to *him*: provided, that the absence of distinct references to his books, which I could not at all times make with truth as designating citations or thoughts actually *derived* from him; and which, I trust, would, after this general acknowledgment be superfluous; be not charged on me as an ungenerous concealment or intentional plagiarism. . . . I regard truth as a divine ventriloquist: I care not from whose mouth the sounds are supposed to proceed, if only the words are audible and intelligible.[37]

The tortured syntax, contradictory assertions, and excessive protesting all point to Coleridge's anxiety regarding charges of plagiarism – charges that passages like this scattered throughout the *Biographia Literaria* and his letters did little to allay.

Schelling himself seems to have been generous toward his English admirer, calling him "the first of his countrymen who grasped and sensibly employed German poetry and science, yet in particular philosophy."[38] Moreover, many of "Effusion XXV"'s original passages display striking resemblances to Schellingianism that predate Coleridge's exposure to German philosophy. The third stanza, for example, begins with another brief acknowledgment of Sara Fricker's presence before quickly moving into more elevated imaginative territory. Lying halfway up a hill, watching the sunbeams play through his "half-clos'd eye-lids," Coleridge reports that he begins to experience "Full many a thought uncall'd and undetain'd,/ And many idle flitting phantasies," which "Traverse my indolent and passive brain,/ As wild and various as the random gales/ That swell and flutter on this subject Lute!" (ll. 36, 39–43).

In this extended simile, the adjectival phrase "subject Lute" takes on a remarkable multiplicity of meanings: it is not only the titular subject of the poem as Coleridge would rename it, but also a subject in its own right, actively emitting sounds even as it is *subject to* the winds that play it. In the same way, Coleridge proposes, his mind asserts itself as a subject paradoxically by becoming subject *to* the thoughts and fantasies that pass through it from the outside. In Schellingian fashion, that is, Coleridge seems suddenly to understand, or more accurately, to intuit that there is no meaningful distinction between nature and humanity, subject and object. An even more radical insight is broached in the next stanza:

> And what if all of animated nature
> Be but organic Harps diversely fram'd,
> That tremble into thought, as o'er them sweeps
> Plastic and vast, one intellectual breeze,
> At once the Soul of each, and God of all? (ll. 44–8)

By phrasing this short stanza as a question, Coleridge avoids assertion in favor of speculative query; in the 1803 revision, moreover, the opening conjunction is changed to "But," thereby presenting what follows as an alternative rather than a continuation of the previous stanza's subject/object dissolution. Nevertheless, we should not be too quick to dismiss the potential ramifications of these lines. Often understood as part of Coleridge's youthful dalliance with "the religion of nature,"[39] to quote Harold Bloom, these lines too anticipate Schelling's nature-philosophy, in which (to quote from the central statement of an 1800 essay) "All dynamic motions have their final ground in the subject of nature itself, namely in the forces of which the visible world is only the support."[40] Borrowing from Fichte (among others), Schelling sees self-positing – the essential, originary moment of absolute becoming – as possible only thanks to "dynamic" motions; likewise, Coleridge here limits the workings of "the One life" to "animated nature."[41] Notwithstanding his exclusion of inanimate nature, this is a hugely encompassing picture of the kind of "speculative physics" Schelling seems to have envisioned.

Yet at the very point where Coleridge might appear to anticipate most closely Schelling's revolutionary philosophy, hints appear of his subsequent backing away from nature-philosophy's most radical ramifications. Even as he invokes a vision in which "all of animated nature" is quite literally moved by the same "intellectual breeze," Coleridge introduces a division that, from Grant's perspective at least, has no place in a Schellingian worldview: a difference in kind, and therefore presumably in origin, between nature's harps and the wind that plays them, which is to say between body and soul or spirit. For in Coleridge's vision, the unconditioned or absolute ground of all thought – "one intellectual breeze" – simply doesn't exist on the same physical plane as everything else; it manifests in and through all other living things, but maintains some kind of identity apart from (if not absolutely prior to) those manifestations. Even at its most radical, in other words, Coleridge's vision diverges from what Grant identifies as the core of Schelling's nature-philosophy: "Ideas conduct ideation *in nature*."[42] For Coleridge, by contrast, the Idea first comes from elsewhere – from an avowedly metaphysical plane that cannot, finally, be accessed or even understood by humans – and only then does it infuse everything else. This is borne out by the earliest "Rugby manuscript" draft version of the poem, in which Coleridge bluntly concludes an extended version of this stanza with the lines: "Thus God the only universal Soul/ Organiz'd Body is the Instrument/ And each one's Tunes are that, which each calls."[43]

In the final stanza of all but the very earliest draft, moreover, even this degree of unorthodox thinking comes under pressure and is rejected. With no transition beyond the oppositional conjunction with which it begins, Coleridge famously credits Sara Fricker for calling him back from such abstruse philosophizing:

> But thy more serious eye a mild reproof
> Darts, O belovéd Woman! Nor such thoughts
> Dim and unhallow'd dost thou not reject,
> And biddest me walk humbly with my God. (ll. 49–52)

The tone here is ambiguous: is Coleridge relieved or annoyed to have had his train of thought derailed by a look from Sara's "more serious eye"? The conventional but awkwardly stressed epithet "O belovéd Woman," combined with the double negative of his reconstruction of her motivation ("*Nor* such thoughts . . . does thou *not* reject" [emphasis added]), suggest the latter. In a sense, Sara is being a more strict materialist than Coleridge himself, for she has drawn his attention back to the people and things who are literally, most concretely present in his life.[44] Yet Coleridge does not appear to see it this way; instead, the stanza doubles down on his rejection of speculative philosophy, denigrating the poem's previous ideas as "These shapings of the unregenerate mind;/ Bubbles that glitter as they rise and break/ On vain Philosophy's aye-babbling spring" (ll. 55–7). Here, the latent double-meaning of the adjective "vain" to describe speculative philosophy as an endeavor both futile and narcissistic is complemented by the comparison of it to an "aye-babbling spring," where "aye" homophonically evokes a self-obsessed "I" as well as a meaningless assent to fashionable but insubstantial ideas. The poem's final lines, in which Coleridge describes himself as "A sinful and most miserable man" when bereft of traditional Christianity's support, tip so far toward self-flagellation that they would seem ironic if their tone were not clearly, even pathetically, sincere. From the heights of his Schellingian vision, Coleridge retreats – with reluctance, relief, or some combination – to "Peace, and this Cot, and thee, heart-honour'd Maid!" (l. 64).

As disappointing as the poem's ending is from an SR perspective, it accurately anticipates Coleridge's eventual disenchantment with Schelling, and confirms (as Thomas Pfau has argued) that the two men's ontological beliefs were never fully compatible, since Coleridge in practice was always "far more inclined to start out deductively, beginning with the micromanagement of empirical phenomena, rather than descending from those remote and uncertain 'stars and nebulae' of transcendent ideas."[45] Pfau's phrase "stars and nebulae" comes from an 1817 letter in which Coleridge refers to Schelling's "Theology and Theanthroposophy" emanating from those celestial phenomena before musing that "In short, I am half inclined to believe that both he and his friend Francis Baader [Franz Xaver von Baader, a contemporary German theologian and philosopher] are but half in earnest – and paint the veil to hide not *the face* but the *want* of one."[46] The return to traditional Christianity in "Effusion XXV"/"The Eolian Harp" is thus less a failure of Coleridge's speculative nerve than a resurgence of his inmost faith in a two-world model unsupported by Schellingian nature-philosophy. Nevertheless, recognizing the extent to which Coleridge was drawn to Schelling's insight into "the necessary conjuncture of matter and intuition, without which experience is inconceivable," allows us to appreciate anew the speculative resonances of his poetic vision of "the one Life."[47]

Coleridge's attraction to Schellingianism – in which divisions between subject and object, humanity and the natural world become visible as anthropocentric projections – persists in several of his other conversation poems. Rajan observes that in these texts – especially "This Lime-tree Bower my Prison" from 1797, and "Frost at Midnight" from 1798 – Coleridge's named addressees are forced to play key roles in ratifying the poet's intimations of "the one Life" by experiencing or bearing witness to it more fully than the poet himself. After the resistance to his speculative vision by Sara Fricker in "The Eolian Harp," in other words, Coleridge chooses more pliable figures to hear and legitimize his thoughts: an absent friend in "This Lime-tree Bower" and his infant son in "Frost at Midnight."[48] In addition to indexing Coleridge's anxiety that he may be merely "an involuntary Imposter," Rajan argues, these figures "poin[t] in turn to the surrogate status of literary signs, which also seek to take the place of the absent and to represent something which they cannot capture."[49] From this deconstructive perspective, then, Coleridge primarily bears witness to language's insufficiencies when, in "This Lime-tree Bower," he must imagine the experiences and feelings of Charles Lamb in order to assert that "No sound is dissonant which tells of Life," or when, in "Frost at Midnight," he must use his infant son as the conduit through which to translate scenes of nature into

> The lovely shapes and sounds intelligible
> Of that eternal language, which thy God
> Utters, who from eternity doth teach
> Himself in all, and all things in himself.[50]

Again, Coleridge's commitment to a two-worlds philosophy reasserts itself in no uncertain terms here, albeit via the safely quiet and involuntarily passive medium of his baby.

As in the previous chapter on Wordsworth's poetry, however, bringing an SR perspective to these poems allows us to see in them something more than merely a "Romantic ideology" gone awry due to inevitable linguistic failure or intellectual bad faith. Just as Wordsworth's retreat from claiming to see fully into the life of things can be seen to echo the object-oriented insight regarding the withdrawal of things, so Coleridge's explicit reliance on others to bear witness to his speculative visions in his conversation poems may be re-viewed as congruent with Schelling's assertion that, in the context of nature-philosophy, traditional subject–object divisions simply do not hold up. It would certainly be a mistake to overlay Schelling's most radical visions entirely onto Coleridge's; the latter's commitment to a primary, non-material Idea aligned with a Judeo-Christian God is simply too strong. But to the extent that Coleridge shares and even anticipates Schelling's insight into "the necessary conjuncture of matter and intuition, without which experience is inconceivable," recognizing this intellectual congruence allows us to appreciate the fine balance Coleridge strikes when, trying to articulate poetically his vision of "the one Life," he draws freely on the resources of others' imagined subjectivities to construct a shared vision of the creative force that animates all things and all thoughts.

Tracking Coleridge's intellectual development via his poetic publication record, as I attempted with Wordsworth in the previous chapter, is difficult. Compared to Wordsworth's, Coleridge's poetic output is notoriously small; increasingly, he preferred to expound his ideas in the prose formats (especially lectures and essays) that came more easily to him and were more lucrative. Moreover, even when Coleridge continued to publish poetry later in his career, it was often material that he had written much earlier but neglected for various reasons to complete or publish at the time; the most famous example is his Gothic verse narrative "Christabel," whose two parts were initially composed in 1797 and 1800 but not published until 1816, by which point it had circulated enough in manuscript form that other poets had borrowed its original rhyme scheme. Similar delays attended the publication of one of his other great fantasy-poems, "Kubla Khan, or, A Vision in a Dream. A Fragment," which was written in late summer or early autumn of 1797 but again withheld from publication until 1816.

   Accordingly, by turning now to "Kubla Khan" – followed by "The Rime of the Ancient Mariner," which Coleridge wrote in early 1798 – I do not mean to imply a decisive break between the conversation poems that began with "The Eolian Harp," and the composition of "Kubla Khan" and "The Rime"; after all, "This Lime-tree Bower" was written the same year as the former, and "Frost at Midnight" the same year as the latter. Nevertheless, there are compelling biographical reasons to look at "Kubla Khan" and "The Rime" as products of a new epoch in Coleridge's life. At the end of 1796, Coleridge settled his new family in a small, seventeenth-century cottage in the village of Nether Stowey, Somersetshire; although hardly luxurious, it suited Coleridge's sensibilities and facilitated a productive period of poetry writing for him.[51] His industriousness during 1797–8 was also spurred by his friendship with William Wordsworth. He and Wordsworth had probably begun corresponding in 1796 – their earliest letters do not survive – but it was not until June 1797 that they met in person. After spending two weeks with William and Dorothy Wordsworth at their home in Racedown, Coleridge persuaded them to return with him to Nether Stowey, and the Wordsworths leased a house three miles away from their new friend.[52] Moreover, the southwest English landscape of Somersetshire soon worked its way into the poetic imagery of each, as is made clear by one of Dorothy Wordsworth's characteristically closely observed journal entries from this period: "There is everything here; sea, woods wild as fancy every painted, brooks clear and pebbly as in Cumberland, villages so romantic; and William and I, in a wander by ourselves, found out a sequestered waterfall in a fell formed by steep hills covered with full-grown timber trees."[53] Finally, it is tempting to conjecture that Coleridge's increasingly heavy use of opium (in the form of laudanum, a liquid tincture) at this time – a March 1798 letter to his brother George describes its effects as creating as "a spot of enchantment" in "the very heart of a waste of Sands"[54] – lent the verse produced in these years not only its heightened imagery but also its (relatively) uninhibited imaginative fecundity. Especially when compared to the orthodox final verses with which Coleridge capped "The Eolian Harp," the original versions of "Kubla Khan" and "The Rime" are refreshingly uncensored.

Ultimately, however, establishing that Coleridge's biography supports the idea of a radical shift in his perspective in 1797–8 is less important than recognizing that "Kubla Khan" and "The Rime" represent less a total shift in philosophical direction for Coleridge and more a surprising intensification of one of the elements that troubles him most in his conversation poems: the possibility of an entirely immanent vision of life, one in which a metaphysical or "two-worlds" ontology holds little or no sway. In this chapter's second half, then, I want to see what happens if we read "Kubla Khan" and "The Rime" as radical experiments in the kind of realism we saw Coleridge fitfully access via Schellingian nature-philosophy's refusal to cordon off the human mind from the natural world. Doing so will also allow us to explore the ideas of Manuel DeLanda, a process-oriented theorist whose relation to SR is that of fellow traveler rather than full-blown adherent, but whose innovative, rigorous interpretations of Gilles Deleuze have won him widespread regard.

A clear intellectual line can be drawn from Schelling's nature-philosophy to what Adrian Johnston calls the "neo-Spinozism" of Deleuze and DeLanda.[55] In his early magnum opus *Difference and Repetition* (1968), Deleuze cites Schelling approvingly several times, even crediting him as a predecessor in the task of outlining the radical potential of difference. Moreover, Deleuze sees Schelling (like Heidegger) as a philosopher of "forces" rather than of "concepts."[56] To be sure, Deleuze's characterization of Schelling as the German idealist who most effectively "brings difference out of the night of the Identical" is not without its problems.[57] As Grant indicates in *Philosophies of Nature*, Deleuze strategically overlooks the fact that Schelling elaborates a "one-world physics," whereas Deleuze builds a "one-world transcendentalism,"[58] as exemplified in passages like the following:

> In terms of the distinction between empirical and transcendental principles, an empirical principle is the instance which governs a particular domain. Every domain is a qualified and extended partial system, governed in such a manner that the difference of intensity which creates it tends to be cancelled within it (*law of nature*). But the domains are distributive and cannot be added: there is no more an extensity in general than there is an energy in general within extensity. On the other hand, there is an intensive space with no other qualification, and within this space a pure energy. The transcendental principle does not govern any domain but gives the domain to be governed a given empirical principle; it accounts for the subjection of a domain to a principle.[59]

The "[e]nergy in general"[60] that Deleuze sees as the common feature of both extensive and intensive spaces – about which we will have more to say below – places him in a philosophical tradition (although Deleuze famously resisted such positions) reaching back from Bergson and Whitehead to Spinoza and the pre-Socratics, in which no "extra-worldly" force or prime mover is needed to explain what exists.[61]

The Deleuzian term that arguably figures largest in his ontology, however, and that needs additional unpacking before we turn more closely to DeLanda (and then back to Coleridge), is *the virtual*. As

Deleuze makes clear, this term is not the opposite of what is real; on the contrary, "the virtual must be defined as strictly a part of the real object – as though the object had one part of itself in the virtual into which it plunged as though into an objective dimension."[62] Deleuze also frequently quotes Proust's definition of a virtual state: "Real without being actual, ideal without being abstract."[63] For DeLanda, however, Deleuze is best understood not via his literary or even his philosophical intertexts but via the scientific and mathematical models he draws upon. According to DeLanda, then, the Deleuzian "virtual" can be specified as the realm of intensities, or properties – like pressure, temperature, and density – that can only be measured indirectly and comparatively. Such intensities only exist "in" other, actual things; but by the same token, "actual" things exist and change only by virtue of alterations at the level of their virtual properties. In this precise sense, the virtual takes ontological priority over the actual.

In his 2002 book, *Intensive Science and Virtual Philosophy*, DeLanda explains that in a Deleuzian ontology, objects must be understood not as unified entities defined or governed by unchanging essences, but rather as dynamic systems. The nature of such systems, he shows, can best be understood with help from differential geometry, a branch of mathematics inaugurated by the publication of Carl Friedrich Gauss's *Theorema Egregia* (*Remarkable Theorem*) in 1828, six years before Coleridge's death. If geometry seems too prosaic a discipline for understanding Deleuze, keep in mind that it was Deleuze himself who declared, in a conversation after the initial publication of *A Thousand Plateaus* (one of the texts he co-authored with Félix Guattari), that "We think lines are the basic components of things and events. So everything has its geography, its cartography, its diagram."[64] Gauss realized that calculus could be used to determine rates of change of geometrical objects based on their points, meaning that two-dimensional lines no longer needed to be fitted onto static axes in order to be measured and plotted. Accordingly, it was now possible to study a surface "*without any reference to a global embedding space.*"[65] Later in the nineteenth century, Bernhard Reimann (to whom Deleuze and Guattari refer explicitly in *A Thousand Plateaus*) went a step further and proved that surfaces could be treated as spaces in their own right, so that there was no longer any need to imagine a space that pre-existed the surface to be considered. In this way, n-dimensional surfaces or spaces – which Reimann called "manifolds" – were born, with no need to posit or presuppose an n +1 space in which to embed them. This is how DeLanda develops his basic understanding of dynamical systems, in which "the dimensions of a manifold are used to represent the properties of a particular physical process or system, while the manifold itself becomes *the space of possible states* which the physical system can have."[66] Thus an object's state at any given moment becomes merely "a *single point* in the manifold," which in turn is now best understood as capturing "not [objects'] static properties but the way these properties change" – that is, the processual nature of all reality.[67]

With the establishment of this mathematical model of the virtual realm, DeLanda helps clarify the major accomplishment of Deleuze's ontology: the formulation of a rigorously conceived materialism that is process-oriented rather than essentialist and immanent rather than idealist. Deleuze himself calls his ontology a "transcendental empiricism," which helpfully distinguishes his position from what he terms "everything that makes up the world of the subject and the object,"[68] but lacks the precision of DeLanda's more scientific version, in which a processual view of the world is the best way to "defend the autonomy of non-human entities (atoms, molecules, cells, species) . . . to account for their mind-independent identity without bringing essences into the picture."[69] DeLanda's invocation of "atoms, molecules, cells, species," while parenthetical, signals the importance for his philosophical method of tying Deleuze's provocative but often abstract formulations to objective, material processes in the biological as well as mathematical spheres. In his earlier *A Thousand Years of Nonlinear History* (1997), for example, DeLanda deploys basic Deleuzian concepts to de-center human beings from accounts of material and planetary change taking place at the energetic, genetic, and linguistic levels. Here, DeLanda displaces traditional, Enlightened assumptions that history can be understood as progress-toward-perfection, since such narratives implicitly posit essences as either the origin or telos of development and therefore remain prescriptive rather than descriptive. Even when focusing on human history, says DeLanda, we can deploy process-oriented, materialist frameworks to re-conceive societies as complex systems: ones that may temporarily obtain stable states but – like their "natural" counterparts – are nevertheless best understood as "*matter-energy* undergoing phase transitions of various kinds . . . for the generation of novel structures and processes."[70]

There is, of course, much more to DeLanda's mathematically oriented re-articulation of Deleuzian process philosophy. We have enough at hand already, however, to shed new light on the surprising realism harbored in two of Coleridge's most famously supernatural poems. The relationship between the natural and the supernatural in Romantic poetry has received no shortage of critical attention, from assessments of the influence of German folk ballads and the Gothic novel to M. H. Abrams's interpretation of Romanticism as a sublimated, secularized theology.[71] In the latter's influential reading, Coleridge's supernatural poems are of a piece with his "poem[s] of ordinary life" insofar as both supposedly articulate what Abrams takes to be Coleridge's investment in an unmistakably Hegelian form of Idealism:

> This is the root-principle of Coleridge's thought: all self-compelled motion, progress, and productivity ... is a generative conflict-in-attraction of polar forces, which part to be reunited on a higher level of being, and thus evolve, or "grow," from simple unity into a "multeity in unity" which is an organized whole.[72]

Such may very well be the tenor of Coleridge's conscious intentions. As we have already seen, however, the materialist dynamic of Coleridge's poetry is far stronger than such descriptions are able to accommodate.

Let us look first, then, at how we can use DeLanda's schemata to re-describe the infamously supernatural imagery of "Kubla Khan." The well-known visionary qualities of this poem are apparent in its highly sensual verses and highlighted by its subtitle, "A Vision in a Dream. A Fragment," which inserts several layers of mediation between the author and his production. In a prose preface, Coleridge famously claims to have composed hundreds of lines of text in his opium-induced slumbers, only to have been interrupted by a visitor, after which he could remember a mere fifty-four lines from his original dream-vision.[73] This claim, not surprisingly, has been questioned more or less since the poem's initial publication, not only because Coleridge never produced the "missing" lines but also because the poem as it stands has long been praised for its masterful combination of technical craftsmanship and impassioned imagination.[74] Given its dreamy, exotic nature, it seems naturally to lend itself to meta-interpretations, a tendency that has remained strong even after the rise of deconstructive and New Historical approaches. For McGann in *The Romantic Ideology* (1983), for example, "Kubla Khan" is a poem about the power of Romantic poetry to "transcend historical divisions by virtue of their links with the Imagination": a core tenet of what McGann identified as the "Romantic ideology" that he claimed previous critics – including Abrams – had uncritically accepted.[75] Accordingly, "Kubla Khan" features prominently in McGann's seminal study as an archetypal Romantic poem insofar as "Coleridge's poem works at all points to sustain its own generative energy at the ideological level, and to drive out the fears which beset [it] . . . Ultimately, then, a poem like "Kubla Khan" operates through symbols because both its style and its subject matter are 'ideal'."[76] McGann's reading of "Kubla Khan" quickly became "critical orthodoxy," as did his more general skepticism regarding Romanticism's claims to access universal and timeless truths.[77] Accordingly, most recent readings of "Kubla Khan" – like many contemporary readings of Romanticism in general, to speak broadly – tend to focus on bringing to light the historical, political, or literary contexts that inform it, albeit mediated in this case by Coleridge's drug-addled imagination.[78]

This mediation, however, has already facilitated a materialist reading of Coleridge's poem that, although different in focus from where SR will take us, sets an important precedent. According to Alan Richardson, both Coleridge's prefatory note and the poem itself should be read in the context of the poet's "long and productive fascination with physiological psychology."[79] Despite Coleridge's dismissals of materialist accounts of the mind which were gaining popularity in his day – and against which his theory of the imagination in *Biographia Literaria* clearly sets itself – the straightforward framing of "Kubla Khan" as an opium-induced, spontaneously composed "vision in a dream" immediately calls into question the mind's isolation from the material world; as Richardson observes, "Not only does opium, a material substance, act on the will; but by acting on the will, it suggests that mental faculties are affected by material changes in the body."[80] Richardson finds the same dynamic at work in the poem itself; likewise, I want now to argue that, with DeLanda's help, we can read "Kubla Khan" as Coleridge's surprisingly candid admission of the material underpinnings of reality as a whole.

Whereas in the conversation poems Coleridge speaks in the first person and is therefore immediately accountable for the views expressed, "Kubla Khan" begins in an omniscient third person that feels immediately liberated from all perspectival constraints:

> In Xanadu did Kubla Khan
> A stately pleasure dome decree,
> Where Alph, the sacred river, ran
> Through caverns measureless to man,
> Down to a sunless sea. (ll. 1–5)

Ranging freely through time and space, and comprehending what exists both above and below ground, the speaker of "Kubla Khan" seems unimpeded by the constraints, physical as well as onto-theological, that elsewhere circumscribe Coleridge's poetic voice. According to McGann's now-classic reading, these opening lines and the stanzas that follow construct a series of oppositions between the human (represented above all by the pleasure dome) and the natural world (represented first by the caverns measureless to man, and later by features like the "deep romantic chasm ... a savage place" [ll. 12, 14]), which the rest of the poem subsequently harmonizes.[81] Literally running through all of this imagery and thereby connecting it is Coleridge's invocation of "Alph, the sacred river." But despite the poem's profusion of concrete, sensuous imagery, the Alph is almost inevitably interpreted allegorically as a reification of human creativity, sexual drive, infinity, or some other abstract force. (McGann even terms the river "symbolic" in parentheses, as if to indicate the obviousness of that register.)[82] Of course, Romanticism in general has long been associated with symbolism, and Coleridge – thanks in large part to his own statements on the subject – has long been deemed the Romantic symbol-maker *par excellence*; in René Wellek's influential opinion, "In Coleridge a theory of symbolism is central; the artist discourses to us by symbols, and nature is a symbolic language."[83] In the case of the river in "Kubla Khan," moreover, a symbolic reading seems authorized by its impossible hydraulics: instead of flowing to the ocean or into another river, it forms a loop which endlessly recycles itself: a flowing version of the ouroboros, an "Alph[a]" with no Omega.

Rather than view the river as a symbol of something else, however, thanks to DeLanda's process ontology we can understand it as embodying the process of material becoming itself. The Khan's river, after all, may not flow according to the usual movement of naturally occurring waterways, but it nevertheless behaves precisely in the way that DeLanda suggests most material things do: as "dynamical systems operating far from equilibrium, that is, traversed by more or less intense flows of matter-energy that provoke their unique metamorphoses."[84] Under normal conditions, such changes occur gradually, but at certain moments – when, for example, a basin of attraction suddenly pulls a manifold into a new phase-state – the changes can be dramatic, resulting in the dynamical system taking on an entirely new set of characteristics. Water, of course, is one of the best-known substances to dramatically change states as different intensities of energy move through it: from its liquid state to a solid (ice) at zero degrees Celsius, and to a gas (steam) at one hundred degrees Celsius. In DeLandian terms, the points at which these phase-transitions take place are its "singularities," but such moments are merely the most obvious kinds of events, since the relative stability of water in any of its three states (solid, liquid, gas) is belied by its constant changes at the virtual level of the differential levels of energy ("intensities") that traverse it.[85]

Of course, the river of "Kubla Khan" does not change states as radically as the water I have just invoked. As represented by Coleridge, however, it enacts a series of dramatic changes that, if they do not reach the level of actual phase-transitions, nevertheless come close. The Alph undergoes several changes of speed, for example: after the condensed description of its complete path in the first stanza, it becomes "a mighty fountain . . . burst[ing]" (ll. 19–20) from underground, then returns to "meandering with a mazy motion" (25) through the Khan's grounds, and then sinks "in tumult to a lifeless ocean" (l. 28) – from which, somehow, it is recycled through the "caverns measureless to man" (ll. 4, 27) until, presumably, it reaches the "deep romantic chasm" (l. 12) through which it will again be "forced" and "flung up" (ll. 19, 24) by an unseen power source. At this point, one could speculate on what that source might be, or which eighteenth-century geological theories might have influenced Coleridge's improbable hydraulic vision; it is possible, for instance, that the Alph's fountain-phase is a geyser, although this would demand specific hydrogeological conditions (including the nearby presence of active magma near the earth's crust) that seem unlikely alongside other features of "Kubla Khan"'s imaginary landscape. It is also possible, indeed tempting, to speculate on how the presence of the "huge fragments" famously sprayed out of the poem's central chasm might relate to the geological strata that DeLanda himself uses as a prime example of how rivers operate as veritable "sorting computers": "highly nonlinear dynamical system[s]" that, among other functions, transport rocks and other earthy materials from eroding mountains to the bottoms of oceans, and in the process "sort" the rocks based on their differing responses to the river flow's intensity (among other factors).[86] In both cases, Coleridge may have been drawing on his knowledge of contemporary geological science, specifically the debate "as to whether water or fire was the agent of earth-origin and geological change," as James McKusick has intriguingly argued.[87] But above and beyond the possibilities that emerge via this kind of historicizing, what an SR perspective makes visible is the way Coleridge's general representation of the river Alph anticipates the two main principles of non-linear – which is also to say, virtual – science as DeLanda articulates them in *A Thousand Years of Nonlinear History*. First, it shows that "without an energy flow of a certain intensity, no system, whether natural or cultural, can gain access to the self-organization resources constituted by endogenously generated stable states (attractors) and transitions between those states"; in other words, whatever causes the river to jet out of the "deep romantic chasm," that energy source embodies the engine of difference that generates the intensities that traverse all systems, organic and otherwise. Second, it demonstrates how "the structures generated by matter-energy flows, once in place, react back on those flows either to inhibit them or to further intensify them" (55): this is the feedback loop, characteristic of all non-linear systems, made literal by the circular flow of the River Alph back onto itself.

Seen in this light, the apparently fantastical nature of Kubla Khan's waterworks becomes visible as a "vision," just as Coleridge promises in the poem's subtitle and again in line 37 – not, however, of the poetical power of the Romantic imagination to build pleasure domes in the air, but rather of what DeLanda specifies are the *intensive* properties of reality: those "continuous and relatively indivisible" properties, like temperature and pressure, that generally remain invisible but in fact form – via the phase-shifting phenomena discussed above – our extensively measurable spaces, like the "twice five miles of fertile ground" (l. 6) that compose the Khan's gardens. DeLanda's process-oriented philosophy allows us to see that, if Coleridge indeed raises the power of the poet above that of the king, he does so by aligning the poet with virtuality itself: "That dome in air," like the impossible river Alph, exists at the level of the virtual intensities that traverse and make possible reality at the level of the actual. What McGann and others have identified as "Kubla Khan"'s poetic celebration of the Romantic imagination becomes visible, in this light, as a celebration of the intensive processes that make possible all acts of becoming, not just the human ones.

The process-oriented vision of "Kubla Khan" laid out above sub-scribes to a largely benevolent view of the world's immanence and the shared becoming of man and nature. It would be remiss to leave off any discussion of Coleridge's ambivalent attraction to materialism, however, without paying due attention to "The Rime of the Ancient Mariner," which dwells on the nightmarish potentials of the same. The "Rime" is probably the most-discussed poem in Coleridge's corpus; since its first publication at the head of *Lyrical Ballads* in 1789 – where it appeared with its original, antiquated spellings as "The Rime of the Ancyent Marinere" – it has elicited strong emotions and opinions from readers and critics alike. In his anonymous review of the volume, Southey complained of "The Rime" that "Many of the stanzas are laboriously beauti-ful; but in connection they are absurd or unintelligible. . . . Genius has here been employed in producing a poem of little merit."[88] Modern critics have long since come to a different conclusion regarding the poem's merit, of course, but questions regarding its thematic coherence have lingered. The Mariner's infamously arbitrary shooting of the Albatross is followed by a series of pun-ishments so horrific as to appear utterly disproportionate to the crime; this is also the case with regard to the grisly fate of all the other crew members, whose only failing appears to be their moral relativism when they first condone and then decry the Albatross's killing. A similar sense of disproportion undercuts the poem's overly pat moral, in which we (along with the Wedding Guest, the Mariner's addressee within the poem) are told that "He prayeth best, who loveth best/ All things both great and small;/ For the dear God who loveth us,/ He made and loveth all."[89] Coleridge himself seems to have been uncomfortable with his poem's lack of providential reassurances; for its 1817 republication, he added an interpretive gloss that mostly succeeds only in intensifying the poem's curious ambiguities.[90] This has not prevented modern critics from doing their best to find order in the poem's narrative welter, a trend exemplified on the one hand by Edward Bostetter's reading of the poem as a troubled Christian allegory, and on the other by Stanley Cavell's finding in "The Rime" a secular ethics in which Coleridge's protagonist "accepts his participation as a being living with whatever is alive."[91] More recently still, such thematic readings have been joined by vigorous historicizings of Coleridge's poem, which tend to hear in its energetic stanzas echoes of contemporary debates over exploration and imperialism.[92]

In this case, I think the deconstructive critics are correct: if a final "meaning" requires the possibility of a stable interpretation, then "The Rime" never achieves full meaning. Indeed, it seems actively to forestall attempts to fit all of its pieces into a durable semiotic framework; it is too grotesque, too full of "slimy, slimy things," too crammed with Death, Life-in-Death and polar spirits to be pinned down to a Christian meaning, yet too invested in the thematics of sin and redemption to be fully pagan. DeLanda's process-oriented philosophy, however, allows us to bypass traditional critical efforts to stabilize the poem's meaning, encouraging us instead to look at how the poem thematizes precisely the impossibility of stability or stasis in a virtual world of intensities and becomings. Work of this kind has already been done on "The Rime," in fact, especially by Morton, who sees an "inhuman core . . . at the heart" of Coleridge's poem.[93] Indeed, "The Rime" seems to have become a touchstone poem for Morton, appearing in a number of his recent books and essays that combine object-oriented philosophy and ecocriticism. This makes sense, since Coleridge's poem unleashes what Amelia England calls "a multitude of nonhuman actors that persist" well beyond the limits of the Mariner's – or the reader's – ability to process their meaning or even fully apprehend their existences.[94]

From Morton's and England's object-oriented perspectives, "The Rime" is best understood as a tale about the necessity – but also the dangers – of accepting intimacy with the radically Other things whose coexistence we cannot fully accept without trauma but cannot deny without causing even greater harm to ourselves and others.[95] Morton himself, however, points out that "The Rime" brings into such vivid focus the viscosity of all the living things it encompasses – especially the water snakes that the Mariner must bless before he can be freed from the Albatross's literal weight around his neck – that it arguably emphasizes the existential "teeming infinity and collectivity" of materiality over object-oriented philosophy's stress on the autonomy of individual things.[96] When the Mariner moans that "a thousand, thousand slimy things/ Liv'd on, and so did I," he is indeed showing "awareness of coexistence" with the water snakes and by extension with the other creatures of the poem, as Morton argues.[97] But there are limits to the Mariner's sympathy: even though he blesses the water snakes as fellow living creatures, he recovers no such fellow-feeling for his dead crew members. As soon as they are rendered "lifeless lump[s]" after Life-in-Death wins her game of dice against Death (l. 218), all of them seem immediately to pass beyond the sphere of commonality recognizable by Coleridge's protagonist. Strangely – if anything in this bizarre poem can be singled out as strange – this lack of sympathy fails to resolve itself even when the dead crew members are re-animated by the seraphs to sail the ship and later to hail the Pilot's rescue boat, for as Amelia England notes, the description of their "limbs" as operating like "lifeless tools" (l. 339) underscores their lack of recognizable vitality.[98] Whatever the crew have become, they are apparently no longer alive in any sense that allows them, like the water snakes, to be counted among "God's creatures." At stake here, I think, are the limits of the vitalism to which Coleridge was attracted throughout his early career. Robert Mitchell has recently demonstrated that in his later philosophical prose Coleridge clearly rejects the simple vitalism of his era, which posited a clear, perceptible division between living and non-living matter, in favor of an understanding of life as expressed via an entity's tendency toward greater unity and complexity.[99] Along these lines, "The Rime"'s sailors remain dead (and therefore beyond the purview of sympathy) even when they are temporarily re-animated because they are now merely collections of parts, unbound by any intensities intrinsic to their arrangements; by contrast, the sea snakes are worthy of being blessed, despite their sliminess, because they exhibit the "dynamism and intensity" characteristic of truly living things.[100]

From a process-oriented ontological perspective, however, even this revaluation of "dead" versus "living" is insufficiently attuned to reality – which is also to say that it remains overly correlationist – because it remains at the level of "things," whereas reality from DeLanda's perspective is truly only composed of matter and energy in perpetual states of becoming. Indeed, from the Deleuzian standpoint that DeLanda elaborates, neither change nor becoming occurs in any significant way at the level of extensive reality (i.e. "things"), but only at the level of matter-energy itself. At this virtual level, "life" is defined by a given system's capacity to generate differential intensities via self-organization (e.g. the river as rock-sorting computer); and as John Protevi indicates, this definition alone is enough to qualify Deleuze as a radical anti-correlationist whose "post-Kantian challenge" consists essentially of "hold[ing] that we have to show the genesis of real experience from within experience," not via "conditions of human rational reflective consciousness."[101]

Yet although Coleridge's interest in Schelling's nature-philosophy may have set him down the materialist path, it would be wrong to read even "The Rime" – Coleridge's most "weird" text – as authorizing anything like a fully immanent vision of life; this would ignore not only the pivotal appearances of the personified figures of Death and Life-in-Death, but also the key role played by the polar spirits who eventually take control of the Mariner's ship. Nevertheless, what is notably missing from every moment of "The Rime" is precisely the "conditions of human rational reflective consciousness" that Deleuzian ontology renders unnecessary for describing life. After the Mariner does "a hellish thing" and shoots the Albatross (l. 91), no explanation is ever given for his impulsive act of violence; furthermore, when he "redeems" himself by blessing the water snakes, Coleridge is even more explicit that the Mariner acts more or less unconsciously, having him twice repeat "And I blessed them *unaware*" (ll. 285, 297; my emphasis). Perhaps most telling, the Mariner remains "in a swound" or "fit" (ll. 392, 393) during the entire time his ship is guided to safety by the polar spirits. Coleridge's seemingly redundant language at this point, in which the Mariner describes how he heard the spirits discussing his fate "ere my *living life* returned" (l. 395; my italics), confirms the Mariner himself is not truly or completely alive during the later stages of his voyage. Mitchell notes that in his prose Coleridge "was suspicious of any form of suspension that affected the will," even as he declared his purpose in *Lyrical Ballads* to be that of encouraging in readers "that willing suspension of disbelief for the moment, which constitutes poetic faith."[102] In "The Rime," however, such suspended animation at the level of the individual organism forms the precondition for real change at the level of immanent life – the latter being the level at which, in Deleuze's words, "The life of the individual gives way to an impersonal and yet singular life that releases a pure event freed from the accidents of internal and external life, that is, from the subjectivity and objectivity of what happens. . ."[103] Temporarily re-absorbed into this "pure plane of immanence,"[104] upon regaining consciousness and attempting to return to his previous "living life" the Mariner finds himself unrecognizable to other humans: as soon as he tries to speak, the Pilot who has come to rescue him "shrieked/ And fell down in a fit" (ll. 560–1), the Pilot's boy calls him "the Devil" (l. 569), and even the holy Hermit wants as little to do with him as possible (see ll. 574–81).

Such stripping away of individuality at the poem's conclusion even extends to its frame narrative, in which the Wedding Guest who has been held captive by the Mariner's "glittering eye" since the poem's opening stanzas (l. 13) is now free to go – yet he leaves, we are told, "like one that hath been stunned,/ And is of sense forlorn" (ll. 622–3). Critics have long pondered why Coleridge characterizes the Wedding Guest's state of mind so ambiguously in the poem's final lines, in which (despite Coleridge's attempt at a clear moral) the Guest – who never enters the wedding, a place of human society – wakes the next morning "a sadder and a wiser man" (l. 624). The perspective opened up by Deleuze's and DeLanda's process-oriented materialism provides an answer, however, for as Deleuze observes, "The indefinite as such is not the mark of an empirical indetermination but of a determination by immanence or a transcendental determinability."[105] Coleridge's representation of life as composed in the first instance by immanent, virtual intensities in "The Rime of the Ancient Mariner" is such that the lives of individual entities are revealed to be utterly superfluous; in this sense, the Mariner's ultimate punishment – he is doomed to wander eternally, forever retelling his tale of woe – is entirely fitting, since he lives a "death-in-life" that is fundamentally indistinguishable from what passes for life itself.

One could, I think, extend this kind of reading to illuminate the non-anthropocentric plane of immanence operating in Coleridge's other great supernatural poem, the Gothic ballad "Christabel" (1816); here, as in "The Rime," much of the action takes place when the eponymous heroine is unconscious or in a trance, such that her individuality is submerged in the flow of virtual intensities from which actual "things" only temporarily emerge. Coleridge, of course, became increasingly uncomfortable with this kind of writing – he wrote the two extant parts of "Christabel" in 1797 and 1800, for example, but could never finish it to his satisfaction – and he eventually left off writing poetry almost entirely in favor of prose essays and lectures that were both more lucrative and more conservative, generically as well as thematically. One of his late poems, "Constancy to an Ideal Object," even seems designed expressly to refute his earlier dalliances with materialism; in it, Coleridge announces in seemingly certain terms that a "yearning Thought" is "The only constant in a world of change."[106] Even as he makes these assertions on behalf of a seemingly unadulterated idealism, however, his metaphorical description of an existence without belief in the power of human thought is striking: without a sustaining, implicitly anthropocentric belief in abstract thought, says Coleridge, even the most peaceful cottage would become "but a becalmed bark,/ Whose Helmsman on an ocean waste and wide/ Sits mute and pale his mouldering helm beside" (ll. 22–4). Here, echoes of his earlier tale of a supernatural journey at sea are unmistakable; although he does not admit it, Coleridge is clearly still haunted by his portrayal in "The Rime" of the literally inhuman forces that compose what exists.

In Chapter 4, we will see how Percy Shelley pushes even farther than Coleridge into the realm of attempting to think what lies outside thought; next, however, I turn to consider the work of a much more self-consciously worldly Romantic poet, Lord Byron, to see a different version of non-anthropocentric, speculative thought at work. But first, let us take one more moment to savor the ambivalence with which Coleridge, even as he attempts to forget once and for all the troubling possibility of a universe that exists regardless of human thought, unavoidably recalls the most haunting images of pure immanence that suffuse his strangest and therefore perhaps his most honest poem – in which a single voice assesses his situation and concludes that he is "Alone alone, all, all alone,/ Alone on a wide, wide sea!" ("The Rime," ll. 232–3).

Notes

1. Samuel Taylor Coleridge, *Biographia Literaria*, ed. Nigel Leask (London: J. M. Dent, 1997), 89–90.
2. Nigel Leask, Introduction to *Biographia Literaria*, by Samuel Taylor Coleridge, xxix.
3. David Simpson, *Romanticism, Nationalism, and the Revolt against Theory* (Chicago: University of Chicago Press, 1993), 8.

4. Coleridge, *Biographia Literaria*, 175.

5. See Leask, Notes to *Biographia Literaria*, 409.

6. See Leask, Notes to *Biographia Literaria*, 409–10.

7. M. H. Abrams, *Natural Supernaturalism: Tradition and Revolution in Romantic Literature* (New York: Norton, 1971), 268–9.

8. See Tillotama Rajan, *Dark Interpreter: The Discourse of Romanticism* (Ithaca: Cornell University Press, 1980), esp. Chapter 5, "Image and Reality in Coleridge's Lyric Poetry," 204–59.

9. Paul Hamilton, *Metaromanticism: Aesthetics, Literature, Theory* (Chicago: University of Chicago Press, 2003), 85.

10. See Seamus Perry, *Coleridge and the Uses of Division* (Oxford: Oxford University Press, 1999).

11. Coleridge, letter to Southey, November 3, 1794, in *The Collected Letters of Samuel Taylor Coleridge*, ed. E. L. Griggs, 6 vols. (Oxford: Oxford University Press, 1956–61), I.122. Quoted in Rosemary Ashton, *The Life of Samuel Taylor Coleridge: A Critical Biography* (Oxford: Blackwell, 1996), 58.

12. Ashton suggests a darker explanation for Coleridge's enthusiastic, visceral response to Schiller's play: he may have been under the influence of opium when he read it. The drug was commonly pre-scribed by doctors at the time, and its addictive qualities were not well understood. Addiction itself was seen as a sinful failing of the will rather than as a biologically based medical condition, and in later years Coleridge struggled greatly with guilt over his opium usage. See Ashton, *Life of Coleridge*, 29.

13. See, e.g., the essays collected in *Romantic Empiricism: Poetics and the Philosophy of Common Sense, 1780–1830*, ed. Gavin Budge (Lewisburg: Bucknell University Press, 2007).

14. For a complete study of the pre-Coleridgean history of German ide-alism's diffusion into British intellectual circles, see Monika Class, *Coleridge and Kantian Ideas in England, 1796–1817: Coleridge's Responses to German Philosophy* (London: Bloomsbury, 2012), esp. 17–48. See also Paul Hamilton, *Coleridge and German Philosophy: The Poet in the Land of Logic* (London and New York: Continuum, 2007).

15. Lee Braver, *A Thing of This World: A History of Continental Anti-Realism* (Evanston: Northwestern University Press, 2007), 3.

16. M. H. Abrams, *The Mirror and the Lamp: Romantic Theory and the Critical Tradition* (New York: Norton, 1958), 58.

17. Monika Class draws attention to the availability of materials by and about Kant prior to Coleridge's direct engagement, including

Friedrich Nitsch's pamphlet, *A General and Introductory View of Professor Kant*, published in 1796 and enthusiastically reviewed by one of Coleridge's Bristol mentors, Thomas Beddoes; see Class, *Coleridge and Kantian Ideas in England*, 2, 25–38.

18. Southey, perhaps seeing the writing on the wall, decided to travel to Spain with his uncle instead; see Ashton, *Life of Coleridge*, 72.

19. Coleridge, "The Eolian Harp, Composed at Clevedon, Somersetshire," in *Poetical Works*, ed. Ernest Hartley Coleridge (Oxford: Oxford University Press, 1969), 100, ll. 1–9. Subsequent citations are given parenthetically in the text.

20. See Class, *Coleridge and Kantian Ideas in England*, 3.

21. For an invaluable comparison of the various manuscript and published versions of this poem, see Paul Cheshire, "The Eolian Harp," *Coleridge Bulletin* New Series 17 (Summer 2001): 1–22, http://www.friendsofcoleridge.com/membersonly/CheshireCB17.html (accessed April 7, 2015). A side-by-side comparison is available as a separate webpage: http://www.friendsofcoleridge.com/membersonly/EH%20Foldout.htm (accessed April 7, 2015).

22. Abrams, *Natural Supernaturalism*, 434.

23. Ibid., 273.

24. Coleridge, *Biographia Literaria*, 94.

25. Slavoj Žižek, *The Indivisible Remainder: On Schelling and Related Matters* (New York and London: Verso, 2007), 14.

26. Iain Hamilton Grant, "Speculative Realism: A One-Day Workshop," *Collapse* 3 (2007): 334, "Speculative Realism" conference special issue, ed. Robin Mackay.

27. Friedrich Wilhelm Joseph Schelling, "Ideas on a Philosophy of Nature as an Introduction to the Study of This Science, 2nd ed. (1803)," trans. Priscilla Hayden-Roy, in *Philosophy of German Idealism*, ed. Ernst Behler (New York: Continuum, 1987), 168–9.

28. See Thomas Pfau's discussion of the relations between Kant, Fichte, and Schelling (and Hegel) in his "Critical Introduction," in *Idealism and the Endgame of Theory: Three Essays by F. W. J. Schelling*, trans. and ed. Thomas Pfau (Albany: State University of New York Press, 1994), esp. 26–9.

29. Schelling, "Treatise Explicatory of the Idealism in the *Science of Knowledge*," in *Idealism and the Endgame of Theory*, ed. Pfau, 71, 75.

30. Grant, "Speculative Realism: A One-Day Workshop," 341.

31. Iain Hamilton Grant, *Philosophies of Nature after Schelling* (London and New York: Continuum, 2006), 2.

32. Ibid., 48.
33. Schelling, "Ideas on a Philosophy of Nature," 181.
34. Grant, *Philosophies of Nature after Schelling*, 182.
35. Ibid., 186.
36. Ibid., 188.
37. Ibid., 94–5.
38. Quoted in Pfau, "Excursus: Schelling in the Work of S.T. Coleridge," in *Idealism and the Endgame of Theory*, 274.
39. Harold Bloom, *The Visionary Company: A Reading of English Romantic Poetry*, rev. ed. (Ithaca: Cornell University Press, 1971), 201.
40. Schelling, from *Universal Deduction of the Dynamic Process* (1800), quoted in Grant, *Philosophies of Nature after Schelling*, 119.
41. For a thorough explanation of Fichtean ontology, see Grant, *Philosophies of Nature after Schelling*, 81–102.
42. Ibid., 109.
43. See the companion "foldout" to Cheshire's "The Eolian Harp," *Coleridge Bulletin*, cited in note 21 above.
44. Thanks to Mike Goode for drawing my attention to this possibility.
45. Pfau, "Excursus: Schelling in the Work of S. T. Coleridge," in *Idealism and the Endgame of Theory*, 275.
46. Ibid., 274.
47. See, e.g., Timothy Morton, *Realist Magic: Objects, Ontology, Causality* (Ann Arbor: Open Humanities Press, 2012), 63: "On this view, what are normally called *subject* and *object* are simply aesthetic properties that are shared in some way between objects."
48. See Tilottama Rajan, *The Supplement of Reading: Figures of Understanding in Romantic Theory and Practice* (Ithaca: Cornell University Press, 1990), 113–19.
49. Rajan, *Dark Interpreter*, 229. Rajan quotes Coleridge from his *Collected Letters*, ed. Griggs, I.379.
50. Coleridge, "Frost at Midnight," in *Poetical Works*, 242, ll. 59–62. The previous quotation is from "This Lime-tree Bower my Prison," in *Poetical Works*, 181, l. 76.
51. "The little cottage, for all its dampness and crampedness and popularity with mice, seemed to be the center of a personal, poetic, and philosophical idyll during that summer of 1797": Ashton, *Life of Coleridge*, 109.
52. For a full account of Wordsworth and Coleridge's tumultuous rela-

tionship, see, e.g., Adam Sisman, *The Friendship: Wordsworth and Coleridge* (New York: Viking, 2007).

53. Quoted in Ashton, *Life of Coleridge*, 104.

54. Quoted in Ashton, *Life of Coleridge*, 126.

55. Adrian Johnston, *Adventures in Transcendental Materialism: Dialogues with Contemporary Thinkers* (Edinburgh: Edinburgh University Press, 2014), 51.

56. Quoted in Grant, *Philosophies of Nature after Schelling*, 195. For an illuminating discussion of Deleuze's oft-obscured debts to Heidegger, see Knox Peden, *Spinoza contra Phenomenology: French Rationalism from Cavaillés to Deleuze* (Stanford: Stanford University Press, 2014), 200–3.

57. Gilles Deleuze, *Difference and Repetition*, trans. Paul Patton (New York: Columbia University Press, 1994), 190–1.

58. See Grant, *Philosophies of Nature after Schelling*, 200–1.

59. Deleuze, *Difference and Repetition*, 241.

60. Ibid., 240.

61. My use of the term "extra-worldly" comes from Levi Bryant, *Difference and Givenness: Deleuze's Transcendental Empiricism and the Ontology of Immanence* (Evanston: Northwestern University Press, 2008), 19. For an alternative genealogy that places Deleuze in a line of philosophical "constructivism," see Steven Shaviro, *Without Criteria: Kant, Whitehead, Deleuze, and Aesthetics* (Cambridge, MA: MIT Press, 2009).

62. Deleuze, *Difference and Repetition*, 209.

63. Ibid., 209. See also Deleuze, *Bergsonism*, trans. Hugh Tomlinson and Barbara Habberjam (New York: Zone Books, 1991), 96. Both instances are cited as the formulation "which Deleuze compulsively repeats in all his writings on virtuality," by Elizabeth Grosz in her *Time Travels: Feminism, Nature, Power* (Durham, NC: Duke University Press, 2005), 106–7.

64. Deleuze, "On *A Thousand Plateaus*," in *Negotiations*, trans. Martin Joughin (New York: Columbia University Press, 1995), 33.

65. Manuel DeLanda, *Intensive Science and Virtual Philosophy* (London and New York: Continuum, 2002), 12.

66. Ibid., 13.

67. Ibid., 13–14. Not surprisingly, Harman finds DeLanda (and by extension all process philosophers) guilty of undermining objects; see, e.g., Graham Harman, "DeLanda's Ontology: Assemblage and Realism," *Continental Philosophy Review* 41 (2008): 367–83.

68. Gilles Deleuze, *Pure Immanence: Essays on a Life*, trans. Anne Boyman (New York: Zone Books, 2005), 25.

69. "Deleuzian Interrogations: A Conversation with Manuel DeLanda, John Protevi, and Thorkild Thanem," *Tamara: Journal of Critical Postmodern Organization Science*. http://www.protevi.com/john/Delanda-Protevi.pdf (accessed February 25, 2015).

70. Manuel DeLanda, *A Thousand Years of Nonlinear History* (New York: Zone Books, 1997), 21.

71. See, e.g., Michael Gamer, *Romanticism and the Gothic: Genre, Reception, and Canon Formation* (Cambridge: Cambridge University Press, 2000); Abrams, *Natural Supernaturalism*.

72. Abrams, *Natural Supernaturalism*, 272, 268.

73. Coleridge, "Kubla Khan, Or, A Vision in a Dream. A Fragment," in *Poetical Works*, 296. Subsequent citations are given parenthetically in the text by line number.

74. For a recent reconsideration of "Kubla Khan" as a "fragment poem," see Andrew Allport, "The Romantic Fragment Poem and the Performance of Form," *Studies in Romanticism* 51.3 (2012): 399–417.

75. Jerome J. McGann, *The Romantic Ideology: A Critical Investigation* (Chicago: University of Chicago Press, 1983), 101.

76. Ibid., 99–101.

77. Nigel Leask, "Kubla Khan and Orientalism: *The Road to Xanadu* Revisited," *Romanticism* 4.1 (1988): 1.

78. See, e.g., Michael Raiger, "Fancy, Dreams, and Paradise: Miltonic and Baconian Garden Imagery in Coleridge's 'Kubla Khan'," *Studies in Philology* 110.3 (2013): 637–55; Kuri Katsuyama, "'Kubla Khan' and British Chinoiserie: The Geopolitics of the Chinese Garden," in *Coleridge, Romanticism, and the Orient: Cultural Negotiations*, ed. Kaz Oishi, Seamus Perry, and David Vallins (London: Bloomsbury, 2013), 191–206.

79. Alan Richardson, *British Romanticism and the Science of the Mind* (Cambridge: Cambridge University Press, 2001), 47.

80. Ibid., 51.

81. See McGann, *Romantic Ideology*, 99–104.

82. Ibid., 98.

83. René Wellek, "The Concept of 'Romanticism' in Literary History," in *Romanticism: Points of View*, ed. Robert F. Gleckner and Gerald E. Enscoe (Englewood Cliffs, NJ: Prentice-Hall, 1962), 209.

84. DeLanda, *A Thousand Years of Nonlinear History*, 28.

85. See DeLanda, *Intensive Science and Virtual Philosophy*, 14–17, for a much fuller account of these processes.

86. DeLanda, *A Thousand Years of Nonlinear History*, 60.

87. James C. McKusick, "'Kubla Khan' and the Theory of the Earth," in *Samuel Taylor Coleridge and the Sciences of Life*, ed. Nicholas Roe (Oxford: Oxford University Press, 2001), 134–51.

88. Robert Southey, anonymous review of *Lyrical Ballads*, *Critical Review* 24 (October 1798), in *Lyrical Ballads: 1798 and 1800*, ed. Michael Gamer and Dahlia Porter (Peterborough, Ont., and Buffalo, NY: Broadview Press, 2008), 149. Rosemary Ashton suggests that even as Southey disparaged "The Rime" publicly, he nevertheless "borrowed" elements of it for a seafaring ballad of his own; see Ashton, *Life of Coleridge*, 162–3.

89. Coleridge, "The Rime of the Ancient Mariner," in *Poetical Works*, 209, ll. 614–17. Subsequent citations are given parenthetically in the text by line number. Although the poem appears in *Poetical Works* in the "1797" section, it is worth noting that the version printed there is *not* the one that originally appeared in *Lyrical Ballads* in 1798, but rather the version Coleridge reprinted with more modern spellings in the 1800 edition of *Lyrical Ballads*, combined with the gloss and other materials he added for its 1817 reprint in his own collection, *Sibylline Leaves*.

90. See, e.g., Rajan, *Dark Interpreter*, 22.

91. Stanley Cavell, *In Quest of the Ordinary: Lines of Skepticism and Romanticism* (Chicago: University of Chicago Press, 1988), qtd. in Timothy Morton, *Ecology without Nature: Rethinking Environmental Aesthetics* (Cambridge, MA: Harvard University Press, 2007), 158.

92. See, e.g., Tim Fulford, Debbie Lee, and Peter J. Kitson, *Literature, Science, and Exploration in the Romantic Era: Bodies of Knowledge* (Cambridge: Cambridge University Press, 2004), 171–3; Siobhan Carroll, *An Empire of Air and Water: Uncolonizable Space in the British Imagination, 1750–1850* (Philadelphia: University of Pennsylvania Press, 2015), 37–42.

93. Timothy Morton, *The Ecological Thought* (Cambridge, MA: Harvard University Press, 2010), 92. In a somewhat different register, Morton also writes about "The Rime" as "kitsch ecology" in *Ecology without Nature*, 157–60.

94. Saara Amelia England, "'The Life of Things': Weird Realisms in Samuel Taylor Coleridge and William Wordsworth's *Lyrical Ballad*," MA thesis, Oregon State University, 2014, 37.

95. See, e.g., Timothy Morton, "Coexistence and Coexistents: Ecology without a World," in *Ecocritical Theory: New European Approaches*, ed. Axel Goodbody and Kate Rigby (Charlottesville: University of Virginia Press, 2011), 168–80: "What makes the poem 'ecological' is what makes it least pantheist: its disturbing, relentless intimacy with the 'it': Death and Life-in-Death, with 'slimy things'" (171).

96. Morton, *Ecology without Nature*, 158.

97. Morton, *The Ecological Thought*, 47.

98. England, "Weird Realisms," 48. England connects this description to Harman's tool-analysis, in which the withdrawn, unknowable aspect of the tool only becomes discernible when it breaks.

99. See Robert Mitchell, *Experimental Life: Vitalism in Romantic Science and Literature* (Baltimore: Johns Hopkins University Press, 2013), 89–93. Mitchell also notes that Coleridge's understanding of "life" was heavily influenced by Schelling's nature-philosophy, which also rejected the idea of "life" as a "force" separate from things.

100. Mitchell, *Experimental Life*, 91.

101. John Protevi, *Life, War, Earth: Deleuze and the Sciences* (Minneapolis: University of Minnesota Press, 2013), 180. Like DeLanda, Protevi is committed to thinking through the materialist ramifications and applications of Deleuze's thought.

102. Mitchell, *Experimental Life*, 60, 43. Coleridge's famous description of his poetic role in *Lyrical Ballads* appears in his *Biographia Literaria*, 179.

103. Deleuze, *Pure Immanence*, 28.

104. Ibid., 26.

105. Ibid., 30.

106. Coleridge, "Constancy to an Ideal Object," in *Poetical Works*, 455, ll. 3–4. Subsequent citations are given parenthetically in the text by line number.

3

Byron, Actor-Network-Theory, and Truth Procedures

The idea that Byron should or even could be read philosophically has not always been well received. As an exceptionally popular poet from the publication of the first two cantos of *Childe Harold's Pilgrimage* (1812), Byron was almost as famous for his life and personality as for his poetry – a conflation he frequently used to his advantage.[1] His immediate legacy was thus to be considered "the definitive non-intellectual Romantic ... a poet of passion but not of thought";[2] Goethe, Matthew Arnold, and T. S. Eliot all contributed to this underestimation of Byron's philosophical aptitude. Yet despite what Emily Bernhard Jackson calls his "spotty" formal education, Byron was at least as well versed in the major philosophical ideas of his time as any of the other Romantics.[3] If (unlike Coleridge) he purposefully downplays his erudition in his writings, this impulse seems to stem more from Byron's aristocratic *sprezzatura* than from any ignorance, much less from the supposed "triviality" of which Eliot posthumously accused him.[4] In a letter to a friend written during his last term at Trinity College, Cambridge, Byron records having read "Paley, Locke, Bacon, Hume, Berkeley, Drummond, Beattie, and Bolingbroke ... [and] Hobbes"; furthermore, Bernhard Jackson notes that catalogue sales of Byron's library record additional volumes by Voltaire, Dugald Stewart, and Adam Smith among others.[5]

Nevertheless, Byron was clearly not as closely engaged with philosophical questions as were Coleridge, Shelley, or even Wordsworth; unlike the first two, he showed little interest in directly tackling philosophical issues in his poetry, and unlike Wordsworth, little desire to formulate an explicit poetic program. Instead, what interested Byron intensely was society. This term, used frequently in his personal letters, usually designates interesting human company or its absence, as when Byron complains to his half-sister, Augusta, that in the village of Southwell, Nottinghamshire (where Byron's mother resided from 1803 to 1809), "There are very few books of any kind that are either instructive or amusing, no society but old parsons and old Maids. . . ."[6] According to the *Oxford English Dictionary*, this usage agrees with the most common definition of society in Byron's era as an "association or friendly interaction with other people; the company of others." In addition to this traditional sense, however, a new, less anthropocentric usage was also gaining currency, thanks in part to the Enlightenment's increasingly empirical approach to natural philosophy; in this more specific context, "society" began to designate the "social organization of a group of animals of the same species; the state or condition of living in a social group." (The *OED* quotes Erasmus Darwin, Charles Darwin's grandfather, on "societies" of rabbits in 1794.) As the above wording of the newer meaning suggests, however, definitions of "society" are frequently so self-referential as to be nearly useless, since designating society as "social organization" simply raises the question of what qualities or characteristics of shared existence count as social in the first place. What if society itself is an effect and not a cause?

Self-consciously looking back to the eighteenth century in matters of interest as well as style, Byron's poetic oeuvre can be read as a sustained investigation into precisely this question. I pursue this reading of Byron by reading some of his key texts in tandem with the basic concepts of today's best-known non-anthropocentric theorists of the social: Bruno Latour and Alain Badiou. This may initially seem a strange pairing on several levels. Although they have both been linked to SR, neither Latour nor Badiou closely identifies with the movement, both having established their careers well before SR's emergence. Furthermore, they seem unlikely to hold much affinity for one another's approaches, since Latour's work on "reassembling the social" seems to fit with the attitude Badiou condemns as today's common-sense "democratic materialism."[7] Nevertheless, there are good reasons to consider both of their theories in tandem with readings of some of Byron's major poems. Chief among these is that both Latour and Badiou consider themselves to be non-dialectical thinkers. Although the latter in particular has engaged consistently with Hegel (in ways that go well beyond the scope of this book), each has striven to create frameworks for thinking about the formation of the social – and in Badiou's case, for how something new emerges from what already exists – without explicit recourse to a dialectical approach. Like the other speculative realists, moreover, both theorists embrace a mind-independent, fully immanent view of reality. Furthermore, both seek to overcome what they see as traditional philosophy's inability to theorize society effectively. The exact cause of this inability, however, is one of the places where Latour and Badiou diverge: whereas Latour sees the conventional Western division of phenomena into separate "natural" and "cultural" spheres as the primary obstacle to understanding how society operates, Badiou seeks a model of communal composition and change that allows for the production of what he calls "truths" alongside those more conventional social elements, bodies and languages. Accordingly, Latour finds resources for his theorizing in anthropology and, more recently, rhetoric; Badiou, by contrast, in modern mathematics.

Byron's poetry, needless to say, draws explicitly on neither anthropology nor mathematics; nevertheless, in this chapter I argue that his poetic output can be productively read alongside concepts from both. Interestingly, although Byron uses a facility with numbers as an insult in the first canto of his satirical epic, Don Juan (1818–24), both his wife and daughter, Ada Lovelace, were highly talented mathematicians; furthermore, as noted above, Byron was certainly familiar with the ideas of key figures who pioneered the modern social sciences. In the first part of this chapter, then, I review the methodological innovations of several of Byron's eighteenth-century Enlightened predecessors as they developed the disciplines we now call anthropology and sociology, before considering how key passages from Childe Harold's Pilgrimage Canto One can be understood in their light and then re-coded in terms of Latour's work surrounding his seminal text We Have Never Been Modern (1991; Eng. trans. 1993). Subsequently, I read several of Byron's middle-period poems with help from the fundamental paradigms of Badiou's increasingly influential philosophy of truth procedures. Finally, I return to Latour to see how his most recent work can be productively compared to Byron's development as a social thinker in the opening canto of Don Juan. As holds true throughout this study, my methods in this chapter are both historicist, insofar as the influence of Enlightened models of sociability on Byron's poems is time-bound, and theoretical, as I am most interested in using Byron's poetry to shed light on the ideas of Latour and Badiou (and vice versa). What is lost in terms of completeness in both cases will, I hope, be compensated by what is gained in critical insight.

Two-thirds of the way through Canto One of *Childe Harold's Pilgrimage*, Byron's eponymous hero finds himself in Cadiz, a port city in southwest Spain, on a Sunday. We know it's Sunday because the previous stanza describes the Christian day of rest as observed in London, Harold's native capital:

> The seventh day this; the jubilee of man.
> London! right well thou know'st the day of prayer:
> Then thy spruce citizen, wash'd artisan,
> And smug apprentice gulp their weekly air:
> The coach of Hackney, whiskey, one-horse chair,
> And humblest gig through sundry suburbs whirl,
> To Hampstead, Brentford, Harrow make repair;
> Till the tir'd jade the wheel forgets to hurl,
> Provoking envious gibe from each pedestrian Churl.[8]

This unorthodox description of Sabbath-day observations maintains the world-weary tone of bemused observation that Byron, via his eponymous mouthpiece, has already deployed in his previous descriptions of southern and western Europe during the Peninsular War. For reasons that remain murky but seem to involve transgressions of a sexual nature, Harold has left Britain for the Continent; Byron himself would do the same in April 1816, fleeing the break-up of his marriage, rumors of incest with his half-sister, and tales of affairs with various men and boys. When Harold calls to mind the Sabbatarian rituals of Londoners, then, he does so from a position of geographical distance but cultural proximity. He knows what all of this hustle and bustle portends:

> Ask ye, Boetian shades! the reason why?
> 'Tis to the worship of the solemn Horn,
> Grasp'd in the holy hand of Mystery,
> In whose dread name both men and maids are sworn,
> And consecrate the oath with draught, and dance till morn.
>   (1.70.706–10)

Far from observing their Sabbath in an appropriately pious fashion, Londoners rush after church to prepare themselves for

"The worship of the solemn Horn": *not* another religious ceremony, despite Byron's ironic use of sacred vocabulary, but a Highgate pub tradition in which the initiate pledges to devote himself to debauchery. Readers of the *Pilgrimage* will not be surprised by this turn of events insofar as it is merely the latest twist in what Harold describes as "Sin's long labyrinth" (1.6.37). At issue, instead, is a local manifestation of the general British hypocrisy that McGann identifies as Byron's consistent target throughout the poem.[9] Moreover, by making explicit the link between these two apparently discrete British practices – a Sunday morning's religious observations, so common as to need little description, followed by a Sunday afternoon's frenzied rush to drink and dissolution – Byron throws into relief the latter's dual function, which may not even be apparent to the practitioners themselves: their hasty retreat to Highgate presumably washes away not only the unpleasant memories of the morning's church service, but also the guilty feelings that accompany perfunctory attendance at religious functions.

As we learn at the start of stanza 71, however, the habit of going from Sunday morning prayers to something far less sacred is not restricted to Britons: "*All* have their fooleries" (1. 71.711; emphasis added). But the Sabbath rituals of western Spain turn out to be more difficult for Harold to decipher than those of his native land. Of course, even when he is still in Britain, Harold does not really feel at home: "Apart he stalk'd in joyless reverie" (1.6.50). Dissolute to the point of ennui, Harold has long been recognized as the prototype of Byron's gloomy, charismatic, peripatetic protagonists. More importantly for our purposes, his perennially estranged attitude means he functions as an observer of the arrangements and practices of early nineteenth-century Europe. Spending most of Byron's poem as the proverbial stranger in a series of strange lands, Harold is perfectly positioned to perform what Latour has recently called "an anthropology of the moderns."[10] Obviously, Byron could not have described his poetic project in such terms. Nevertheless, he would have been familiar with one of the most influential new intellectual methodologies of his day: stadial history. Emerging from the Scottish Enlightenment, stadial history can be thought of as a synthesis of two related developments in knowledge production: stadial theory and conjectural history. The former – developed by seminal thinkers like David Hume, Adam Smith, and Adam Ferguson – held that all societies progress according to a step-wise pattern of evolution based primarily on their modes of production. Once identified, these stages – usually hunting, pasturage, agriculture, and industry – were used to describe the degree of "progress" attained by a given society, speculate on past transitions and even origins (as in Hume's theory that political order has its beginnings in violence),[11] and make policy recommendations (as in Smith's famous, albeit widely misunderstood, prescriptions for national and international economic growth). Furthermore, stadial theory provided the conceptual framework for conjectural history, a methodology by which the gaps and blanks of the historical record could be filled according to inferences made via the previously described stages. Together, stadial theory and conjectural history revolutionized the way writers were subsequently able to find patterns in human history – sometimes constructing what they could not find, to be sure – and to discover meaning in otherwise unfamiliar human practices and rituals.[12]

With their willingness to consider all potential participants in a given event, and their resistance to arbitrary distinctions between the natural and the cultural, the Scottish Enlighteners who preceded Byron invented and deployed stadial history in the service of enquiries that set the groundwork for our modern disciplines of anthropology and sociology.[13] I want now to suggest that they also anticipated the work of one of today's best-known interdisciplinary theorists and practitioners: Bruno Latour. A philosopher by schooling, an anthropologist by training, and a sociologist by profession, Latour rose to prominence by documenting and analyzing methods of knowledge production in various scientific communities.[14] But as Latour himself frequently asserts, he is best understood neither as a postmodernist nor as a social constructionist but as a diagnostician of modernity's central contradictions. In his best-known text, *We Have Never Been Modern*, Latour lays out the conceptual framework distilled from his earlier texts. Modern Western society is characterized by two related but antithetical patterns: a powerful determination to (attempt to) separate nature and culture, which Latour calls "purification," and an equally strong drive to create hybrids of natural and cultural phenomena, which he calls "translation." Ironically, although we have been obsessed with the former, we have failed to recognize the extent to which our knowledge production consistently depends on the latter. Latour's goal in *We Have Never Been Modern* is thus not to reconcile translation with purification but to make explicit their inevitable imbrication:

> So long as we consider these two practices of translation and puri-fication separately, we are truly modern – that is, we willingly sub-scribe to the critical project, even though that project is developed only through the proliferation of hybrids down below. As soon as we direct our attention simultaneously to the work of purification and the work of hybridization, we immediately stop being wholly modern, and our future begins to change. At the same time we stop having been modern, because we become retrospectively aware that the two sets of practices have always already been at work in the historical period that is ending.[15]

If we have never been modern, it has not been for lack of trying – but our efforts, for the most part, have made matters worse rather than better, muddier rather than clearer. Accordingly, as Latour asserts near the end of *We Have Never Been Modern*, recognizing that "Nature and Society are not two distinct poles, but one and the same production of successive states of societies-natures, of collectives" is the only way out of the mess we have inherited from modernity (and without becoming stuck in a cynical, compulsively self-reflexive postmodernism that, for Latour, is "a symptom, not a solution").[16] In this vision, the role of humanity is best under-stood as a kind of "morphism": the endless, but also endlessly creative "work of mediation."[17]

The first canto of *Childe Harold's Pilgrimage* can be read as an early, literary version of the kind of socio-anthropological work that the Scottish literati anticipate and that Latour promotes. If the English seek solace in Highgate taverns immediately follow-ing Sunday morning services, and if this practice allows them to maintain a religious façade while not actually absorbing the Church's putative lessons, then what form of entertainment do Spaniards seek on a Sunday afternoon, and what function does it serve? Byron strategically declines to tell readers immediately what Harold is describing in stanzas 71–81 of Canto One, so that although we can tell that a public spectacle is about to unfold – "Then to the crowded circus forth they fare/ Young, old, high, low, at once the same diversion share" (1.71.718–19) – we are forced to deduce the nature of the event in question from the evidence presented. Even when the central participants begin to enter the scene, colorfully mounted on horseback with lances, Byron withholds the exact nature of what they have come to do. Only once one of the figures is named "the light limb'd Matadore" (1.74.738) can we be sure that Harold is witnessing a bullfight.

Ritualistic slayings of bulls have featured in various world traditions for millennia; in its modern form, the Spanish bullfight dates from the 1720s and follows the style of fighting pioneered by Francisco Romero.[18] Yet Byron provides neither this nor any "insider" information of the kind that Spaniards themselves would likely have used to explain the fight's stages and meanings to themselves (for example, the precise style of bullfighting being employed, comparisons between this fight and previous ones). Instead, the poet sticks primarily to an "outsider" account that conveys only what Harold himself presumably sees and understands of the event.[19] Byron had attended an actual bullfight on July 30, 1809, just across the bay from Cadiz at Puerto Santa Maria.[20] Yet his description of it in *Childe Harold* remains notably generic. Packed to capacity, the arena is described only in general terms, such that it comes to represent *every* Spanish bullring. The audience quiets expectantly before the first "Four cavaliers" on "gallant steeds" appear, with the matador himself on foot among them, "eager to invade/ The lord of lowing herds" (1.73.728–30; 1.74.740–1). The ensuing spectacle unfolds with a combination of realism (including descriptions of blood pouring from the bull's flanks as it is repeatedly pricked, and of the mangled carcasses of the toreadors' horses, one of which is "unseamed" by the bull's horns) and attention to the sort of ritualistic details that would strike a keen observer: trumpets sound precisely three times when it is time for the matador to take charge, for example, and later the characteristic red cloak of the bullfighter is noted (1.75.746; 1.78.779). As each of these details is given, a clearer picture is created – a picture, to put it in the terms Latour develops in his quasi-textbook, *Reassembling the Social: An Introduction to Actor-Network-Theory* (2005), of the multitude of "actants" that make up the event called a bullfight. As Latour readily admits, the term "actant" is borrowed from structuralist literary theory, and simply designates anything or anyone that acts or is made to act. This last clause is important, furthermore, because it allows Latour to distinguish between "actant" and "agency": not all actants exercise their own agency, but all agency comes from actants of some sort.[21] Actor-Network-Theory (ANT) thus allows for "the tracing of associations" in a way that does not rely on reifying "the social" as an explanation; on the contrary, society is what happens when various actants associate, modify, use, transform, or otherwise interact with each other. As Latour puts it, "social does not designate a thing among other things . . . but *a type of connection* between things that are not themselves social."[22]

What "things" become visible when we use ANT to describe Byron's bullfight? The humans actants are clear: the bullfighters and audience, firstly, but also those whose presence in the text is unmentioned but implicit, including (at a minimum) ticket-takers, assorted vendors, and the bull's owners and handlers. Where ANT truly challenges traditional sociology, however, is that it requires us also to account for the non-human actants that play important, albeit often overlooked, roles in almost every event we call "social." In this case, the non-human bullfight actants include not just the most obvious candidate – the bull itself – but also the combatants' costumes, their weapons, and the bullring in which all of these actants gather. Additionally, an actant such as the bull does not simply connect the fighters and the spectators, but is what Latour calls a "mediator," an actant that clearly "exceeds its conditions"; although presumably raised in a field and brought to the city to be killed for entertainment, the bull – as we will see in a moment – produces effects that go far beyond its prosaic, even humble conditions of existence.[23]

As the bullfight moves toward its bloody conclusion, Byron's tone does not remain entirely objective. The poet's sympathies clearly lie with the animal actants: both the fighters' horses and the bull are celebrated with adjectives like "gallant" and "furious," whereas the human fighters are "conynge" (cunning) and callous as they "play" around the dying bull (see 1.73–8). Furthermore, when the bull is finally dead, Byron's famed irony appears to resurface in his description of its corpse loaded atop a specially "decorated car" as a "sweet sight for vulgar eyes" (1.79.789). I say "*appears* to resurface," however, because in some sense he is also being entirely accurate. Although it is more straightforward to read the bullfighting scene as a critique either of chivalry in general or of this bloodsport in particular, viewing it via Latour's Actor-Network-Theory makes a different effect visible. For Latour, the important question to ask of any event is not "Is it natural or constructed?" – the query which obsessed the Moderns – but rather "Is it well constructed or poorly constructed?"[24] In this case, that means asking, not "Does Byron see the bullfight as good or bad?" but rather "What effects does Byron see the bullfight producing?" Superficially, he appears to condemn the bullfight for seeming to encourage bloodthirstiness and high passions, which in turn (he suggests) leads to internecine fighting among Spanish villagers:

> Such the ungentle sport that oft invites
> The Spanish maid, and cheers the Spanish swain.
> Nurtur'd in blood betimes, his heart delights
> In vengeance, gloating on another's pain.
> What private feuds the troubled village stain! (1.80.792–6)

This sounds disapproving, but – and here we must simply take Byron at his word with regard to such effects – it turns out that producing and maintaining a high level of bloodthirstiness in the Spaniards has definite advantages too. For after several more passages, Byron spends the remaining nine stanzas celebrating Spain's national vigor and martial spirit – precisely what was needed, at the time, to resist Napoleon's forces during the brutal Peninsular War.

Indeed, after noting the "strange" fact that the Spaniards have continued to put up an impassioned resistance to Napoleon even after their king and prince have abdicated (1.86.882–5), Byron explains this state of affairs with reference, once again, to the Spaniards' supposedly inherent love of fighting and thirst for revenge:

> Ye, who would more of Spain and Spaniards know,
> Go, read whate'er is writ of bloodiest strife:
> Whate'er keen Vengeance urg'd on foreign foe
> Can act, is acting there against man's life: (1.87.891–4)

Notably, the terms with which Byron celebrates Spain's ability to resist the French occupiers echo those he earlier asserted were produced, encouraged, and inculcated at the bullfight. The Spaniards' previously noted nonchalance with regard to dying animals reappears as admirable resolution in the face of "bloodiest strife"; the "delight in vengeance" nurtured by the brutal spectacle of the bullring finds its proper outlet in their ongoing, increasingly vicious guerilla war. Further, what previously sounded like a hint of disapproval concerning the very mixed crowd in the arena – the "vulgar eyes" observing the bull's carcass – is also transformed, since it is precisely Spain's commoners who continue to resist the French long after their sovereigns' abdications. The bullfight, as Byron shows through Harold's eyes, is a typically Spanish event not because it *is* Spanish in some kind of essential way, but because it produces Spanishness – the blend of bloodthirstiness, vengeance, and passion that Byron believes is necessary to roll back the Napoleonic tide.

In his recent "Attempt at a 'Compositionist Manifesto'," Latour reasserts his long-held position that traditional modes of critique have "run out of steam," and that we need alternatives, not merely critiques of critique. As he puts it, somewhat polemically:

> To be sure, critique did a wonderful job of debunking prejudices, enlightening nations, and prodding minds, but, as I have argued elsewhere, it "ran out of steam" because it was predicated on the discovery of a true world of realities lying behind a veil of appearances. . . . With critique, you may debunk, reveal, unveil, but only as long as you establish, through this process of creative destruction, a privileged access to the world of reality behind the veils of appearances. Critique, in other words, has all the limits of utopia: it relies on the certainty of the world *beyond* this world. By contrast, for compositionism, there is no world of beyond. It is all about *immanence*.[25]

One may certainly quarrel with Latour's characterization of critique; its utopian horizon, moreover, may be precisely its most valuable quality. Nevertheless, Latour is convincing that methods, like ANT and compositionism, which seek to account for the real variety of actants in a given network are essential if we wish to help "compose the common world" in which we all must live.[26] We may no longer be fighting the Napoleonic Wars, as Britain was when Byron wrote *Childe Harold's Pilgrimage*. But if indeed we have entered the age of the Anthropocene, we may have a much greater battle on our hands, one in which humans and the planet together occupy all sides of the battlefield simultaneously.[27] Then it will no longer be a matter of seeing how national characters are produced, but seeing how humanity as a whole has produced a situation that may well alter the course of human history even more substantially than did Napoleon when he tried to occupy the Iberian peninsula and was resisted by those bloodthirsty, bullfight-attending Spaniards – with Childe Harold looking on and taking notes.

The initial two cantos of *Childe Harold's Pilgrimage* made Byron's poetic reputation; as recorded by his friend Thomas Moore, after the first edition sold out in three days, Byron reported that he "awoke one morning and found myself famous."[28] The comment's flippant tone belies the work that Byron put into both his poetry and his self-image; as Tom Mole has shown, even Byron's body (which he molded according to the latest dieting fads) was carefully crafted.[29] Alongside his celebrity came increased scrutiny of his personal life, which eventually led Byron, after a failed marriage and a very public divorce, to abandon England in favor of life abroad. Even before his self-imposed exile began in 1816, however, he seems to have initiated an imaginative change of focus; whether by plan or by instinct, his poetry became more introspective. Although the so-called "Oriental Tales" of 1813–15 outwardly maintain the peripatetic, adventure-oriented narrative structure of the first two cantos of *Childe Harold's Pilgrimage*, content-wise they turn away from the latter's social commentary toward more traditionally philosophical themes of love, identity, and the meaningfulness (or lack thereof) of human existence. Formally, too, Byron became more innovative, branching out from fixed forms like the *Pilgrimage*'s technically challenging but repetitive Spenserian stanzas to a host of new forms, fixed and otherwise.

This combination of increased attention to poetic form and a newly apparent interest in using poetry to investigate explicitly philosophical themes, I will now argue, makes Byron's middle-period poetry particularly well suited to viewing through the optic of Alain Badiou's rigorously formal philosophical system. Although he has been writing in French since the 1960s, it was not until the later 1990s that Badiou's work began to appear regularly in English. Since then, he has rightly taken his place as the most important, original, and systematic thinker in the French theoretical tradition since the declines of post-structuralism and deconstruction. In many ways, Badiou is an outlier in SR, not least because even his mature work predates its emergence. To the extent that he has become associated with SR, this is at least partially via association: his most famous pupil, Meillassoux – whose ideas I examine in the next chapter – is one of the original Speculative Realists. Since Meillassoux's basic philosophical orientation is inherited from Badiou (albeit, as we will see, with significant differences), convergences run deeper than mere degrees of separation. Indeed, Badiou recognizes their shared interest in investigating the possibilities of a mind-independent reality, confirming that "The rupture with the idealist tradition in the field of philosophic study is of great necessity today."[30] Idealism is a capacious term, of course, but here Badiou clearly means those forms of thought that assume the impossibility of a mind-independent reality. For Badiou, as for the other SR thinkers, overcoming these "philosophies of access," as Harman calls them, is the starting point for any genuine contemporary ontology.

Nevertheless, Badiou differs from the rest of the SR movement on many other significant points. For one thing, his philosophical vision is deeply informed by his radical political commitments. Perhaps more importantly for our purposes, Badiou favors a mode of describing reality that we have not yet encountered: modern mathematics, more specifically set theory and category theory. It is neither my intention nor within my ability to give a full account of Badiou's understanding of mathematics as "first philosophy."[31] Instead, the link between Badiou's radical politics and his philosophical use of mathematics can be made clear by foregrounding one of his most basic concepts: the One is not. The main tradition of Western philosophy, by contrast, is based on the opposite affirmation: from at least Plato onward, oneness and wholeness or consistency have been celebrated as the natural state of things, whereas multiplicity and difference have been seen as abnormal or unnatural deviations from the One. In his magnum opus *Being and Event* (1988; Eng. trans. 2005), however, Badiou uses set theory to confirm his assertion that reality is essentially multiple ("devoid of any instance of the one, radically withdrawn from all possible unifications," in the words of one commentator),[32] and that the appearance of unity or oneness is only because a concealed prior action – the "count-as-one" – has made it so. What is normally thinkable in any situation is thus circumscribed by the rules governing the count that has made a given set of things appear and be presented as a unity. The "count-as-one" not only hides or covers over its own mechanism and any inconsistencies within the set, but also attempts to mask the ubiquitous presence of what it is founded upon: "the void," which in set theory is "the empty or numberless set . . . to which no elements belong," and which is necessarily a subset of every other existent set.[33] As "the unrepresentable point of being" – because even to name it "void" is to count it as one in order to present it – the void is "that on the basis of which an infinity of multiples structures itself."[34]

With the establishment of this ontology – which, as set out in *Being and Event* and related texts, is much more detailed and nuanced than my all-too-brief description can take in; it also includes, for example, "the state of the situation," which is the way a given count-as-one is itself counted, or re-presented – the next goal of Badiou's philosophical system is to demonstrate how it is possible, in a given situation, to think or do something new, that is, something that does not already conform to the pre-existing logic of the count-as-one. This "something" is what Badiou calls an "event": an unprecedented thought or act that momentarily "opens" the set in question to other possible arrangements or even to its dissolution as an apparent unity. The onto-mathematical basis for this is the *"theorem of the point of excess,"* which Badiou introduces in "Meditation Five" of *Being and Event* and then applies to the concept of the void in the seventh meditation. Since it belongs to itself but is not included in itself (for if the void set contained anything it would no longer be void), the structure of the void retains the excessiveness of the inconsistent multiple that the count-as-one attempts to curtail. A legitimate event, according to Badiou, activates this latent inconsistency – the void – of a given set. Furthermore, events do not happen on their own, even if their origins remain obscure. Instead, every event must successfully call together – or "convoke," to use one of Badiou's favorite terms – individuals who become faithful to it and proceed to re-configure the situation in light of the event. This is the process whereby a new truth comes into the world.

There are only four general domains, or conditions, under which a new truth can appear: love, politics, science, and art. (Philosophy, for Badiou, is not itself a truth condition; rather, it is the means by which truth processes in those other domains can and must be understood.) For a truth not only to exist but also to become present, however, it must be taken up and promoted by individuals who commit themselves to it. Individuals who effectively pledge themselves to the new truth that has emerged in a given domain, shattering the previous situation, become *subjects*, in Badiou's terminology, precisely insofar as they commit themselves to being subject to the truth in question. This double-sided process of "forcing" a truth helps explain why Badiou has lately taken to calling his system a "materialist dialectic." Badiou's philosophy is thoroughly materialist because its truth processes are entirely immanent to the worlds in which they appear; further, it is dialectical to the extent that a subject's emergence and a truth's appearance are radically intertwined. (The move from the ontology of being to the logic of appearance is formulated much more rigorously than will be accounted for here in *Logics of Worlds* [2006; Eng. trans. 2009], Badiou's long-awaited sequel to *Being and Event*; the mathematics at his system's core, however, remains essentially unchanged.) Badiou's philosophical system is thus committed to thinking what we might call "immanent novelty" – the apprehension of something new without recourse to a separate realm of truth – as standing in opposition not only to traditions of phenomenology ("always too pious") and analytic philosophy ("always too sceptical") but also forging a third way between what Badiou calls "the diktats of authenticity" and "the humilities of Critique."[35] It is a system that claims not to privilege the human, or at least not the individual subject, in its picture of reality; although elsewhere Badiou shows himself no friend to those who see no essential differences between humans and other animals, he is also quite clear that "the individual is not the author of this thought ["as immanence to the True"] but merely that through which it passes" as a new truth establishes its universality or trans-worldly applicability.[36]

This Badiouian insight – that the individual is less significant than the truth to which she is called to be faithful – provides fitting entry into the first of Byron's major poems to be written in the wake of *Childe Harold*'s success: *The Giaour* (1813). Critics have long remarked on the ways in which this poem's unnamed but eponymous protagonist – the "giaour" (pronounced "jower"; its meaning will be discussed below – bears more than a passing resemblance to Byron himself, or rather to the Byronic persona of the charismatic, darkly handsome, guilt-ridden young man that the poet had begun to cultivate. As a result, whatever truths are revealed or, better yet, convoked over the course of the poem issue not from the title character himself but from the voices brought together by the poem's ingenious format. In what follows, I argue not only that *The Giaour* articulates a view of subjectivity that is strikingly similar to Badiou's, but also that its form embodies the principle of excess that Badiou identifies as the precondition for a new truth to emerge from a given situation. As we will see, however, the poem also puts pressure on one of Badiou's truth conditions, love, such that it moves toward an outcome Badiou himself seems unlikely to endorse.

The Giaour is infamous for its confused chronology and fragmented narrative structure, yet its plot is relatively straightforward: Leila, a concubine in Hassan's harem, is murdered by
him after becoming romantically involved with the Giaour, who
subsequently ambushes and murders Hassan before retiring to a
monastery. As Byron relates the narrative – which he claims in a
note to have heard while on his Levantine travels, although he also
encouraged the rumor that it was based on his own experiences
– it takes on layers of complexity by being told through the
limited perspectives of a series of characters, culminating in a
monologue by the Giaour himself. This formal structure is sometimes dismissed by critics as merely an attempt to enliven or
perhaps obscure the relatively conventional love triangle at its
heart, as well as to lend an air of mystery to its brooding, guilt-
ridden central character.[37] Presented as "A Fragment of a Turkish
Tale,"[38] Byron's poem clearly participates in the well-known
Romantic interest in fragmented form. As a genre, the Romantic
fragment's self-conscious incompleteness is usually understood as
an attempt to invoke an impossible, even transcendent wholeness;
Friedrich Schlegel's *Athenaeum Fragments* (1798) are exemplary
in this regard, and spawned a philosophical tradition extending through Nietzsche to Benjamin and Adorno.[39] Just because
something is fragmented, however, does not mean it is condensed;
whereas Coleridge's supposed fragment "Kubla Khan" (discussed
in the previous chapter) contains only three sections, *The Giaour*
grew from its original 1813 edition of 684 lines to almost double
that length by the time Byron finished adding to it a year later.
The final published version of the poem boasts over twenty-five
discrete sections, many of them separated typographically by lines
of asterisks that seem to represent missing or yet-to-be-added
sections.

In the editorial notes to his Oxford edition, McGann suggests
that *The Giaour* should be read allegorically as a continuation of
Byron's critique in *Childe Harold* of Napoleonic-era European
ideology.[40] This makes sense on a thematic level, perhaps – but
what about on a formal level? Here, I submit that the poem can
be read as a corollary of Badiou's basic argument that "mathematics is ontology." Especially given the poem's unusual publication history, in which Byron continued to add to and expand its
discrete sections without ever calling it complete (which is to say
without ever altering its status as a fragment), it seems possible to

re-conceive *The Giaour* as a poetic version of a potentially infinite set – a set, moreover, built around and out of a void. Each time a new section begins or a different narrator picks up the thread of Leila's murder and the Giaour's subsequent revenge on Hassan, the elements of the set – the parts of the poem itself – increase in number. Yet even as these elements increase, they fail to cohere. Indeed, the poem's gaps and uncertainties not only persist despite its accumulations, but even seem to multiply, engendering new questions at every turn. How long has the Giaour been in the monastery by the poem's end? How did Leila become one of Hassan's concubines, and how did she meet the Giaour? What is the latter doing in Turkish-ruled Greece to begin with? How does he come by the fortune he eventually donates to the monastery in return for sanctuary? These questions are both unaccounted for by the poem's narrative and – since they are generated by the poem itself – literally uncountable in the set-theoretical sense of being potentially limitless; even if Byron were to have continued adding additional sections from new narrative perspectives, these presumably would have had a net effect of generating more questions to be answered, prompting more sections of verse, and so on.

If *The Giaour* finally gestures toward closure and an end to the potentially infinite succession of its sections, we might expect it to do so according to Badiou's understanding of Romantic aesthetics, that is, via a historicizing gesture: "In the deployment of its Romantic figure, the infinite becomes the Open for the temporalization of finitude and, because it is in thrall to History, it remains in thrall to the One."[41] History indeed is powerful in Byron's poem, which opens with a relatively long, unbroken passage spoken by a disembodied narrator whose descriptions of Greece's dilapidation under Ottoman rule allude, as McGann suggests, to a historically determined frame for the woeful tale that follows. This narrative voice, which describes Greece first as a "Clime of the forgotten brave!" and mourns that "'Twere long to tell, and sad to trace,/ Each step from splendor to disgrace," would seem to be Byron's own; as such, we might expect it to operate as the authorial equivalent of the mathematical "count-as-one" that would make the poem's otherwise heterogeneous parts into a complete set. In narrative terms, this typically requires the same authorial voice to return at the poem's end, framing the poem and thus closing off its contents to further alteration. In *The Giaour*, however, this final gesture is so scanty that it is almost parodic:

following the Giaour's instructions regarding his eventual burial, there are just six further lines of verse – in many printings not even separated from the Giaour's speech by a line break – which merely confirm that the reader will never learn the contents of the Giaour's final, deathbed confession. It is not even entirely clear whether the speaker of these final lines is the same as that of the opening passages: there, Byron employs the first person, but the poem's concluding lines use the third.

As if these obfuscating gestures were not sufficient, Byron adds a host of other paratextual elements that mediate between readers and the narrative itself: an epigraph by his friend and fellow poet Moore, a dedication to his friend Samuel Rogers, an "Advertisement," and a series of lavish notes explaining many of the poem's exotic and abstruse details. Rather unexpectedly for a text whose poetic tone is relentlessly serious, moreover, these notes are frequently tinged with irony and skepticism regarding the superstitions and traditions which the poem contains, and which lend it much of its famously exotic, mysterious atmosphere. The surprising effect is to undermine the profundity on which both the poem's content and its form would otherwise seem to insist. To take merely one example, during one of his many descriptions of his protagonist's remorse over Leila's death, Byron makes an extended comparison between the Giaour's self-inflicted misery and a legend concerning scorpions' supposed instinct to turn their stingers on themselves when death by fire seems imminent (ll. 422–38). Byron's appended note to this intense passage, however, reads as follows:

> Alluding to the dubious suicide of the scorpion, so placed for experiment by gentle philosophers. Some maintain that the position of the sting, when turned toward the head, is merely a convulsive movement; but others have actually brought in the verdict 'Felo de se' [a felon on himself]. The scorpions are surely interested in a speedy decision of the question; as, if once fairly established as insect Catos, they will probably be allowed to live as long as they think proper, without being martyred for the sake of an hypothesis.

The multiple ironies of this passage undercut both the solemnity of the Giaour's suffering and the poem's philosophical pretensions; "Gentle philosophers" turn out to be anything but gentle as they sacrifice other living creatures "for the sake of an hypothesis," the

scorpions' "interest" in resolving this question is made comical
by understatement, and the horror of violent death – a recurrent
theme of the entire poem – is unmistakably trivialized.

To see what Byron is up to here, let's return to his poem's
unusual title. "Giaour," according to one of Byron's early notes,
is a Turkish term for "infidel." As the *OED* confirms, the etymol-
ogy of "infidel" is the Latin *infidēlis*, which means "unbeliever"
in religious contexts but translates literally as "unfaithful." Both
meanings apply to Byron's protagonist: the Giaour is called such
by several of the poem's Eastern narrators for his Western origins
and lack of belief in Islam, and he appears equally alienated from
traditional Christian belief, as made clear when a fellow inhabit-
ant of his monastery gossips that "never at our vesper prayer,/ Nor
e'er before confession chair/ Kneels he, nor recks he when arise/
Incense or anthem to the skies" (ll. 802–5). (In a nod to convention, the Giaour ultimately requests a Christian burial.) Yet the
second meaning of infidel – "unfaithful" – is fitting in a secular
sense, too. From Hassan's perspective, of course, the Giaour is
unfaithful by virtue of his illicit love affair with Leila. Furthermore,
Badiou's philosophical system allows us to see a deeper relevance.
For Badiou, we recall, a new truth is initiated with the occurrence
of an event, but it will only become sufficiently present or manifest
if individuals commit themselves to it:

> If I claim – as an individual, a body, and an element of the situation
> – to be within the truth procedure inaugurated by that event, I have
> to assume the consequences as tenaciously as possible: those of the
> event, of its nomination and of the engagement I've taken. ... The
> consequences need to be unfolded and don't unfold all by themselves.
> Fidelity consists in being in the subjective element of those conse-
> quences. This means, basically, that one accepts to participate in the
> new subject made possible by the event.[42]

This succinct and accessible definition of becoming a "subject to
truth" appears, perhaps not coincidentally, in one of Badiou's
recent expositions of what it means to fall authentically in love
– love being one of the four conditions from which Badiou says
a new truth can emerge. And love is certainly the driving force
behind the Giaour's actions in Byron's poem, as he declares during
his final extended monologue:

'Yes, Love indeed is light from heaven –
A spark of the immortal fire
With angels shar'd – by Alla given,
To lift from earth our low desire.
Devotion wafts the mind above,
But Heaven itself descends in love –
A feeling from the Godhead caught,
To wean from self each sordid thought – (ll. 1131–8)

Although its religious vocabulary is at odds with Badiou's declared atheism (and, for that matter, with the suspicion toward institutionalized religion which the Giaour displays elsewhere), the sentiments unexpectedly coincide with Badiou's own. What might sound like self-centeredness in Byron's hero's experience of love – he values it because it purifies him – is transmuted in Badiou's philosophical system into something more selfless via his insight (shared with one of his theoretical masters, Jacques Lacan) that love is less about the formation of a couple than about how authentic love provides each partner with the opportunity to see the world anew, by committing themselves to a partnership that is nevertheless something other than a complete fusion:

Love is not that which from a Two taken as structurally given creates a One of ecstasy . . . for the ecstatic One can be inferred to be beyond the Two only as a *suppression of the multiple*. . . . [Secondly,] Love does not involve prostrating the Same before the alter [*sic*] of the Other. I will argue that love is not even an experience of the other, but an experience *of the world*, or of the situation, under the postevental condition that there are Two.[43]

For Badiou, togetherness-in-disjunction is the hallmark of the authentically loving couple. Their willingness to face every new situation from this new vantage point is what guarantees the truth brought into being by their love; for both, the world is radically changed as a result of their commitment to seeing and acting within it together. In Badiou's words, "Love is an enquiry into the world from the vantage point of the Two."[44]

Turning back to *The Giaour*, however, we see that Byron's vision of his protagonist's experience of the truth of love darkens after Leila's death. The Giaour is indeed faithful to their love inasmuch as he never takes another lover; at least, none is mentioned in the text. And although we learn almost nothing regarding what the relationship was like while it lasted, the Giaour powerfully describes his sense of loss in the wake of Leila's murder: "She was my life's unerring light –; That quench'd—what beam shall break my night?" (ll. 1145–6). But his faithfulness leaves him with nothing to lose as well as with nothing more to hope: "Who falls from all he knows of bliss,/ Cares little into what abyss" (ll. 1157–8). Presumably, such feelings of abandonment and hopelessness are not Badiou's ideal outcome of fidelity. He does say, however, that after the "partial decentering" of the self via the "new orientation of experience" brought about by love's truth, there is no complete return to normalcy: "Putting an end to love is always disastrous. Even if you can accept, even desire, this disaster, the rupture remains, nonetheless, intrinsically disastrous."[45] So what happens to the faithful subject of love when the other element of the Two no longer exists? *The Giaour* makes quite clear that its protagonist experiences neither remorse nor redemption following his killing of Hassan, but rather continues to feel responsible for Leila's death, suffering spectral visions and longing for the quiet of the grave.

Yet even a quiet death for the Giaour seems less than guaranteed, given the strange passage prior to his final speech in which Byron unexpectedly takes up the perspective of Hassan's mother, who learns of her son's murder and curses the Giaour in terms both vivid and specific. He will go to hell eventually, she claims,

"But first, on earth as Vampire sent,
Thy corse shall from its tomb be rent;
Then ghastly haunt thy native place
And suck the blood of all thy race,
There from thy daughter, sister, wife,
At midnight drain the stream of life;
Yet loathe the banquet which perforce
Must feed thy livid living corse; (ll. 755–62)

Putting aside this passage's hints of incest (a theme to which I will return when discussing *Manfred*), what is most remarkable here is the vision of the Giaour's punishment as a kind of earthly damnation – one, moreover, in which his faithfulness to Leila is mutated into a faithless breaking of the bonds that are supposed to hold between family members. Even as he avoids the scandal of homoeroticism by leaving male kin out of the familial cast of characters that the Giaour sucks, Byron neatly reverses the directives of Badiou's schema of amorous truth: the vampire feels no love as he bites others, only hunger and need; far from respecting the alterity of the bitten, his bite converts the Other to the Same; and of course the vampire necessarily fails to be changed for the better by the encounter. Although Hassan's mother's prophecy goes unrealized, Byron's protagonist certainly endures a version of such empty subjectivity, bereft of past and future alike: "My memory now is but the tomb/ Of joys long dead—my hope—their doom" (ll. 1000–1). Finally, is it merely a coincidence that the author of one of the first vampire tales published in English, John Polidori, was Byron's personal physician – and later claimed to have based the title figure of his novella *The Vampyre* (1819) on the poet himself?

The Giaour is not usually read along the philosophical lines I have sketched above. By contrast, Byron's later closet drama, *Manfred* (1817), has lent itself to philosophical readings almost all too readily; McGann's observation that it is "Byron's most Nietzschean work" is typical in this regard.[46] Begun in the spring of 1816 while Byron was on vacation in the Alps, the play's compositional origins lie in the same Gothic, sublime geography that produced *The Vampyre* and Mary Shelley's more famous meditation on monstrous subjectivity, *Frankenstein; or, The New Prometheus* (1819). Accordingly, *Manfred* has frequently been read as a subject-centered work, "an exploration in the meaning, even the possibility, of integrity and selfhood," to quote McGann again. The application of a Badiouian rather than a Nietzschean lens, however, allows us to see that Byron's verse drama does not take for granted the presence of a subject that precedes its investments in truth procedures; instead, as Badiou would have it, the subject is what emerges from such a process – if, that is, it can remain faithful to the truth-event in which it has participated. The difficulties of such fidelity, already on display (as we have seen) in *The Giaour*, are also central to *Manfred*.

Initially, it is not difficult to discern the reasons for the critical consensus connecting *Manfred* to proto-Nietzschean thought. From the play's opening scene, its protagonist is presented as an exceptional individual, one who not only literally lives high above most of humanity in his Alpine castle but also has mastered every mortal knowledge,

Philosophy and science, and the springs
Of wonder, and the wisdom of the world,
I have essayed, and in my mind there is
A power to make these subject to itself –
But they avail not:[47]

What "philosophy and science" cannot do, as the rest of this passage and subsequent scenes insinuate, is erase Manfred's guilt concerning the suicide of his sister, Astarte, following her recognition of his incestuous love. Given the scandalous nature of both Manfred's desire and Astarte's suicide, the text itself is never this explicit; by refusing to disclose the precise nature of either, moreover, Byron knowingly stokes the rumors surrounding his affair with his half-sister, and invites readers to reach their own conclusions.[48] More important for my purposes, however, Manfred characterizes himself as possessing the "power" to subject both "wonder" and "wisdom" to the dictates of his own consciousness. It is statements like this – as well as subsequent claims on Manfred's part that he is effectively "beyond good and evil," to paraphrase both Byron and Nietzsche – that have led many critics to christen Manfred a proto-*übermensch*.[49]

To identify in Manfred a figure closer to that of the Badiouian subject-in-making than that of the Nietzschean over-man, however, we may begin by heeding Badiou's recent critique of the latter. In truth, Nietzsche does not generally play a large role in the latter's thought, except perhaps as a foil against which to position himself, as in the following:

> There is a secret philosophical complicity between the theories that root meaning in the intentionalities of consciousness (to cut to the chase, let's call these the phenomenological orientations) and those, by all appearances entirely inimical, which make life into the active name of being (let's call these the vitalisms: Nietzsche, Bergson, and Deleuze). This complicity rests on the axiomatic assumption of a term which has the power to transcend the states that deploy or unfold it, such that every singularity of being can be rigorously thought only in the most refined possible description of the unique act that constitutes and relates it to the One, of which it is a transitory mode.[50]

Badiou is describing another form of what Harman would call overmining, locating a homology between phenomenological approaches that reduce individual acts to effects of intentional consciousness, and vitalist approaches that reduce individual entities to momentary upheavals in the current of life itself. The problem with both approaches – and we might also include existentialism, broadly understood via the Sartrean dictum "existence precedes essence" – is actually two-fold. First, as the above quotation implies, they take for granted what they should be explaining: the supposed existence of a unified or unitary subject or force to which individual events or entities are referred. Second, they both implicitly rely on a concept of dissolution as the necessary inverse of what Badiou calls the "constituent movement" of the subject or entity, which is figured as a momentary singularity of a larger, "originary over-existence." Accordingly, Badiou concludes, "We can thus say that the term common to phenomenology and vitalism . . . is death, as the attestation of finite existence, which is simply a modality of an infinite over-existence, or of a power of the One which we only experience through its reverse."[51] Not surprisingly, Badiou is unsatisfied with such formulations, which he finds intrinsically onto-theological inasmuch as they ultimately depend upon "a secularized or sublimated God operat[ing] in the background . . . We're always dealing with Him, this underlying infinite whose terrestrial writing is death."[52]

God does not play a role in *Manfred*, even if Byron's "sacramental vision of nature" has occasionally been identified elsewhere.[53] Death, however, is omnipresent; it is both what Manfred wants to conquer – the climactic scene of the closet drama involves his conjuring of Astarte's ghost, in order to hear whether it forgives him – and what he longs for, in the hopes that it will grant him some sort of respite. All of this is quite well established. Yet Manfred's final words, spoken after he has successfully fought off a horde of demons attempting to drag him to hell, should give us pause; turning to the only witness of his demise, he famously cries "Old man! 'tis not so difficult to die" (3.4.151). Byron's point, it would seem, is that death is not the difficult part of existence; it is life itself – in Badiou's terms, trying to become a subject – that is the real challenge. This is where Badiou's concept of the subject as a process, not a product, seems most germane. In his first major theoretical treatise, *Theory of the Subject* (1982; Eng. trans. 2009), Badiou had not yet hit upon mathematics as the basis of his ontology, but was already moving toward his later conception of the subject as something that comes into being only by becoming and then remaining faithful to a truth process. Let's consider only a few of Badiou's early theses, which appear at the start of the last section of *Theory of the Subject*, regarding what he calls, in tellingly formal language, the "the subject-effect":

> 1. The subject-effect is the split articulation of a structural vacillation around an empty place and a forced excess over this place. . . .
> 5. The subject-effect is only the divisible unity of subjectivization [destruction of the empty place] and the subjective process [recomposition at the place of excess]. Each of these moments is abstract. It is not acceptable to speak of the subject except in light of a process of destruction-recomposition, which in turn is referred, in a second articulation, to the dialectic of lack and excess.
> 8. The subject-effect is integrally designated in the topology of the four concepts: anxiety, courage, justice, and superego [terror]. . . .
> 10. A subject is nowhere given (to knowledge). It must be found.[54]

The plotting of the subject's emergence here is topographical rather than purely mathematical; in that sense, it is closer to the spirit of *Logics of Worlds* than to Badiou's formulation in *Being and Event* of subjectivization as a process of fidelity to the emergence of a truth that is produced from the void of a given situation.

Nevertheless, the main points outlined above can serve well to unearth a proto-Badiouian sense of subject formation in *Manfred*. Somewhat ironically, Manfred initially presents himself as a powerful, unified subject; as if it were not enough that his very name begins with the generic "Man," he consistently asserts his control over powers both natural and supernatural as evidence of his essential subjective coherence. Speaking to the seven spirits he conjures in the opening scene, for example, Manfred proclaims: "Slaves, scoff not at my will!/ The mind, the spirit, the Promethean spark,/ The lightning of my being, is as bright,/ Pervading, and far-darting as your own" (1.1.153–6). Yet although he can command spirits, his early attempts to learn from them whether Astarte forgives him prove useless. On the brink of committing suicide by throwing himself off an Alpine cliff, however, something holds him back: "I feel the impulse – yet I do not plunge; . . . There is a power upon me which withholds/ And makes it my fatality to live" (1.2.20, 23–4). Effectively empty inside – in the next lines, Manfred describes how "[I] wear within myself/ This barrenness of spirit, and [am]/ My own soul's sepulcher" (1.2.25–7)

– Manfred is also held back by a "power" which exerts its force on him from without. Most directly, Byron here references the curse placed on Manfred at the end of the previous scene by those spirits who wish to extend his torments; at the same time, however, this profile of Manfred's psyche strongly echoes Badiou's conception of the subject-effect as oscillating between "an empty place and a forced excess over this place." More, the two axes that describe this profile – anxiety–courage and justice–terror – describe very well the competing vectors of Manfred's fluctuating affective state.

Since the subject must be "found" rather than "given to knowledge," the pertinent question for the rest of Byron's verse drama thus becomes: does Manfred succeed in finding his subjectivity? More specifically, to return to the language of Badiou's terminology in *Being and Event*, does he succeed in locating a truth process to which he can commit himself? The answer must be that he does not. In the play's second act, two new figures appear, each of whom offers Manfred a possible way forward: the Chamois Hunter and the Witch of the Alps. To approximate Byron's own Romantic vocabulary, these two represent the virtues of "natural man" and "supernatural woman," respectively, but Manfred cannot accept the truths they represent, despite the fact that the Chamois Hunter in particular embodies much of what McGann identified several decades ago as Romantic ideology. Manfred is not blind to the attractions of the Hunter's existence, which he recognizes as encompassing "Thy humble virtues, hospitable home,/ And spirit patient, pious, proud and free" (2.2.64–5); he simply cannot see their relevance to his own situation. His admonition to the Hunter – "actions are our epochs" (2.2.52) – directly indexes his sense of responsibility for Astarte's suicide, to be sure, but it also reminds us of Badiou's insistence that subjectivization requires the individual to commit to a truth-event, even or perhaps especially in the absence of certain knowledge of its outcome. Manfred claims to be above all human concerns, yet he is continually torn by a guilt that can only be the product of his involuntary investment in the social norms that deemed his love unacceptable and led to Astarte's suicide. In other words, although he is aware that there are other multiplicities within his situation that could potentially be counted differently, in such a way as to alter the coordinates of the situation itself (and therefore by extension his position within it), Manfred cannot commit himself to this new count. He accepts, for example, this mockery and rejection by the Witch of the Alps:

And for this –
A being of the race thou dost despise,
The order which thine own would rise above,
Mingling with us and ours, thou dost forgo
The gifts of our great knowledge, and shrink'st back
To recreant mortality – Away!" (2.2.121–6)

Translating Byron's mystical-Romantic language into Badiou's terminology, the Witch offers Manfred a version of immortality not dissimilar to that which Badiou says can effectively be attained by humans only via the process of incorporation into the body of a truth. It is this ability to become part of something greater than what already exists that for Badiou offers the individual the opportunity to become "Immortal" – not in the sense of transcending death, as the Witch of the Alps appears to offer, but of becoming eternally joined to a new immanence: "Point by point, a body [of truth] reorganizes itself, making appear in the world ever more singular consequences, which subjectively weave a truth about which it can be said that it will render eternal the present of the present."[55]

Although the above quotation is specifically about the truth domain of politics, there's no reason it should not apply to the other domains in which a new truth may emerge. The irony of *Manfred*, however, is that it ultimately brings Badiou's truth conditions into conflict with each other. As the Witch of the Alps realizes, Manfred is unable to accede to the immortality offered him by the spirit world because of his loyalty to Astarte's memory. Such immortality would presumably enable Manfred to become the great leader he has always dreamed of being, but he is held back by the ever-present guilt he feels. Since politics is the realm of emancipatory collective projects, and love is the domain wherein (as we saw in *The Giaour*) "the Two" remain separate even as they face the world together, then Manfred effectively finds himself torn between their competing demands for his fidelity. Similarly, his guilt over Astarte's death holds him back from breakthroughs in the realms of art and science – realms of which Manfred claims to be thoroughly tired due to his overarching world-weariness. The philosophical apex of this poem, then, lies neither in Manfred's acts of conjuration nor in the pyrrhic victory of his final resistance to a demon horde, but rather in his first-act recognition that humanity is by definition caught between opposing domains:

> Beautiful!
> How beautiful is all this visible world!
> How glorious in its action and itself;
> But we, who name ourselves its sovereigns, we,
> Half dust, half deity, alike unfit
> To sink or soar, with our mix'd essence make
> A conflict of its elements . . . (1.2.35–41)

For Byron, it seems, humans are themselves already composed of multiplicities – hence our "mix'd essence" – that resist being formed or counted as a coherent set. Belonging to no single sphere, partaking of multiple conditions without fully inhabiting any of them, how can we imagine we could be dissolved into the body of a new truth? In this light, Manfred's stubborn decision to resist the demons who come to claim him in the drama's final scene can only be read as resistance to what Badiou calls "a protocol of incorporation."[56] At the same time, however, Manfred thereby comes to represent precisely Badiou's assertion that "the creator is a vanishing cause": as the author of his own tragedy, so to speak, the play must conclude with Manfred's demise, since neither redemption, nor forgiveness, nor transcendence is forthcoming, and (literal) incorporation into a truth not of his own making is unacceptable to him. Accordingly, we can now appreciate more fully Manfred's final insight of the drama in which he stars, that it is not as difficult to die as we might suppose. Indeed, as *Manfred* memorably dramatizes, it is living as a Badiouian subject that is truly difficult – perhaps impossible.

Don Juan, which Byron began in 1818 and left unfinished at his death in 1824, is almost unanimously considered as the work in which he discovered once and for all his proper genre and voice. Gone are both the dark, tormented poses and the philosophical investments (not to say pretensions) of the Oriental Tales and closet dramas. What remain are, first, strong traces of Byron's early masterpiece, *Childe Harold's Pilgrimage*, with its geographic fluidity, political topicality, socio-cultural curiosity, and narrative digressiveness; and second, a freedom of thought and expression that Byron finally seems to have felt fully comfortable articulating. He was also at a point in his life where, both professionally and personally, he felt he had nothing more to lose. Writing from Venice to his friend and publisher John Murray after sending the latter the second canto of *Don Juan*, Byron warned Murray not to make additional edits:

> But I will permit no curtailments except those mentioned about Castlereagh & the two *'Bobs'* in the introduction [referring to scathing attacks on Viscount Castlereagh, who had negotiated the controversial Peace of Vienna, and Robert Southey, the Poet Laureate] – You shan't make *Canticles* of my Cantos. The poem will please if it is lively – if it is stupid it will fail – but I will have none of your damned cutting & slashing. – If you please you may publish *anonymously*[;] it will perhaps be better; – but I will battle my way against them all – like a Porcupine.[57]

To this prickly statement Byron adds a significant addendum:

> So you and Mr Foscolo etc. want me to undertake what you call a 'great work' an Epic poem I suppose or some such pyramid. – I'll try no such thing – I hate tasks – and then 'seven or eight years'! God send us all well this day three months – let alone years . . . And works too! – is Childe Harold nothing? you have so many *'divine'* poems, is it nothing to have written a *Human* one?[58]

By "divine poems," Byron is probably referring to those making use of supernatural characters and elements; he may even be thinking of his own *Manfred*. In this context, *Don Juan* is a "human" poem merely by virtue of its being free from such paraphernalia. In what remains of this chapter, however, I would like to begin to consider what it might mean to think of *Don Juan* as a "human" poem in another, more contemporary way: as a poem that ponders what it means to be human in a non-anthropocentric manner. We can do this, moreover, by returning to Latour, especially to his more recent work, which he calls "an anthropology of the moderns."

As we know, throughout his career Latour has worked to overturn the deeply ingrained assumption that nature and culture, or – to put it in SR terms – objects and subjects, occupy inherently different ontological planes of existence. Recently, however, he has admitted that Actor-Network-Theory is insufficiently nuanced to describe effectively the variety of ways in which modern habits of thought have attempted to carry out the purification of the natural from the cultural (even while consistently creating hybrids of them). With *An Inquiry into Modes of Existence* (2012; Eng. trans. 2013), Latour has begun the process of attempting to document the variety of patterns that characterize different modern modes of being. In doing so, he has moved far beyond the concept of networks that initially informed his method. Indeed, "network" is now only one of fifteen (or twelve, depending on how you count them) modes that Latour identifies as composing the panoply of modern discursive-institutional practices of truth-making; these include well-established and generally agreed upon domains like religion, politics, and law, as well as more obscure (but potentially no less important) modes like habit, technology, and fiction.[59]

This welter of modes can be problematic not only in terms of its sheer number but also its apparent arbitrariness; some modes are really ways of combining elements, such as networks, whereas others are more clearly domains of thought and action.[60] For our purposes, however, the great contribution of Latour's rhetoric of modern modes is that it throws into relief the greatest difficulty of composing a common world: the "crossing" of modes is absolutely necessary, since we must talk to each other in a common language if we are ever to act in concert, yet it is simultaneously nearly impossible, since different modes both encode and produce different sets of values. This is so, moreover, regarding not only Latour's original categories of nature/culture and object/subject, but also even such basic concepts as what counts as a fact or a good. Latour's hope is that by delineating the different modes and their common institutional "moves" in the greatest possible detail, it will be possible "to bridg[e] the abyss that separates what the Moderns say from what they do" and hence to attempt to "institute the Moderns [i.e., ourselves] in habitats that are, if not stable, at least sustainable and reasonable."[61]

Let us now consider, briefly, how a version of Latourian inquiry is enacted – but also, I want to suggest, critiqued – in the first canto of *Don Juan*. Leaving aside the hilariously barbed dedication, which was not published until after Byron's death, the poem begins with the poet's ironic call for a protagonist worthy of his time and attention – or at least one who can bear the burden of being the vehicle of his wide-bore social critique:

I want a hero: an uncommon want,
    When every year and month sends forth a new one,
Till, after cloying the gazettes with cant,

The age discovers he is not the true one;
Of such as these I should not care to vaunt,
   I'll therefore take our ancient friend Don Juan,
We all have seen him in the pantomime
Sent to the devil, somewhat ere his time.[62]

"Cloying the gazettes with cant": with this allusion to the copious periodical advertising of his era, Byron rhetorically inserts his poem into the circuits of print culture that made up media reproducibility in the Romantic era.[63] Beyond being a material object and commodity in its own right, that is, *Don Juan* as a text is also extraordinarily self-conscious in its internal deployment of a whole host of both popular and underground codes and jargons.[64]

Putting this in the Latourian terms introduced earlier, we can immediately say that *Don Juan* both delineates and participates in a number of the networks that produce the social effects they represent. But adding *An Inquiry into Modes of Existence* allows us to be more precise. Here, Latour recognizes that his previous focus on networks has had the unfortunate side effect of making every assemblage of actants sound similar, usually to the dismay of the human participants themselves: "we understand this now, this method has retained some of the limitations of critical thought: the vocabulary it offers is liberating but too limited to distinguish the values to which the informants cling so doggedly" (*Inquiry*, 64). Accordingly, his *Inquiry* sets out a new framework in which all networks – denominated [NET] – need to be understood according to the "various *trajectories* of veridiction or malediction" – prepositions, or [PRE] – against and through which they operate. Likewise, I want now to suggest that *Don Juan* represents a similar advance over *Childe Harold's Pilgrimage*: whereas that early poem is mostly restricted to doing what Latour says ANT is good at doing – namely, "making it possible to follow the liaisons of humans and nonhumans, and especially . . . transforming the notion of "the social" and society into a general principle of free association" (64) – the later poem traces a number of different modes of being that may have superficially similar arrangements, but ultimately adhere to quite different sets of conditions for producing their particular truths, beings, and domains of knowledge. I do not wish to claim that *Don Juan* somehow foresees or adheres to all of the modes delineated by Latour; instead, I want to suggest that we can use the variegated framework of Latour's *Inquiry* as a window through which to view the poem's first canto in order to gain additional insights into the operations and relations of some of its various modes. Byron's generic and thematic experimentations in *Don Juan* allow for crossings of the various chains of association in and through which we live; tracking these modal intersections, moreover, helps "define what is specific about" each mode and thereby establishes the grounds for illuminating "the often tortuous history of their relations" (63).

If there is a base or background mode of *Don Juan*, it is [NET] itself: the poem's formal constitution as a self-conscious, increasingly diffuse set of character studies, scenes, reflections, and adventures. Byron's unwillingness to be hemmed in by the usual conventions of long-form poetry is already on display in the later cantos of *Childe Harold*, which phase out their eponymous protagonist in favor of a more direct narrative voice that allows Byron more freedom to range imaginatively across time and space. This rejection of the requirements of the classical epic is made explicit at the start of *Don Juan*, where he foregoes beginning his poem *in medias res* by proclaiming with humorous bluntness that "That is the usual method, but not mine –/ My way is to begin with the beginning" (1.7.49–50). Nicholas Halmi cites this as one of many places where Byron "honors epic norms as much in the breach as in the observance," and goes on to conclude that Byron's ambivalence toward his poem's generic identity is not only highly self-reflexive – later in Canto One, for example, Byron jokes that "My poem's epic and is meant to be" (1.200.1592) before cataloguing the generic requirements that each book will supposedly meet – but also an integral component of its fitness for its task: "Don Juan adapts its various literary models . . . for the purposes of an extraordinary capaciousness of view, and precisely in the renunciation of any pretension to *una visione unitaria del mondo*."[65] In Latourian terms, we can say that by transforming the epic into a vehicle for open-ended reflections on his society, Byron effectively renders long-form poetry capable of tracking modernity's multiple modes of existence.

Several of these modes are made visible early in Canto One, which introduces Juan's infamously dysfunctional family. From a biographical perspective these opening stanzas can be interpreted primarily in *roman à clef* fashion; historicist critics, by contrast, have sought to locate in Byron's representations of Juan and his family various representations (coherent or otherwise) of the norms of Byron's day. A Latourian modal analysis, however, allows us not only to go far beyond the (psycho)biographical – an interpretive mode that Byron seems to have invited, and which for that very reason we should perhaps eschew – but also to make sense of the contradictions that have led more historically minded critics to condemn Byron's supposed confusion regarding matters of ideology.[66] Indeed, bringing Latour's modes to bear on *Don Juan* suggests that its uneasy jumbling of contradictory perspectives and discourses may be one of its greatest strengths. Juan's father, for example, is clearly a being of what Latour calls "the most common, the most familiar of all" modes of existence (*Inquiry*, 265): habit ([HAB]). If habit is indeed "the patron saint of laid-out routes, pathways, and trails," then Don Jóse, whom Byron describes as "a mortal of the carless kind,/ With no great love for learning, or the learn'd" (1.19.145–6), is a devotee of the highest order. Without second thoughts, he falls back on his respectable lineage and equally time-honored habit of taking mistresses – a habit that Byron wryly suggests is inherited, since Don José behaves as if he were "a lineal son of Eve" (1.18.143).

Soon, however, a new character is introduced who clearly belongs to a different mode: Donna Inez, Juan's mother. Her primary mode, we learn quickly, is the religious ([REL]), which brings with it a different set of norms than Don José's carelessly patriarchal habits. According to Latour, unfolding the network and defining the prepositions of [REL] have little to do with either recovering or debunking some sort of authentic spirituality; rather, like the other significant modern modes – especially politics, law, technology, and "Double Click" (in which, like the impatient user of a computer mouse, information is expected to be accessed immediately and unproblematically) – what counts for the beings of religion is less the specific content of what is thought and said than *how* one speaks and behaves in a religious context. In this way, the "beings of religion" bear the most resemblance to those of the more general category of reproduction ([REP]), which includes everything from chairs and electrons to bodies and languages; in both cases, "Continuity over the long term is obtained . . . by a particular form of discontinuity that we have called persistence" (*Inquiry*, 311). Let us note, too, that the specific type of discontinuity or "hiatus" that enables the reproduction of the religious mode of existence is the "break in time," which can be experienced as conversion, apocalypse, salvation, or (re)incarnation.

Doubtless, Byron intended to mock his estranged wife when he gave Juan's mother characteristics he associated with her, including a faultless memory, a facility with mathematics, and a high degree of moral superiority: "She made the cleverest people quite ashamed,/ And even the good with inward envy groan,/ Finding themselves so very much exceeded/ In their own way by all the things that she did" (1.10.77–80).[67] But reading Donna Inez as a Latourian being also sheds light on less obvious elements of her character. When Byron reports, for example, that "her conversation was obscure/ Her thoughts were theorems, her words a problem/ As if she deem'd that mystery would ennoble 'em" (1.13.102–4), [REL] helps us realize that her obscurity of speech is likely involuntary, since religious beings (at least Christian ones; it's unclear whether Latour's model works outside the Judeo-Christian tradition) replicate by undergoing periodic temporal discontinuities that make them "gradually become incomprehensible in [their] own eyes" (*Inquiry*, 313). Less a hypocrite than a walking contradiction, Donna Inez's self-defeating manner – "To others' share let 'female errors fall',/ For she had not even one – the worst of all" (1.16.127–8) – remains opaque even to her. More problematic still, between her mathematical cast of mind and her religious mode of being Donna Inez believes she has access to modes of truth-seeking that are universal, yet the truths she produces or accesses – and as should be clear by now, very much in contrast to Badiou, these are essentially undifferentiated activities for Latour – are for this very reason completely incomprehensible to the rest of her family. Accordingly, although Byron seems to think he is being purposefully disingenuous when he claims not to know why Donna Inez and Don José argued (see 1.23.177–8), he is accurate inasmuch as the characters themselves, fully immersed in their different modes of existence, necessarily view one another's actions and values with complete incomprehension and therefore scorn.

But what of Juan himself, the "hero" of his own epic? As critics have long noted, he begins the poem as an archetypal naïf – Byron's satirical inversion of the famous seducer, now himself repeatedly pursued and seduced – and only slowly (and perhaps always incompletely) assumes the world-weary persona that Childe Harold perennially embodies. Juan enters life full of juvenile vitality – "A little curly-headed, good-for-nothing,/ And mischief-making monkey from his birth" (1.25.193–4) – only to be spoiled by his parents while simultaneously left in the dark about the source of their conflict. After his father's death, moreover, Juan remains ignorant, by his mother's decree, about all matters sexual:

> But that which Donna Inez most desired,
> And saw into herself each before all
> The learned tutors whom for him she hired,
> Was, that his breeding should be strictly moral; [. . .]
> Arts, sciences, no branch was made a mystery
> To Juan's eyes, excepting natural history. (1.39.305–8, 311–12)

As readers of the poem well know, this strategic omission in his educational program causes Juan no small amount of confusion in other areas of his studies; he has no idea what to make of Greek mythology and the classical authors, for example, until he finds his tutors have placed all the expurgated passages in an appendix, "Which saves, in fact, the trouble of an index" (1.44.351). The Bible remains an even greater mystery – indeed, it is literally a closed book to Juan, since his mother keeps the family Bible to herself and gives Juan another, presumably expurgated, version to read instead. Thoroughly confused by this partial education, Juan is subsequently utterly unprepared to withstand the advances of his mother's friend, the highly attractive Donna Julia.

The irony by which Juan's enforced ignorance leads directly to his first seduction is undeniably Byron's main point in Canto One. Once more, however, I want briefly to show how viewing Juan through the lens of what we can call Latour's "grammar of modes" can shed additional light on his status as an archetypal modern being. In fact, Juan in Canto One arguably, albeit involuntarily, inhabits the most insidious of modern modes: "Double Click" ([DC]). This is the mode of being that, more than any other, Latour decries as dangerous, even "devil[ish]," because information must come readily, even immediately, for it to count as information at all. Such a mode is dangerous not only because it leaves [DC] ignorant of anything that does not already fit her worldview, but also because whatever information [DC] *does* manage to access is treated as "pure" and unmediated (*Inquiry*, 93–4). As a result, the beings of [DC] instinctively reject any networked account of knowledge and its transmission as mere relativism, not realizing (says Latour) that they themselves have fallen into the worst kind of epistemological absolutism. This might seem an overly harsh description of Juan's attitude in Canto One, especially since his ignorance is hardly his own fault; rather, his simplistic attitude toward "truth" is arguably overdetermined by his being the product of a literal crossing of his father's ([HAB]) and mother's ([REL]) modes – a clear recipe for disastrous oversimplification. But if it exaggerates the malevolence of his illusions and ignorance, seeing Juan in the early cantos as an embodiment of [DC] throws into relief how his enforced partial education anticipates the ills of today's double-clickers, whose mode "threatens ... to efface, to obliterate one by one the types of veridiction necessary to the exercise of their civilized life" in the name of an illusory, immediate access to "pure" information and truth (94). Byron, it seems safe to say, would not have subscribed to such a view;[68] accordingly, his depiction of Juan's inability to make the necessary connections when he and Julia suddenly become embarrassed in each other's company (see, e.g., 1.70.559–60) becomes visible as a first sign of the proliferation of [DC] as the prevailing attitude of our current moment.[69]

Granted, there is nothing hidden about the fact that Juan's ignorance sets the stage for the rest of the epic; likewise, the near-total incomprehension that governs Donna Inez and Don Jóse's interactions prior to the latter's death exists on the epic's surface. But as Latour himself frequently points out, the goal of his work – and this holds true for ANT as well as for what we might call his grammar of modes – is not to critique, much less to add anything to or take anything away from the arrangements, institutions, or representations under scrutiny; instead, it is to re-describe behaviors and relations in such a way that those involved in them would agree with those descriptions while simultaneously better understanding what they are doing and why they are doing it.[70] In other words, even if applying Latour's modal framework to Byron's poem did nothing more than provide a new way of describing the fact that Donna Inez and Don José are incapable of comprehending each other, then it would still be valuable for allowing us to re-describe that incomprehension in a manner that sheds light on its causes while remaining recognizably "true" to the characters' own perceptions of themselves (although of course in the case of fictional beings their assent to our descriptions cannot be ascertained). Yet it does more than this, I want to argue, precisely because it illuminates the extent to which Byron's poem is already engaged in unpacking the ramifications of the fact that, thanks to astute observers like Latour, our modern modes of existence can be categorized in the first place. Aside from working out which specific modes are being represented or invoked at any given time or in any particular character/being, in other words, a Latourian reading of *Don Juan* underscores the fact that what is deeply wrong with modernity goes far beyond the flaws, limitations, or ideologies of any particular mode of existence. To be sure, a similar conclusion can also be drawn from *Childe Harold's Pilgrimage*: the world is a mad place because the people who run it have mad values or none at all. But with the help of Latour's grammar of modes, what becomes unmistakable in *Don Juan's* first canto is that the most significant "problem" with the untotalizable mesh of networked relations we call "society" does not lie with any single or even multiple set of harmful or misguided modes of existence against which other, more productive or benevolent modes might be arrayed; rather, it lies in the difficulty experienced by each mode when its beings try to interact and communicate with other modes' beings in mutually beneficial ways. This difficulty, as Latour shows throughout *An Inquiry into Modes of Existence*, stems not just from each mode having its own "rules" for producing its truth conditions – "rules" of which its beings are frequently only partially aware, if at all – but also from each mode's conviction that it alone proceeds logically and authentically. In this sense, Latour's catachrestic summary of the prototypical modern attitude toward so-called fetish worshippers – "We believe that we know. We know that they believe" (*Inquiry*, 173) – applies equally well to each mode of existence's attitude *vis-à-vis* all of the others. This is not a matter of false consciousness, as the original forms of Marxian critique would have it, because it is not merely a representation that exists at a distance from some material reality it is disguising (see *Inquiry*, 153). Likewise, although it bears some relation to Mikhail Bakhtin's concept (well known to literary critics) of heteroglossia,[71] it extends beyond the traditional literary critical focus on language to include, crucially, the powerful effects of different assemblages of behaviors, institutions, truth procedures, and worldviews. Accordingly, the "anthropologist of the moderns" must parse, describe, and delineate each mode's operations in such a way that its mechanisms are laid bare for those who operate within it as well as outside it. Only by doing so, Latour argues, can we move beyond critique toward something more positive, which he has lately taken to calling "compositionism": the active composing of our common world.[72]

How, finally, might this be undertaken most effectively? Happily for literary critics, Latour reserves a special place for fiction as an institution that lends itself readily to modal description. Already in *Reassembling the Social*, Latour names fiction as one of the places to which sociologists can always turn to find "occasions where th[e] momentary visibility" of networked associations can be brought into relief for the purposes of careful delineation: "when everything else has failed, the resource of fiction can bring . . . the solid objects of today into the fluid states where their connections with humans may make sense."[73] In his *Inquiry*, moreover, Latour devotes an entire chapter to what he now dubs "the beings of fiction": "these entities encountered everywhere that weigh on us with a quite particular weight of reality" (238). Here, fiction does not merely "freeze" associations so that we can get a clearer picture of them; it also provides evidence for Latour's diagnosis of the ontological confusions of the Moderns. Fictional beings provide the perfect vehicle through which Latour can pursue his goal of troubling the Moderns' unrelenting but misguided desire to separate "what is true" from "what is constructed" or "fabricated." Nobody doubts the existence of characters like Don Juan or Donna Inez, for example, but nobody tries to claim they are somehow natural. Yet the beings of fiction have been forced to pay a substantial price for their modern acceptance by being reduced to purely "imaginary creatures," "phantoms" who are said by the Moderns to originate only in the "human mind" (240). But to accept this, Latour points out, is to reinstate the "Bifurcation" between "words and the world," reality and fiction, that is merely another version of the endless modern attempt to purify the natural and the cultural. Understood properly, however – which is to say, understood as they actually function in the networks of human and non-human associations we misleadingly call "society" – the beings of fiction reveal once again the gap between what the Moderns say about themselves, and what they actually do. To use the example of Byron once more, his fictional creations – not just Childe Harold, the Giaour, Manfred, Don Juan, and the rest of his poetic characters, but also the Byronic persona that George Gordon developed over the course of his life – had, and arguably continue to have, much greater (i.e. longer lasting and more widespread) effects in the so-called "real world" than most of us, as "living" mortal persons, will ever have. As Latour observes, "Such works populate the world" (241) – a statement that is entirely realistic, once one comes round to seeing "the world" as Latour encourages us to see it, made up of relations and modes of being rather than of truly phantasmic abstractions like Nature, Society and Language (241–2). If, as we saw Manfred put it, to be human is indeed to be "half dust, half deity," then Latour's greatest achievement to date is to help us see that each of these components is equally real.

Notes

1. See, e.g., Tom Mole, *Byron's Romantic Celebrity: Industrial Culture and the Hermeneutics of Intimacy* (Basingstoke: Palgrave Macmillan, 2007).

2. Anthony Howe, *Byron and the Forms of Thought* (Liverpool: Liverpool University Press, 2013), 1. As his title makes clear, Howe is paraphrasing this perspective, not condoning it.

3. Emily A. Bernhard Jackson, *The Development of Byron's Philosophy of Knowledge: Certainty in Uncertainty* (Basingstoke: Palgrave Macmillan, 2010), 14.

4. Quoted in Anne Barton, "Byron Lives!," *The New York Review of Books* 40.11 (June 10, 1993), www.nybooks.com/articles/archives/1993/jun/10/byron-lives/?insrc=toc (accessed May 2, 2014).

5. Bernhard Jackson, *Byron's Philosophy of Knowledge*, 14.

6. Byron, *The Works of Lord Byron: Letters and Journals*, vol. 1, ed. Rowland E. Prothero (1898), http://www.gutenberg.org/cache/epub/8901/pg8901.html (accessed July 15, 2014).

7. I'm thinking here of the apparent affinity between Badiou's derisive summary of the default position he calls "democratic materialism" – *"There are only bodies and languages"* – and Latour's early thesis that "The principle of reality is other people." See Alain Badiou, *Logics of Worlds: Being and Event 2*, trans. Alberto Toscano (London and New York: Continuum, 2009), 1; Bruno Latour, "Irreductions," in *The Pasteurization of France*, trans. Alan Sheridan and John Law (Cambridge, MA: Harvard University Press, 1988), 166.

8. Byron, *Childe Harold's Pilgrimage*, in *The Major Works*, ed. Jerome J. McGann (New York: Oxford University Press, 1986), 44, I.69.692–701. Subsequent citations are given parenthetically in the text.

9. See McGann, "Introduction" to *The Major Works*, esp. xv–xvi.

10. Bruno Latour, *An Inquiry into Modes of Existence: An Anthropology*

of the Moderns, trans. Catherine Porter (Cambridge, MA: Harvard University Press, 2013).

11. See, e.g. David Hume, "On the Origin of Government," in *Essays: Moral, Political, and Literary*, ed. Eugene Miller (Indianapolis: Liberty Fund, 1985), 37–41.

12. Elsewhere, I have argued that the theoretical paradigms of the Scottish Enlighteners set the modern framework for understanding global modernity; see Evan Gottlieb, *Romantic Globalism: British Literature and Modern World Order, 1750–1830* (Columbus: Ohio State University Press, 2014), Chapter 1.

13. See, e.g., Christopher Berry, *Social Theory of the Scottish Enlightenment* (Edinburgh: University of Edinburgh Press, 1997); John D. Brewer, "Putting Adam Ferguson in his Place," *British Journal of Sociology* 58 (2007): 105–22; Fania Oz-Salzberger, *Translating the Enlightenment: Scottish Civic Discourse in Eighteenth-Century Germany* (Oxford: Clarendon Press, 1996); Frank Palmeri, "Conjectural History and the Origins of Sociology," *Studies in Eighteenth-Century Culture* 37 (2008): 1–21; and many of the essays in *The Cambridge Companion to the Scottish Enlightenment*, ed. Alexander Broadie (Cambridge: Cambridge University Press, 2003).

14. See, e.g., Bruno Latour and Steve Woolgar, *Laboratory Life: The Construction of Scientific Facts* (New York: Sage, 1979); Latour, *Science in Action: How to Follow Scientists and Engineers through Society* (Cambridge, MA: Harvard University Press, 1987).

15. Bruno Latour, *We Have Never Been Modern*, trans. Catherine Porter (Cambridge, MA: Harvard University Press, 1993), 11.

16. Ibid., 139, 74.

17. Ibid., 137, 139.

18. See the entry "Bullfighting" on Wikipedia, http://en.wikipedia.org/wiki/Bullfighting (accessed June 20, 2014).

19. Harold is a consummate observer, as Stanza 84 makes clear (the context here is no longer the bullfight specifically, but the description is accurate nonetheless): "Still he beheld, nor mingled with the throng;/ But view'd them not with misanthropic hate" (*Childe Harold's Pilgrimage* I.84.828–9).

20. See Fiona MacCarthy, *Byron: Life and Legend* (London: Faber and Faber, 2003), who writes that "the bullfight . . . aroused mixed emotions in Byron: excitement at the drama, horror at the torments of the toreador's dying horse" (96).

21. Bruno Latour, *Reassembling the Social: An Introduction to Actor-*

Network-Theory (Oxford: Oxford University Press, 2005), 54–5. For a detailed survey of Latour's career through the mid-2000s, plus an object-oriented critique of his ontology, see Graham Harman, *Prince of Networks: Bruno Latour and Metaphysics* (Melbourne: re.press, 2009).

22. Latour, *Reassembling the Social*, 5.
23. For Latour's definition of "mediation" (as opposed to a mere "intermediary"), see p. 307 in the very useful glossary near the end of his *Pandora's Hope: Essays on the Reality of Science Studies* (Cambridge, MA: Harvard University Press, 1999).
24. Bruno Latour, "An Attempt at a 'Compositionist Manifesto'," *New Literary History* 41 (2010): 474.
25. Ibid., 474. For the earlier argument to which Latour refers, see his "Why Critique Has Run Out of Steam: From Matters of Fact to Matters of Concern," *Critical Inquiry* 30.2 (2004): 225–48.
26. Latour, "Compositionist Manifesto," 485.
27. Among the many recent books on this subject, see especially McKenzie Wark, *Molecular Red: Theory for the Anthropocene* (New York and London: Verso, 2014). Latour's own book on ecology – a revised, expanded version of the Gifford Lectures he delivered at the University of Edinburgh in 2013 – is currently only available in French but is forthcoming in English as *Facing Gaia* (Polity, 2017).
28. Quoted in Annette Peach, "'Famous in my time': Publicization of Portraits of Byron during His Lifetime," in *Byron: The Image of the Poet*, ed. Christine Kenyon-Jones (Newark, DE: University of Delaware Press, 2008), 57.
29. See Mole, *Byron's Romantic Celebrity*, 74–5.
30. Badiou, Interview with Ben Woodard, in *The Speculative Turn: Continental Materialism and Realism*, ed. Levi Bryant, Nick Srnicek, and Graham Harman (Melbourne: re.press, 2011), 19.
31. For a selection of Badiou's accounts of his own mathematical methods, see, e.g., "Philosophy and Mathematics," in *Conditions*, trans. Steve Corcoran (London and New York: Continuum, 2008); *Number and Numbers*, trans. Robin Mackay (Cambridge and Malden, MA: Polity, 2008); *Mathematics of the Transcendental*, trans. A. J. Bartlett and Alex Ling (London and New York: Bloomsbury, 2014).
32. Alex Ling, "Ontology," in *Alain Badiou: Key Concepts*, ed. A. J. Bartlett and Justin Clemens (Durham: Acumen, 2010), 49.
33. Ibid., 52. Ling points to the importance of "the axiom of the power set" for Badiou's ontology, since it is here – in the count of all the possible subsets of a given set – that the void (set) always subsists.

34. Badiou, *Logics of Worlds*, 86, 92.

35. Ibid., 7.

36. Alain Badiou, *Second Manifesto for Philosophy*, trans. Louise Burchill (Cambridge and Malden, MA: Polity, 2011), 109.

37. See, e.g., Mary Hurst, "Byron's Catholic Confessions," *The Byron Journal* 40.1 (2012): 37.

38. Byron, *The Giaour: A Fragment of a Turkish Tale*, in *The Major Works*, ed. McGann, 207–47. Subsequent citations are given parenthetically in the text by line number.

39. For an introduction to Schlegel's use of the fragment, see Otabe Tanehisa, "Friedrich Schlegel and the Idea of Fragment: A Contribution to Romantic Aesthetics," trans. David Boyd, *Aesthetics* 13 (2009): 59–68; on the influence of the fragment form in subsequent philosophical thought, see, e.g., David Cunningham, "The Futures of Surrealism: Hegelianism, Romanticism, and the Avant-Garde," *SubStance* 34.2 (2005): 47–65, esp. 53–6.

40. See Byron, *The Major Works*, ed. McGann, 1034, note to p. 207.

41. Badiou, "Philosophy and Mathematics," 99.

42. Alain Badiou with Fabien Tardy, *Philosophy and the Event*, trans. Louise Burchill (Cambridge and Malden, MA: Polity, 2013), 48.

43. Alain Badiou, "What is Love?," in *Conditions*, trans. Steve Corcoran (London and New York: Continuum, 2008), 181–2.

44. Ibid., 193. We may note in passing that Badiou's notion of the couple's necessary disjunction has nothing to do with sexual differentiation on the basis of biology, but rather on the basis of "masculine" and "feminine" positions that may be occupied by persons of any gender. See *Philosophy and the Event*, 62–3.

45. Badiou with Tardy, *Philosophy and the Event*, 49.

46. Byron, *The Major Works*, ed. McGann, 1038, note to p. 274.

47. Byron, *Manfred: A Dramatic Poem*, in *The Major Works*, ed. McGann, Act 1, scene 1, lines 13–16. Subsequent citations are given parenthetically in the text by act, scene, and line numbers.

48. On the question of the nature of Byron's relationship with his half-sister, Augusta Leigh, see Duncan Wu, *Thirty Great Myths about the Romantics* (Malden, MA, and Oxford: Wiley Blackwell, 2015), 132–9.

49. E.g., "Good, or evil, life,/ Powers, passions, all I see in other beings/ Have been to me as rain unto the sands": *Manfred*, 1.1.21–3.

50. Badiou, *Logics of Worlds*, 267.

51. Ibid., 268.

52. Ibid., 268.

53. See, e.g., Gavin Hopps, "Shades of Being: Byron and the Trespassing of Ontology," in *Byron's Ghosts: The Spectral, the Spiritual and the Supernatural*, ed. Gavin Hopps (Liverpool: Liverpool University Press, 2013), 48–82. The classic work on Byron and religion remains Edward Marjurum, *Byron as Skeptic and Believer* (New York: Russell & Russell, 1962); for two more book-length studies on the general subjects of Byron and belief, see also Robert Gleckner, *Byron and the Ruins of Paradise* (Baltimore: Johns Hopkins University Press, 1967), and Wolf Hirst, *Byron, the Bible, and Religion* (London and Toronto: Associated University Presses, 1991).

54. Alain Badiou, *Theory of the Subject*, trans. Bruno Bosteels (London: Bloomsbury, 2013), 277–8. When Badiou returns to his four-point scheme of the affects that structure the subject-effect in *Logics of Worlds*, "terror" is replaced by "superego"; see *Logics of Worlds*, 86–7. Here, Badiou is very clear that they are not to be opposed merely in a conventional way, with courage–justice privileged over anxiety–terror: "All the affects are necessary in order for the incorporation of a human animal to unfold in a subjective process" (87).

55. Badiou, *Logics of Worlds*, 503.

56. Badiou with Tardy, *Philosophy and the Event*, 71.

57. Byron, Letter to John Murray, April 6, 1819, in *The Major Works*, ed. McGann, 998.

58. Ibid., 998. Byron's better-known description of *Don Juan*, in a letter to his friend Douglas Kinnaird, works a similar angle: "it may be bawdy – but is it not good English? it may be profligate – but is it not *life*, and is it not *the thing*? Could any man have written it – who has not lived in the world?"

59. The two-page chart listing all of the modes and their various perturbations is printed without pagination at the back of the book. The *Inquiry* also exists as an interactive website; see www.modesofexistence.org (accessed September 30, 2014).

60. I owe this observation to Graham Harman; see his *Bruno Latour: Reassembling the Political* (London: Pluto Press, 2014), esp. 81–107.

61. Latour, *An Inquiry into Modes of Existence*, 21, 23. Subsequent citations are given parenthetically in the text.

62. Byron, *Don Juan*, in *The Major Works*, ed. McGann, 378, Canto 1, Stanza 1, ll. 1–8. Subsequent citations are given parenthetically in the text by canto, stanza, and line number.

63. See, e.g., Hadley J. Mozer, "'I WANT a Hero': Advertising for an Epic Hero in *Don Juan*," *Studies in Romanticism* 44 (2005): 239–60.

64. On Byron's use of slang ("cant") in *Don Juan*, see especially Gary Dyer, "Thieves, Boxers, Sodomites, Poets: Being Flash to Byron's *Don Juan*," *PMLA* 116.3 (2001): 562–78.

65. Nicholas Halmi, "The Very Model of a Modern Epic Poem," *European Romantic Review* 21.5 (2010): 592, 597.

66. This is not to say that psychoanalytic critical methods have not produced important works of scholarship on Byron; see, in particular, Peter J. Manning's *Byron and his Fictions* (Detroit: Wayne State University Press, 1978). For an example of recent historicist criticism that (perhaps not surprisingly) finds Byron guilty of ideological confusion in *Don Juan*, see Eric Strand, "Byron's *Don Juan* as a Global Allegory," *Studies in Romanticism* 43 (2004): 503–36.

67. See also 1.12.89–92: "Her favourite science was the mathematical,/ Her noblest virtue was her magnanimity,/ Her wit (she sometimes tried at wit) was Attic all,/ her serious saying darken'd to sublimity ..."

68. For an extended reconstruction of Byron's epistemological perspectives, see Bernhard Jackson, *Development of Byron's Philosophy of Knowledge*.

69. For more popular studies of this attitude, see e.g. Nicholas Carr, *The Shallows: What the Internet is Doing to our Brains* (New York: Norton, 2010); Jarrod Lanier, *You are Not a Gadget: A Manifesto* (New York: Knopf, 2010); Evgeny Morozov, *To Save Everything Click Here: The Folly of Technological Solutionism* (New York: Public Affairs, 2013).

70. For a critique of Latour's reluctance to engage in critique, however, see Benjamin Noys, *The Persistence of the Negative: A Critique of Contemporary Continental Theory* (Edinburgh: Edinburgh University Press, 2010), 80–95.

71. See M.M. Bakhtin, *The Dialogic Imagination: Four Essays*, trans. Michael Holquist and Caryl Emerson (Austin: University of Texas Press, 1982).

72. See, e.g., Latour, "Compositionist Manifesto." Again, for Latour the great project on which humanity must embark in common – before it is too late – is a change in attitude toward the planet, its climate, and its resources; see the forthcoming publication of his modified and expanded 2013 Gifford Lectures, entitled *Facing Gaia* (Polity, 2017).

73. Latour, *Reassembling the Social*, 80, 82.

4

Shelley, Nihilism, and Speculative Materialism

In April 1811, a few months shy of his twentieth birthday, Percy Shelley was expelled from the University of Oxford. This was no surprise; days earlier, he and a friend had mailed an incendiary pamphlet of Shelley's devising to the bishops and heads of every college. Entitled *The Necessity of Atheism*, it begins with a telling epigraph by Sir Francis Bacon: "The human mind cannot accept at all as true that which has no clear and obvious demonstration."[1] In the pamphlet, Shelley returns to this theme almost immediately, restating it as a judgment on the importance of tangible evidence to any investigation: "A close examination of the validity of the proofs adduced to support any proposition is the only secure way of attaining truth, on the advantages of which it is unnecessary to descant."[2] The young radical then declares that "God is an hypothesis and, as such, stands in need of proof: the onus probandi [burden of proof] rests on the theist" (35). Given Oxford's notorious conservatism in the early nineteenth century, this alone would probably have warranted expulsion, but Shelley continues:

If we wish to explain our ideas of the Divinity we shall be obliged to admit that, by the word God, man has never been able to designate but the most hidden, the most distant and the most unknown cause of the effects which he saw; he has made use of [t]his word only when the play of natural and known causes ceased to be visible to him; as soon as he lost the thread of these causes, or when his mind could no longer follow the chain, he cut the difficulty and ended his researches by calling God the last of the causes, that is to say, that which is beyond all causes that he knew; thus he but assigned a vague denomination to an unknown cause, at which his laziness or the limits of his knowledge forced him to stop. Every time we say that God is the author of some phenomenon, that signifies that we are ignorant of how such a phenomenon was able to operate by the aid of forces or causes that we know in nature. (37)[3]

Combining the language of empiricism – cause and effect – with the rationalism of the Enlightenment, Shelley appears to reach a definitive conclusion that no sufficient proof of God exists; the burden of proof has not been met. Yet this must be understood in light of a key distinction Shelley makes directly before the above passage: "This negation must be understood solely to affect a creative Deity. The hypothesis of a pervading Spirit co-eternal with the universe remains unshaken" (31).

Needless to say, the Anglican heads of Oxford were not appeased. From an SR perspective, however, Shelley appears guilty less of atheism – after all, he expressly affirms his belief in a "pervading Spirit" whose existence and coevality with the universe is beyond question – than of the two-worlds metaphysics that has constrained philosophy since at least Kant. It was Kant himself who made room for a divine principle within a philosophically conceived universe by setting limits to humanity's knowledge of reality; in Braver's concise summation, the Kantian paradigm "consists in a single type of transcendental subject forming components of reality which are then known in the same way by everyone."[4] Whatever components of reality might exist outside human thought – Kant's noumena – are thus perceptible only by "an absolute subject," which is to say by God. On the strength of Shelley's youthful pamphlet alone, we might conclude that he hewed to some version of this schema, in which the limits of human reason mark the starting point of the divine.

As Paul Hamilton reminds us, however, it is dangerous to generalize about Shelley's beliefs on the basis of his many "striking quotations," especially when taken out of context. Shelley was certainly well acquainted with the materialist thinkers of his day, including Lucretius, Spinoza, and the French *philosophes*, as well as the Anglophone tradition (Bacon, Locke, Hume). Yet he also was attracted to Platonism, as evidenced by his repeated allusions to Plato's famous Allegory of the Cave, as well as his praise in *A Defence of Poetry* (written in 1821) of the classical philosopher as "essentially a poet": the highest praise Shelley could bestow.[5] In the unfinished essay "On Life" (written ca. 1820), Shelley figures his intellectual development as a movement from the first to the second of these positions: "The shocking absurdities of the popular philosophy of mind and matter, and its fatal consequences in morals ... had early conducted me to materialism. ... But I was discontented with such a view of things as it afforded" (506). Yet this self-narrative is at least partially belied by the inclusion of clearly metaphysical elements in Shelley's earliest poems.[6] Instead of hewing to a rigidly progressive view of Shelley's philosophical development, then, in this chapter I contend that Shelley's most visionary poems contain evidence of both his attraction to materialism and his belief that something may exist beyond the merely material. To pursue this fully, we must move beyond the line of interpretation, influentially promoted by Paul de Man and characteristic of much deconstructive criticism, that Shelley's poetry epitomizes the simultaneously arbitrary and inexorable power of language itself.[7] More specifically, I will argue that the inherent duality of Shelley's thought and language – caught between materialism and idealism, the arbitrary and the necessary, the secular and the spiritual – invites us to read his work alongside the ideas of two of the original Speculative Realists: Ray Brassier and Quentin Meillassoux. Brassier's "eliminative nihilism" uses contemporary materialism as the grounds for embracing a nihilism so complete that there is no remainder; for Brassier, only the thought of extinction at every level allows us to recognize the core truth that "there is a mind-independent reality, which, despite the presumptions of human narcissism, is indifferent to our existence. . ."[8] Brassier's conclusions, interestingly, almost directly contrast with those of Meillassoux, whose "speculative materialism" also supports reality's mind-independent status, but as the springboard from which to launch not nihilism but a philosophy of absolute possibility. In other words, as Peter Gratton observes, Brassier and Meillassoux begin from similar positions – philosophy must be brought into line with the findings of science (more specifically, in Meillassoux's case, with mathematics) – but differ greatly in their methods for pursuing this realignment and their conclusions regarding what happens "after the finitude of our own existence" is established.[9] Some of Percy Shelley's most influential writings, I want to demonstrate, not only anticipate what these two SR thinkers have in common – that is, their desire to align philosophy (or, for Shelley, poetry) with science – but also exhibit further tendencies that effectively showcase the "problems" as well as the "prospects" (to borrow the key terms of Gratton's subtitle) of Brassier's and Meillassoux's positions. In particular, I will argue that Shelley

courts but ultimately rejects nihilism in favor of a radically contingent ontology that is strikingly similar to Meillassoux's. In this
way, I hope to put an SR-style spin on Humphry House's decades-
old judgment that "We do not go . . . to Shelley . . . for a system, or
for a final answer about anything, but for an experience."[10]

Like his fellow "second-generation Romantics" (Byron and Keats),
Shelley mostly missed the initial tide of optimism among British
radicals that accompanied the start of the French Revolution.
Instead, Shelley – born in 1792 to a family of some lineage but
unsteady fortune – grew up in a decade that Richard Holmes
describes as "an age of upheaval, in which the Revolutionary and
then Napoleonic wars, although not fought on British soil, coin-
cided with equally revolutionary changes in scientific, artistic, and
political thought."[11] By the time he entered Eton College in 1804,
Shelley had already garnered a reputation for conducting chemical
experiments apt to go spectacularly wrong; moreover, Holmes's
portrayal of the young Shelley's attitude toward the natural sciences as "speculative and imaginative" rather than empirical resonates with Leone Vivante's description of Shelley's subsequent
poetry as "research" carried out in verse rather than a laboratory.[12]

Shelley's own statements about the role and value of poetry are,
if anything, even more ambitious. His *Defence*, to take only the
most prominent example, asserts that "poetry is at once the centre
and circumference of knowledge; it is that which comprehends
all science, and that to which all science must be referred" (531).
Here, however, Hamilton's warning not to take Shelley's quotations out of context is again relevant, since the preceding sentence
of the *Defence* asserts that "Poetry is indeed something divine,"
once more defying hard distinctions between the physical and the
metaphysical, the material and the immaterial, the natural and the
supernatural. Indeed, the *Defence* mixes empirical and theological
imagery in nearly equal proportions; after likening "the mind in
creation" to "a fading coal which some invisible influence, like an
inconstant wind, awakens to transitory brightness" (531), Shelley
describes the act of poetic composition in more spiritual terms: "It
is as it were the interpenetration of a diviner nature through our
own; but its footsteps are like those of a wind over a sea, which
the coming calm erases, and whose traces remain only as on the
wrinkled sand which paves it" (532). What both passages share,
of course, is the image of wind – breath, inspiration – that moves

or shapes the mind's productions, just as in Coleridge's "Eolian Harp" (whose titular music machine Shelley deploys on more than one occasion).[13] But while he is generally certain that inspiration comes from outside the human mind, Shelley is less certain about *which* outside it comes from. Is it immanent to the ontological plane of human existence, or does it hail from elsewhere? If the former, then Shelley is indeed a materialist, albeit one who occasionally invokes "the divine" – frequently called Spirit or Power in his poetry – as a metaphor for describing how the material world interfaces with the human mind to produce effects that sometimes seem to exceed their causes.

Given the intensity and frequency of his poetic engagements with such ontological questions, it is not surprising that Shelley has already received critical attention from SR perspectives. Before accounting for these, however, we may do better to see how a radical undecideability energizes Shelley's ontological perspective from nearly the start of his career. *Queen Mab; A Philosophical Poem* was conceived as early as December 1811, although not published until 1814. Its plot is hugely ambitious, as Shelley takes the Shakespearean fairy invoked by Mercutio in *Romeo and Juliet* (1.4.53–94) and transforms her into a spirit of almost unlimited knowledge and power who visits the sleeping Ianthe (modeled on Harriet Westbrook, Shelley's first wife) and takes her soul on a transcendent voyage through time and space. Shelley himself described the immensity of *Queen Mab*'s scope in no uncertain terms: "The Past, the Present, & the Future are the grand & comprehensive topics of this Poem."[14] Given its vast temporal scope, critics have understandably tended to focus on the politics of the poem's depictions of human history. This is a mistake, however, and not just because, as Monika Lee asserts, *Queen Mab* "is much more than a political manifesto. It is a lyrical enactment of the world's potential spiritual and political liberation through imaginative desire."[15] The poem's radical character stems not merely from its progressive politics and vision of a world set free by "imaginative desire," but also from the ways it repeatedly throws the limitations of our usual human-centered perspective into relief. Although its latter cantos are certainly brimming with references to tyrants who have fallen and warnings to "priests[s], conqueror[s], or prince[s]!" to mend their "errors" before it's too late (4.237, 257), these descriptions and admonitions are themselves placed in contexts that radically relativize their importance.

At certain points, this radical recontextualizing occurs in ways that may remind us of Morton's meshwork or DeLanda's Deleuzian framing of the earth as a dynamical system. This is the case, for example, when Mab reminds Ianthe (and, by extension, the reader) that an anthropocentric perspective on planetary life is sorely blinkered:

"How strange is human pride!
I tell thee that those living things,
To whom the fragile blade of grass,
That springeth in the morn
And perisheth ere noon,
Is an unbounded world;
I tell thee that those viewless beings
Whose mansion is the smallest particle
Of the impassive atmosphere,
Think, feel, and live like man . . . (2.225–34)

Drawing on up-to-date research concerning microscopic creatures, Shelley clearly anticipates Jakob von Uexküll's theory of the radically different *umwelts*, or perceptual environments, inhabited by diverse organisms.[16] By implication, we have sorely overestimated the uniqueness of our capacity to think and feel; could we see the world we inhabit at a higher resolution, so to speak, we would not privilege our human existence so highly. This insight is articulated again by Queen Mab in Canto IV, now infused with a strong pan-psychic dynamic: "Every grain/ Is sentient both in unity and part,/ And the minutest atom comprehends/ A world of loves and hatreds" (4.143–6). Similarly, Mab demonstrates on several other occasions that when seen from enough of a distance, humanity is merely one element of a planet in a galaxy that in turn is only one of a vast universe. This perspective first becomes visible, quite literally, when she takes Ianthe's spirit with her up beyond the Earth's atmosphere:

The magic car moved on.
Earth's distant orb appeared
The smallest light that twinkles in the heaven;
Whilst round the chariot's way
Innumerable systems rolled,
And countless spheres diffused
An ever-varying glory. (1.249–55)

To this description of what is subsequently called an "interminable wilderness/ Of world, at whose immensity/ Even soaring fancy staggers" (1.265–7), Shelley adds a long note which reads, in part, as follows: "The plurality of worlds, – the indefinite immensity of the universe is a most awful subject of contemplation. He who rightly feels its mystery and grandeur, is in no danger of seduction from the falsehoods of religious systems, or of deifying the principle of the universe."

This kind of imaginative movement, in which Shelley turns from considering the fullness of the microscopic worlds that exist beneath the threshold of unaided human perception to considering the tininess of the Earth as a whole when seen from the perspective of the universe, is not restricted to *Queen Mab*. It recurs in several of Shelley's other poems, most notably the last act of *Prometheus Unbound* (which I discuss later in this chapter) and the "Ode to Heaven," written in 1820. The latter poem articulates three levels of increasingly objective perspectives on our planet. First, a "Chorus of Spirits" proclaims the grandeur of Heaven as seen from Earth, calling the sky a "Palace-roof of cloudless night,/ Paradise of golden lights" (ll. 1–2). This viewpoint is quickly ironized, however, when Shelley pulls back in the second and third stanzas to reveal the sheer multitude of heavenly bodies, including "green worlds that glide along,/ And swift stars with flashing tresses,/ And icy moons most cold and bright/ And mighty suns, beyond the Night,/ Atoms of intensest light!" (ll. 14–18). Then "A Remoter Voice" responds, providing a neo-Platonist perspective wherein even the most gorgeous and awe-inspiring visions of this life pale in comparison to the clear view of perfect things that will become available after death: "But the portal of the grave,/ Where a world of new delights/ Will make thy best glories seem/ But a dim and noonday gleam/ From the shadows of a dream" (ll. 32–6). Yet even this voice is superseded by "A Louder and Still Remoter Voice," which chastises the neo-Platonic perspective by underscoring its naïve anthropocentrism. The power of this voice is worth reproducing in full:

Peace! The abyss is wreathed with scorn
At your presumption, Atom-born!
What is Heaven? And what are ye
Who to its brief expanse inherit?
What are suns and spheres which flee

With the instinct of that spirit
Of which ye are but a part?
Drops which Nature's mighty heart
Drives through thinnest veins. Depart! (ll. 37–45)

The "Remoter Voice" follows up this stinging rebuttal with a stunning vision of the entire universe's relative insignificance:

What is Heaven? A globe of dew,
Filling in the morning new
Some eyed flower whose young leaves waken
On an unimagined world.
Constellated suns unshaken,
Orbits measureless, are furled
In that frail and fading sphere
With ten million gathered there
To tremble, gleam, and disappear! (ll. 46–54)

Here, Shelley brilliantly brings together the microscopic and the macroscopic in a singular, startling vision of multiple universes: not just "a World in a grain of sand," as William Blake famously wrote,[17] but the universe in a drop of dew collecting momentarily in a flower growing on some distant planet.

As we will see, Shelley's recognition of humanity's inconsequentiality in the face of the universe's vastness (even, potentially, its multiplicity) is moderated by several countervailing beliefs. But if we now turn to Brassier's philosophical defense of nihilism, we can begin to note some of its affinities with Shelley's expressions of non-anthropocentrism. Brassier's major contribution to SR is his 2007 book, *Nihil Unbound: Enlightenment and Extinction*. Although its title echoes Shelley's *Prometheus Unbound*, Brassier wants to sweep away the illusions he claims have prevented us from accepting the full ramifications of the Enlightenment's discoveries regarding the true nature of the universe. Although he agrees with Horkheimer and Adorno's famous diagnosis that modernity has disenchanted the world, Brassier thinks this accomplishment has too frequently been decried as "a calamitous diminishment" when in fact it should be understood as "an invigorating vector of intellectual discovery."[18] Brassier's basic position, defended vigorously from a variety of angles throughout *Nihil Unbound*, is thus quite clear: "Nihilism is not an existential quandary but a speculative opportunity," one that is derived from accepting and appreciating the consequences of the facts, not only that "there is a mind-independent reality," but also that this reality is "indifferent to our existence and oblivious to the 'values' and 'meanings' which we would drape over it to make it more hospitable" (*Nihil*, xi).

We can already observe a striking overlap between Brassier's rhetoric and Shelley's, inasmuch as the former's image of humanity's "drap[ing]" our "'values' and 'meanings'" over reality in order to "make it more hospitable" (presumably to ourselves; the charge of anthropocentrism is implied, especially given the scare quotes around "values" and "meanings") is anticipated by Shelley's consistent use of veiling imagery throughout his poetic corpus. Many decades ago, Richard Fogle wrote convincingly that Shelley's "most characteristic imagery embodies an attempt to establish the relationship between the finite and the infinite," pointing to recurring veils in *Queen Mab*, *Alastor* (1816), and *Prometheus Unbound*; more recently, Forest Pyle has connected the veiling imagery in *The Triumph of Life* (published posthumously in 1824) to a politically active form of Walter Benjamin's notion of "aura."[19] Similar imagery also pervades "Mont Blanc," which I examine in more detail below. But to my mind, Shelley's most telling use of veil imagery – and the usage that puts him closest to Brassier's – occurs in his posthumously published sonnet, "Lift not the painted veil," which begins:

> Lift not the painted veil which those who live
> Call Life; though unreal shapes be pictured there
> And it but mimic all we would believe
> With colours idly spread, – behind, lurk Fear
> And Hope, twin Destinies, who ever weave
> Their shadows o'er the chasm, sightless and drear. (ll. 1–6)

Initially, the neo-Platonism of these lines seems clear: what we perceive and experience here on earth is no more than a "painted veil" whose "unreal shapes" merely imitate the pure realm of Ideas from which they derive. Yet on closer inspection the sonnet turns out to offer nothing by way of reassurances that the Platonic ideal truly exists; even if "we would believe" in such a realm, what menacingly "lurks" behind the veil of reality is only "the chasm, sightless and drear," a potentially infinite nothingness. The latter half of the sonnet clarifies that whoever has the audacity to lift the veil of appearances will only be disappointed: "I knew one who had lifted it . . . a Spirit that strove/ For truth, and like the Preacher, found it not" (ll. 7, 13–14). Nevertheless, although the veil of Life may be nothing more than "shadows" woven by Hope and Fear, in Shelley's rendering it is all we as humans have.

For Brassier, by contrast, tearing away that veil is the only route to a true understanding of our existential situation. Accordingly, the first part of *Nihil Unbound* interrogates the ideas of several philosophers in order to test the limits of what Wilfrid Sellars influentially calls "the manifest image" of the human: the common-sense notion we have of ourselves as "rational agents engaged in pursuing various purposes in the world" (*Nihil*, 6). Whereas Sellars finds this image useful despite its shaky onto-logical support, Brassier champions the alternative that Sellars himself presents: the "scientific image" of humanity predicated on such materialist frameworks as "elementary particles, neuropsy-chological mechanisms, evolutionary processes, etc." (Sellars qtd. in *Nihil*, 7). Brassier thus endorses the "eliminative materialism" of Paul Churchland, who has denounced at length "our common-sense conception of psychological phenomena" as "a radically false theory . . . fundamentally defective," and argued instead that "completed neuroscience" will provide "a theory we may expect to be more powerful by far . . . and more substantively integrated within physical science generally" (qtd. in *Nihil*, 9–10).[20] As several other philosophers of mind indicate elsewhere, their work "cannot impede the progress of neuroscience. Indeed, it should facilitate it – by excluding nonsensical questions, preventing misconceived experiments, and reducing misunderstood experimental results."[21] Brassier, however, argues that in reducing but not eliminating the role of "folk-psychology" in our understanding of what it means to be human, such philosophers have not gone far enough to reject idealism in its various guises. After enumerating some of the con-tradictions and hidden assumptions embedded in Churchland's vectorial model of mind (*Nihil*, 18–26), Brassier thus draws what he thinks is the necessary conclusion: rather than "wast[ing] time trying to effect some sort of synthesis or reconciliation between the manifest and scientific images" of the mind, philosophy should proceed "in expediting science's demolition of the manifest image by kicking away whatever pseudo-transcendental props are being used to shore it up or otherwise inhibit the corrosive potency of science's metaphysical subtractions" (26). Only by coming to terms with the real inconsequentiality of human consciousness, in other words, can we put ourselves in a position to take full advantage of the intellectual possibilities that come with accepting our existential insignificance; or, as Brassier puts it in his introduction, "Thinking has interests that do not coincide with those of living" (xi).

Just how far, then, does Shelley travel down Brassier's nihilistic road? Only part of the way – but that part is significant. In the sixth canto of *Queen Mab*, Shelley again keenly recognizes the vastness of the cosmos in which all activity unfolds:

> Throughout these infinite orbs of mingling light,
> Of which yon earth is one, is wide diffused
> A spirit of activity and life,
> That knows no term, cessation, or decay;
> That fades not when the lamp of earthly life,
> Extinguished in the dampness of the grave,
> Awhile there slumbers . . . (6.146–52)

Again, both the neo-Platonism and the vitalism of these lines are hard to miss: human activity may transpire on merely one of an "infinite" number of planets, but it shares with the universe a "spirit of activity and life" that transcends humanity. Although this perspective might align Shelley with Schelling's nature-philosophy, and thus with one strand of the Romantic worldview, it does not correspond with Brassier's contention that "Nature is not our or anyone's home, nor a particularly beneficent progenitor" (*Nihil*, xi). Neither does the ending of *Queen Mab*, which redeems the potential anti-humanism of its fantastic cosmic and transhistorical visions first via Mab's concluding speeches, which counsel Ianthe to "Let virtue teach thee firmly to pursue/ The gradual paths of an aspiring change" (9.147–8), and then by the narrative itself, which resolves with a touchingly intimate vision of Ianthe awaking from her dream to behold her young son, "Watching her sleep with looks of speechless love,/ And the bright beaming stars/ That through the casement shone" (9.238–40). Although the reappearance in these final lines of celestial imagery potentially recalls the vastness of the poem's previous anti-anthropocentric vistas, here such stars are transformed into a mere source of illumination for the scene of familial affection with which the poem concludes. If a standard Marxian reading of a novel is to see how it abandons political problems in favor of personal resolutions, *Queen Mab* seems to abandon cosmic knowledge in favor of human feeling.

A cluster of now-famous poems that Shelley wrote and published between 1815 and early 1817 exhibits continued tension between a cosmological nihilism that approaches Brassier's philosophy, and a desire to find in humanity's mindfulness and creativity evidence of something metaphysical. "Mutability," the shortest of these texts, is a strong statement of Shelley's recognition that the folk-psychological version of the human mind – the common-sense view that we each have a stable, extra-material "personality" – is untenable at best and damaging at worst. Each of the poem's opening quatrains is structured around an extended comparison highlighting how humanity's only consistent characteristic is changefulness:

> We are as clouds that veil the midnight moon;
> How restlessly they speed, and gleam, and quiver,
> Streaking the darkness radiantly! – yet soon
> Night closes round, and they are lost for ever: (ll. 1–4)

The next stanza draws on the same Eolian Harp imagery that so captivated Coleridge, but Shelley specifies that he is interested in "forgotten lyres" (l. 5), adding an additional sense of ephemerality to his comparison. In each stanza, the mind is clearly far less stable than it imagines itself to be. Yet Shelley also consistently suggests that, despite our constituent evanescence, there is something potentially valuable in humanity's existence, especially with regard to our interactions with the natural world; whether we are "streaking the darkness radiantly" as in the first stanza, or "[g]iving various response to each varying blast" (l. 6) as in the second, our interchanges with the world around us create real effects, however transitory. This ambivalence extends into the poem's final stanzas, where the drawbacks of our ever-changing existences – "A dream has power to poison sleep"; "One wandering thought pollutes the day" (ll. 9–10) – are counterbalanced by the potentiality our lack of stability consistently generates: "Man's yesterday may ne'er be like his morrow;/ Nought may endure but Mutability" (ll. 15–16).

In this reading, mutability is not an obstruction against which humanity struggles to achieve something enduring; rather, it is the condition of humanity's freedom *from* the perceived necessity of creating anything that will endure. Somewhat unexpectedly, this insight corresponds to Brassier's closing remarks in *Nihil Unbound* that "Senselessness and purposelessness are not merely privative; they represent a gain in intelligibility" (238). His immediate frame of reference here is the Freudian death drive "understood as a repetition of the inorganic" that forms "the trace of aboriginal death," which Brassier argues haunts all living things; Shelley, as we will see, usually repudiates such absolute nihilism – even a nihilism, like Brassier's, recuperated for use by human intelligence – with his faith in a vital Spirit that exceeds the material limitations of human embodiment. Nevertheless, with Brassier's help, it becomes possible to draw a line from the resignation of "Mutability" to the triumphant cynicism of one of Shelley's most famous sonnets, "Ozymandias," in which the decline of Ramses II's civilization ("'Look on my Works, ye Mighty, and despair!'/ Nothing beside remains.") indexes the inevitability of freedom from tyranny due to the radically inhuman timescale that governs all life and death.

"Ozymandias" (1818) is a slightly later poem in Shelley's oeuvre. More typical of his earlier work is another poem written during the 1815–17 period: *Alastor; or, The Spirit of Solitude*. Published as the title poem of the 1816 collection that also included "Mutability," *Alastor* relates the sublime adventures of its eponymous hero-poet, who after being granted a vision of ideal beauty, pursues it unto death. Harold Bloom, who describes *Alastor* as "a blank verse rhapsodic narrative of a destructive and subjective quest," ultimately concludes that it represents "a dead end" in Shelley's poetic development.[22] Along these lines, it has become a critical commonplace to read the poem's poet-hero as a figure for Wordsworth, with whom Shelley was becoming increasingly disillusioned. (Another sonnet in the same collection, "To Wordsworth," harshly denounces the older poet's perceived betrayal of his youthful iconoclasm.) But it is equally possible to view *Alastor*'s protagonist as Shelley's own alter ego, and thus as a kind of vanishing mediator, one whose vain quest Shelley needed to write in order to overcome his own attraction to a totalizing idealism.

The poem begins with Shelley exhorting "Earth, ocean, air, beloved brotherhood!" (l. 1) as the sources of his "natural piety" (l. 3), but it is precisely these earthly, material phenomena that Alastor increasingly disregards in his reckless quest for pure knowledge and inspiration. In the midst of his unending travels "[t]o seek strange truths in undiscovered lands" (l. 77), our protagonist experiences a vision of sublime intensity while sleeping "in the vale of Cashmire [Kashmir]" (l. 145), an Orientalist setting highly reminiscent of Coleridge's Xanadu. Here, he dreams of a "veiled maid" who sings to him of "Knowledge, and truth and virtue ... And lofty hopes of divine liberty,/ Thoughts the most dear to him, and poesy,/ Herself a poet" (ll. 151, 158–61). Subsequently, the "joy and exultation" (l. 144) he has always experienced in the presence of earthly wonders, whether human or natural, are no longer available to him; instead, he becomes obsessed with seeking on earth the ideal truth and beauty presumably contained in the "ineffable tale" (l. 168) related by the dream maiden. Not coincidentally, the specific contents of her tale are never revealed, and Shelley's language leaves little doubt regarding the vanity (in both senses of the word) of Alastor's quest: "thus driven/ By the bright shadow of that lovely dream,/ ... He fled" (ll. 232–4, 237). Nevertheless, the narrative follows Alastor's fruitless wanderings for several hundred more lines. Why? Jerrold Hogle proposes that the poem is best read as a "critical parody" of the idealist philosophies and Wordsworthian poetics to which Shelley gravitated in his youth, although its gorgeous language reveals it to be "a critique still attracted to what it parodies ... a tug of war between contradictory verbal inclinations."[23] This may be true, but Shelley's prose preface to *Alastor* gives little evidence of parody; instead, when it tells us that "The picture is not barren of instruction to actual men," I think we are meant to heed the poem's warning that dedication to a pure Ideal is dangerously self-defeating. Accordingly, Alastor's senseless death – apparently from exhaustion – without ever finding in "real life" the object of his dream is presented neither cynically nor parodically, but pathetically. Despite his considerable assurance that he will eventually find his vision's source or original, Alastor makes no such discovery. Yet even in his last direct speech he clings to hope: not the metaphysical hope that perfection exists but the Wordsworthian (i.e., anthropocentric) hope that there is an immanent fit between humanity and the natural world; addressing a "[w]anton and wild" stream he has been following (l. 495), he still claims that it "imagest my life. Thy darksome stillness,/ Thy dazzling waves, thy loud and hollow gulphs,/ Thy searchless fountain, and invisible course/ Have each their type in me" (ll. 505–8).

The poem's conclusion initially seems to honor this kind of

idealism, claiming that after Alastor's death nothing is the same: "when all/ Is reft at once, when some surpassing Spirit/ Whose light adorned the world around it, leaves/ Those who remain behind" are rendered speechless by their grief (ll. 713–16). Yet on closer reading, the poet-hero's untimely and frankly unnecessary death confirms Brassier's assertion – which concludes his reading of the iconoclastic contemporary French (non-)philosopher François Laruelle[24] – that "it is no longer realism which is naïve, but rather the compulsive idealism" that has dominated Western philosophy since Kant (*Nihil*, 129). Although the poem ends by claiming that after Alastor's passing things "are not as they were," it is in fact the preceding lines' description of everything that has not changed that remains uppermost in readers' minds: "Nature's vast frame, the web of human things,/ birth and the grave" (ll. 719–20) obviously remain intact, despite the poet-hero's narcissistic self-destruction. This "honoring" of Alastor's conception of his own self-importance is not immediately or obviously ironic, especially in light of the narrator's opening lines in which he describes himself in unmistakably Wordsworthian terms as a poet whose "strain" or song

> May modulate with murmurs of the air,
> And motions of the forests and the sea,
> And voice of living beings, and woven hymns
> Of night and day, and the deep heart of man. (ll. 46–9)

Nevertheless, although these lines superficially resemble Alastor's self-conception, the difference is instructive: whereas Alastor indulges the correlationist fantasy that the real world will eventually divulge the origin of his dream-vision, Shelley-as-narrator recognizes that whatever correspondence exists between himself, his poetry, and nature must be created and maintained artificially through creative effort. Such faith may become a fatal contradiction for critical theorists like Horkheimer and Adorno, as Brassier argues in *Nihilism Unbound*'s second chapter, but for Shelley it merely marks the point beyond which he does not travel farther down Brassier's path of nihilistic enlightenment.

There is one more poem from Shelley's prolific 1815–17 period that I want to consider, one that at first appears to counterbalance my previous assertion that Shelley shares Brassier's deep skepticism regarding idealism. Shelley wrote "Hymn to Intellectual Beauty" during the summer of 1816 while staying with Byron on Lake Geneva. "Intellectual" here means "nonmaterial,"[25] as the poem's first lines attest: "The awful shadow of some unseen Power/ Floats though unseen among us" (ll. 1–2). It then addresses itself to the "Spirit of BEAUTY" that Shelley credits with having inspired him, "While yet a boy" (l. 49), with poetic insight and energy. This "Spirit" is explicitly not related to traditional religious belief, however, as Shelley recalls how "I called on poisonous names with which our youth is fed;/ I was not heard – I saw them not –" (ll. 53–4). Such atheism cannot be missed, especially following a stanza in which Shelley critiques "the name[s] of God and ghosts and Heaven" (l. 27) for being nothing more than "[f]rail spells – whose uttered charm might not avail to sever,/ From all we hear and all we see,/ Doubt, chance, and mutability" (ll. 29–31). Consequently, Pyle notes the irony of Shelley's decision to call the poem a "hymn": "To sing this godless, but still sacred hymn is to give worship to the absent spirit of beauty and every form and thought it consecrates."[26]

Shelley's "Hymn," in other words, declares a faith that is not traditionally metaphysical as much as self-consciously aware of the doubtful ontological status of its subject – a status that can only be maintained by purposeful cultivation on the part of the poet. This is the burden of the sixth stanza:

> I vowed that I would dedicate my powers
> To thee and thine – have I not kept the vow?
> With beating heart and streaming eyes, even now
> I call the phantoms of a thousand hours
> Each from his voiceless grave . . .
> They know that never joy illumined my brow
> Unlinked with hope that thou wouldst free
> This world from its dark slavery,
> That thou – O awful LOVELINESS,
> Wouldst give whate'er these words cannot express. (ll. 61–5, 68–72)

This is not the "second nature" of critical theory that Brassier critiques for its nostalgia, nor is it untinctured idealism, since Shelley is absolutely clear that the Spirit of Beauty must be summoned ("call[ed]") by human imagination. Once invoked, moreover, it does not create or define what it intends, as per phenomenological accounts of human agency; instead, it unexpectedly approaches the point that Brassier identifies as the vector of Laruelle's contribution to (non-)philosophy: "a precarious point of equilibrium between the competing claims of transcendental critique and metaphysical construction . . . that transcends the sum of its influences" (*Nihil*, 119). Furthermore, the "dark slavery" that describes the world when bereft of loveliness is unmistakably political as well as ideological in its implications, Britain having recently abolished the slave trade (but not slavery itself) in 1808. What Shelley is invoking and paying tribute to, then, is what Pyle identifies as "the aesthetic": not merely "sensuous beauty," but "the comings and goings of the spirit of beauty" which "by its very inconstancy . . . generates the binding force of love" that ultimately unites "all human kind" (l. 84), as the poem's final line articulates.[27]

It is his commitment to aesthetics that finally separates Shelley's approach, with all its radical skepticism, from Brassier's nihilism. There is no room in the latter's philosophy for such considerations; in extreme contrast to Harman's and Morton's object-oriented view that "aesthetics is first philosophy," for Brassier there can be no such thing. Whereas the object-oriented philosophers see causality as essentially aesthetic (i.e., about relations between things, as discussed in Chapter 1), Brassier sees it as a matter of mathematical or scientific processes; as he puts it in a recent interview, thanks to "the emergence of modern science . . . intelligibility has become detached from meaning: with modern science, conceptual rationality weans itself from the narrative structures that continue to prevail in theology and theologically inflected metaphysics."[28] From Brassier's perspective, any discussion of aesthetics is merely another attempt to impose or project "meaning" onto a world whose essential contours can be understood perfectly well – better, even – without it. But although Brassier is willing to concede that science harbors its own metaphysical assumptions,[29] he staunchly refutes that anything other than "mathematized science" could be permitted to add intelligibility – much less meaning – to the universe. By drawing such distinctions, however, Brassier could be accused of harboring his own metaphysical or at least disciplinary assumptions about which types of knowledge count and which do not. This is in contrast not only to the practitioners of OOP but also to Shelley, whose *Defence of Poetry* is full of statements testifying to the power of aesthetic perceptions that are irreducible to merely subjective or secondary effects. Indeed, far from agreeing with Brassier's contentions that mathematized science offers the only objective perspective on the universe's intelligibility (to say nothing of his belief that neuroscience is on its way to fully explaining the brain's functions in purely material terms), Shelley strongly asserts the priority of the aesthetic over the scientific: "Poetry . . . is at once the centre and circumference of knowledge; it is that which comprehends all science, and that to which all science must be referred. It is at the same the time the root and blossom of all other systems of thought" (531).

Like Brassier, then, Shelley shares a commitment to what, near the end of "Hymn to Intellectual Beauty," he calls "the truth/ Of nature"; unlike Brassier, however, Shelley's truth includes an aesthetic element that is objectively "there." As the final stanza of "Hymn" begins,

> The day becomes more solemn and serene
> When noon is past – there is a harmony
> In autumn, and a luster in its sky,
> With through the summer is not heard or seen,
> As if it could not be, as if it had not been! (ll. 73–6)

If there is a subjective element to these observations, it is so dispersed through the world's entities as to render inoperable the subject–object distinction that Brassier – who has lately rejected the SR moniker altogether and taken to calling his approach "transcendental naturalism"[30] – implicitly endorses when he rules out all philosophical methods that account for qualitative experiences. Indeed, for Brassier it is probably not too much to say that the real and the metaphysical are absolutely mutually exclusive – so absolutely, in fact, that Brassier's warrant for the total dismissal of the latter seems itself ungrounded in anything quantitative or objective. This point will be made more rigorously in the second half of this chapter, in my consideration of Meillassoux's speculative materialism. For now, however, I want merely to note that in the penultimate lines of Shelley's "Hymn" quoted above, "solemn" and "serene" describe the afternoon regardless of whether anyone is present to observe these qualities: they are inherent elements of the phenomena being described, just like the sky's luster, which is present throughout the year even if it is only sensible in autumn. Were Shelley to read Brassier, he might very well repeat the judgment he passes on his own contemporaries in the final pages of his *Defence*: "We want [lack] the creative faculty to imagine that which we know" (530).

In late 1816, Percy and Mary Wollstonecraft Shelley returned to England from their first extended stay on the Continent. Mary was carrying with her the manuscript that would become *Frankenstein, or, The Modern Prometheus* (1818), while Percy had in his possession the ambitious poem with which I will begin this chapter's second half: "Mont Blanc." The immediate impetus for the poem was the Shelleys' experience of the Alps in July 1816. Chamonix, Switzerland, was only beginning to become a popular tourist destination, and still required a good deal of effort to be reached by intrepid travelers. As they did for many British travelers, the Alps repeatedly astonished the Shelleys, as Percy recorded in a letter to his friend Thomas Peacock:

> Pinnacles of snow, intolerably bright, part of the chain connected with Mont Blanc shone through the clouds at intervals on high. I never knew I never imagined what mountains were before. The immensity of those ariel [*sic*] summits excited, when they suddenly burst upon the sight, a sentiment of extatic [*sic*] wonder, not unallied to madness.[31]

Richard Holmes is clearly not exaggerating when he calls the visit "something close to a religious experience" for Shelley.[32]

Similarly, Bloom minces no words in his interpretation of "Mont Blanc," writing that "The poem's subject is the relation between individual mind and the universe, and also the problem of what rules the universe, and to what moral end."[33] Of course, Shelley was not the only Romantic-era author to be inspired to ask after such questions by the Alps in general and Mont Blanc in particular; Coleridge, among others, had already written his own poem of praise to the mountain, "Hymn before Sun-rise, in the Vale of Chamouni" (1802). This relatively conventional poem shares several features with Shelley's later work; where Coleridge describes the river Arve that flows down the mountainside as "Rav[ing] ceaselessly,"[34] for example, Shelley describes how "a vast river/ Over its rocks ceaselessly bursts and raves" (ll. 10–11). Both poets are also fascinated by the paradoxical combination of changefulness and timelessness the mountain river seems to embody; Coleridge asks "Who called you forth from night and utter death,/ From dark and icy caverns called you forth/ Down those precipitous black, jagged rocks,/ For ever shattered and the same forever?"[35] while Shelley addresses the ravine by describing how "Thou art pervaded with that ceaseless motion,/ Thou art

the path of that unresting sound –" (ll. 31–2). Whereas Coleridge
has a single, orthodox answer to these and other questions regarding origins and agency – "God" appears no less than four times,
including as the poem's final word – Shelley does not follow suit.
Instead, as Earl Wasserman observes in his classic close reading
of "Mont Blanc," Shelley maintains an "ambiguous philosophical position" on the question of external reality's relationship to
the human, one that allows him to craft a poem that is "not lyric,
but dramatic; not a static set of elaborations on a fixed theme,
but a dynamic and consistently evolving course of discovery."[36]
While this description is generally accurate, however, to reach it
Wasserman imports a dubious metaphysical proposition. Drawing
on Shelley's fragmentary essay "On Life," Wasserman extrapolates
from its discussion of "intellectual philosophy" to posit Shelley's
belief in a universal mind, which he then applies to his reading of
"Mont Blanc." In fact, however, "On Life" questions the idealism
that Wasserman assumes it endorses; describing sarcastically its
"most refined deductions" and "subtle . . . conception[s]," Shelley
also notes that idealism's mantra of "[n]othing exists but as it is
perceived" fails to explain what causes "mind" to exist in the first
place. Furthermore, even if we (like Wasserman) ignore the ironies
of Shelley's essay, nowhere in the poem itself does Shelley refer
to the "One Mind" that Wasserman claims resolves the problematic relationship between "thoughts" and "things" that concerns
Shelley throughout "Mont Blanc." Consider its startling opening
stanza:

> The everlasting universe of things
> Flows through the mind, and rolls its rapid waves,
> Now dark – now glittering – now reflecting gloom –
> Now lending splendor, where from secret springs
> The source of human thought its tribute brings
> Of waters, – with a sound but half its own,
> Such as a feeble brook will oft assume
> In the wild woods, among the mountains lone,
> Where waterfalls around it leap for ever,
> Where woods and winds contend, and a vast river
> Over its rocks ceaselessly bursts and raves. (ll. 1–11)

Consisting of a single virtuosic sentence, Shelley immediately
establishes the theme noted by both Bloom and Wasserman: the

relation between the human mind and external reality. It is a relationship neither of mutual exclusivity – for "the everlasting universe of things/ Flows through the mind," which in turn "its tribute brings" to those things – nor of dependency, since both external things and the mind exist equally. How, then, are we to understand the relationship between the two? This question takes on additional urgency when we consider that, as Morton observes, Shelley is quintessentially a poet of relations.[37]

For Quentin Meillassoux, one way to pursue an answer is by returning to a distinction that many philosophers have long deemed obsolete: the distinction between primary and secondary qualities. As delineated by John Locke (but already found in Descartes' *Meditations*), primary qualities are those that inhere in things themselves, whereas secondary qualities are those that perceiving subjects experience of things. Meillassoux's example in the first chapter of his principal book to date, *After Finitude: An Essay on the Necessity of Contingency*, is a candle. If we put our finger in a flame we feel pain, but we do not attribute that pain to the flame itself, as an intrinsic or primary quality. But neither do we treat the pain – or, for that matter, any other sensible quality – as a "perpetual and arbitrary" hallucination injected by us into things; such secondary qualities are really present, but only in the *relation* between ourselves and things.[38] As Meillassoux points out, nobody debates this last point any longer; instead, the very distinction between the qualities that inhere in things and the "sensible" qualities that "are not in the things themselves but in my subjective relation to the latter" (*After Finitude*, 2) has been discarded. Especially after phenomenology, *all* qualities have been understood to be secondary, that is, relational: dependent on the correlation between the perceiving subject and the world.[39]

We have now arrived at Meillassoux's most significant contribution to SR: naming "correlationism" as the shared attribute of the main varieties of post-Kantian philosophy, Continental as well as analytical. In one of Meillassoux's clearest definitions, correlationism amounts to the philosophical "decision," stated or unstated, "that there are no objects, no events, no laws, no beings which are not always already correlated with a point of view, with a subjective access."[40] For the other Speculative Realists and their associates, this designates a useful way to apprehend the dogmatic nature of most modern philosophy, but as we have seen in previous chapters, it does not present an especially insurmountable problem. Each in their own ways, Harman, Morton, Grant, DeLanda, Badiou, Latour, and Brassier generally bypass what Harman calls "philosophies of access," be they linguistic or phenomenological. For Meillassoux, by contrast, correlationism represents a compelling philosophical position that must be dealt with on its own terms. To this end, his opening move in *After Finitude* is a thought experiment involving the question of what he calls "ancestrality." Thanks to scientific techniques like carbon dating and starlight observation, we now can say with relative certainty that our universe is nearly 14 billion years old, our planet is roughly 4.5 billion years old, and organic life on Earth appears in the fossil record around another billion years later. The earliest signs of humanoid activity, however, are only 2 million years old. In other words, we have physical evidence of life that vastly precedes the appearance of anything remotely resembling consciousness, human or otherwise. Accordingly, Meillassoux's question for the correlationists is as follows: what is the status of these "ancestral statements"? Their answers, as Meillassoux definitively shows, boil down to asserting that all such statements must be qualified by the phrase "for us": the knowledges that science purports to obtain, like all statements that claim to say anything about mind-independent reality, can be considered "truths" only in the (Kantian) sense that they are intersubjectively agreed upon (*After Finitude*, 15); furthermore, they tell us nothing true about what occurred in the past, only about what is given to us in the present (16). As a result, Meillassoux points out that the correlationist is led to defend staunchly what is in fact "a rather extraordinary claim: *the ancestral statement is a true statement*, in that it is objective, but *one whose referent cannot possibly have actually existed in the way this truth describes it*" (16–17; italics in original).

For Meillassoux, the fact that this paradoxical, self-canceling position forms the basic framework of most contemporary philosophy and critical theory is troubling on a number of counts. It not only renders philosophers and theorists unable to work meaningfully with their counterparts in the scientific community, but also puts correlationism on the same footing as various religious fundamentalisms, which similarly deny the validity of any scientific claim that contradicts their interpretive frameworks. Perhaps most distressingly, correlationism has cut philosophy off from being able to say anything meaningful about the world outside of our human access to it. In Meillassoux's words, "contemporary philosophers have lost *the great outdoors*, the *absolute* outside of precritical thinkers: that outside which was not relative to us . . . that outside which thought could explore with the legitimate feeling of being on foreign territory – of being entirely elsewhere" (7). It is precisely thought's ability to think the absolute – understood as that which exists regardless of whether it exists for us – that Meillassoux is invested in recovering.

Before considering some of the specific proofs Meillassoux adduces in order to break the "correlationist circle" from within, let us pause to note how Shelley's "Mont Blanc" is equally invested in testing thought's ability to think the great outdoors, quite literally. Can Shelley, limited by his own perceptions and trapped within his individual consciousness, say anything objectively true about the mountain which stands before him in this poem, impassive and seemingly timeless?[41] What, if anything, can the poet know about the mountain as it exists and not merely as it is given to him? The beginning of the second stanza starts to answer these questions by addressing a feature of the mountain to which Shelley repeatedly returns over the poem's course: the ravine down which the mountain's river flows.

> Thus thou, Ravine of Arve – deep, dark Ravine –
> Thou many-coloured, many-voiced vale,
> Over whose pines, and crags, and caverns sail
> Fast cloud shadows and sunbeams: awful scene,
> Where Power in likeness of the Arve comes down
> From the ice gulphs that gird his secret throne,
> Bursting through these dark mountains like the flame
> Of lightning through the tempest; . . . (ll. 12–19)

Like many passages in Shelley's poem, this one begins by describing the secondary qualities of its subject matter – here, the ravine's colors and sounds – before attempting to apprehend its primary qualities, which exist "regardless of whether we are thinking about it or not," as Meillassoux puts it in *After Finitude* (7). But although Shelley recognizes that *something* exists regardless of whether a consciousness is present to perceive it,[42] he stops short of claiming it can be described in terms of its primary qualities. Instead, he produces a remarkably backward simile: as opposed to likening the ever-rushing Arve to an image of Power, which would reduce it to his perception of it, he upends our expectations by telling us that it is Power itself that flows down the mountainside "in likeness of the Arve." This is rendered as a statement of fact, but a necessarily speculative one, since "Power" remains both objectively present and impossible for us to apprehend directly. We cannot even know its origin, since Power/the river descends from a "secret throne," presumably the mountain's peak: its most inaccessible, inhuman part, and therefore the one to which Shelley returns almost obsessively throughout the poem. The comparison at the end of this passage between the river, which again is described as "burst[ing]" down the dark mountain, and lightning that momentarily illuminates a storm intensifies Shelley's assertion that he is in the presence of something that holds at least the promise of an enlightenment or clarification that exceeds the human.

The conviction that *something* exists apart from or in excess of our human access to it initially seems to align Shelley with those thinkers whom Meillassoux denominates "weak correlationists," Kant foremost among them. Whereas strong correlationists deny altogether thought's ability to think what lies outside the correlation (*After Finitude*, 30–1), weak correlationists like Kant retain a belief in noumenal things-in-themselves, but maintain that since we cannot know anything meaningful about them beyond the universal truths that they must exist and be non-contradictory (because according to Kant it would be contradictory for there to be appearances without things that appear; see *After Finitude*, 31), we should turn our attention to the phenomenal world as mediated by our senses, language, logic, conventions, etc. For the weak correlationist, in other words, the thing-without-us is thinkable but not knowable, whereas for the strong correlationist it is neither thinkable nor knowable. Although the weak (Kantian) version of the correlationist circle initially appears more likely to facilitate thought's escape from the human–world correlate, it actually locks thought firmly into it, absolutizing some portion of the correlation and then claiming that whatever lies outside it is unknowable. Recently, Meillassoux has further categorized weak correlationists into two subdivisions: realists, who believe that something is out there but that we cannot know precisely what, and "speculative idealists," who project the correlation onto some segment of reality, and then claim its absolute necessity.[43] For Meillassoux, this latter camp includes most twentieth-century philosophers, from Husserl and Levinas (who absolutize different forms of intersubjective relations) to Bergson and Deleuze (who absolutize different versions of perception/intensity and Life). All weak correlationist positions are self-canceling, however, because they have no way of verifying from the outside that the particular correlation they have seized upon is necessary rather than contingent. In other words, whatever portion of reality the weak correlationist claims makes up the correlationist circle cannot be claimed to be absolutely necessary, without violating the terms of the correlation in the first place. Weak correlationism, despite all its variations, is a dead end.

Somewhat surprisingly, then, for Meillassoux the strong correlationist position holds the key to deducing certain knowledge of what lies outside consciousness.[44] He begins with the insight that since strong correlationism absolutely denies our ability to know anything outside the human–world correlate, including whether there even is anything "outside," it cannot give any reason for itself – the very ground of the correlation must, by strong correlationism's own reckoning, remain unknowable. Strong correlationism thus proceeds implicitly on the "facticity" of the correlation: it must be taken as a fact, but no reason for its existing thus and not otherwise can be provided or deduced. Indeed, strong correlationism renders it impossible to give *any* final reason for why anything is the way it is, which enables Meillassoux to make a decisive philosophical move from facticity to the principle of "factuality": if no reason can be given for the existence (or non-existence) of anything, we must admit the absolute contingency (or non-necessity) of everything, up to and including the laws of nature themselves. For the same correlationist circle that prevents us being able to ascertain any necessity in the universe – since the most the strong correlationist can allow is the existence of an entity that seems necessary for us, without of course being able to know why – allows Meillassoux to produce "the absolute truth of a *principle of unreason*. There is no reason for anything to be or to remain the way it is; everything must, without reason, be able not to be and/or be able to be other than it is" (*After Finitude*, 60). To put this even more succinctly (and with apologies to Wallace Stevens): the principle of factuality establishes that the only necessity is the necessity of contingency.

What roles, then, do factuality, contingency, and thought's ability to think the absolute play in Shelley's meditations on Mont

Blanc? As mentioned above, Shelley's poem has already garnered a fair bit of attention from SR perspectives, so let us first consider two of these treatments.[45] Steven Shaviro reads the poem as torn between correlationist and speculative perspectives: even as it hews to a traditional "subject–object binary," it increasingly suggests that "all our mental impressions refer and belong to already-existing things." In Shaviro's view, then, "Mont Blanc" has more in common with the quasi-panpsychism of Harman's OOP than with Meillassoux's speculative materialism, which Shaviro argues treats the "great outdoors" as essentially "lifeless, mindless, and inert, and that operates entirely mechanistically."[46] This description is based on Shaviro's distrust of Meillassoux's belief that if we are to have specific, non-correlationist knowledge of the universe, it will have to come from mathematics (see, e.g,. *After Finitude*, 115, 126) – an important point of overlap between Meillassoux's and Brassier's versions of SR, but one that Shaviro finds untenable for the same reason he critiques the distinction between primary and secondary qualities: at bottom, they are always humanly mediated.[47] By contrast, Greg Ellermann finds the ontology of "Mont Blanc" to be in line with Meillassoux's speculative materialism. In Ellermann's ingenious interpretation, Shelley's poem should be read neither as an articulation of skepticism, as in Wasserman's classic reading, nor as an idealist paean to the powers of the human mind to produce sublimity from meaninglessness, as Frances Ferguson influentially argued.[48] Rather, says Ellermann, the famous question with which Shelley ends his poem – "And what were thou [Mont Blanc], and earth, and stars, and sea,/ If to the human mind's imaginings/ Silence and solitude were vacancy?" (ll. 142–4) – is simply a version of Meillassoux's radicalization of the correlationist circle. As Ellermann points out, the poem is interested in ontological questions: precisely the kind of questions that twentieth-century literary theory after the linguistic turn was committed to deferring endlessly. By focusing especially on those moments in "Mont Blanc" that attempt to discern the mountain's essence (rather than merely describe its appearance) as pure Power, however, Ellermann argues for a congruence between Shelley's Power and Meillassoux's necessity of contingency. When Shelley opines that "All things that move and breathe with toil and sound/ Are born and die; revolve, subside, and swell./ Power dwells apart in its tranquility/ Remote, serene, and inaccessible" (ll. 94–7), for example, Ellermann notes that the poet is dichotomizing what exists in actuality and what exists as pure potentiality – a potentiality that Meillassoux associates not only with the necessity of contingency ("everything must, without reason . . . be able to be other than what it is") but also, in a more recent essay, with the pure iterability of the linguistic sign.[49]

My own sense of "Mont Blanc" is that its philosophy is neither as purely object-oriented as Shaviro argues nor as radically speculative materialist as Ellermann would have it. Although the former's invocation of the role of "aesthetics as first philosophy" in the poem is compelling, Shelley's repeated denomination of "Power" as something that exceeds both our human access *and* the mountain itself differentiates it from Harman's and Morton's OOP, which retains little place for an entity like Power that both really exists (in the world of Shelley's poem) yet has no sensual profile apart from the immanent forms it temporarily assumes. Even Morton's concept of the hyperobject does not precisely describe the mountain, which is not entirely graspable by human senses yet is clearly localized: "Mont Blanc yet gleams on high" (l. 127). But Ellermann's argument that Shelley's "Power" is synonymous with Meillassoux's contingency is not entirely convincing either. Meillassoux always maintains that his derivation of the necessity of contingency should not be mistaken for a statement about what actually exists: "What is strange in my philosophy is that it's an ontology that never speaks about what is but only about what can be. Never about what there is, because this I have no right to speak about."[50] Shelley may or may not believe in the contingency of what is – my discussion of *Prometheus Unbound*, below, explores this question further – but in "Mont Blanc" what he calls "The secret strength of things/ Which governs thought" (ll. 139–40) is absolutely present: it "inhabits" the mountain (l. 141), a verb that affirms its existence even as it denies our complete or unmediated access to its essence.

Nevertheless, Ellermann's attention to the poetic features of Shelley's poem, especially the sibilant consonants that proliferate in its final section, points in an intriguing interpretive direction: the aesthetic. More specifically, I think Ellermann's focus on Shelley's diction can be supplemented by William Keach's careful accounting of the poem's occluded end rhymes. Drawing on the work of several earlier scholars, Keach notes that although "Mont Blanc" initially appears to be written in unrhymed iambic pentameter – blank verse – its heavy use of enjambment and imperfect rhymes conceals a rhyme scheme that is in fact "extensive" and astonishingly resourceful, sometimes employing couplets, at other times spanning many lines and even sections (especially when the rhyming words are homonyms or even occasionally repetitions).[51] Yet Keach also notes that three words remain entirely unrhymed in "Mont Blanc" – "forms," "spread," and "sun" (ll. 62, 65, 133) – creating an effect that "is sufficiently irregular to help evoke the 'untameable wildness' Shelley spoke of [in his note to the poem]," and keeping the poem "open, partly unresolved."[52] Accounting for the unprecedented, irregular form of Shelley's poem – not as blank as it appears, but not perfectly formed either – helps us appreciate Shelley's reluctance to subscribe absolutely to any of the speculative realisms his poem approaches but does not completely accept. It follows that the poem's famous final question should remain open too. "And what were thou, and earth, and stars, and sea,/ If to the human mind's imaginings/ Silence and solitude were vacancy?" is usually understood to be asked rhetorically, especially by critics who assume Shelley puts full faith in the imagination's powers to create meaning where none exists naturally. The indeterminacy of "Mont Blanc"'s formal structure, however, suggests that Shelley's final question should not be understood absolutely either. The mountain and its accouterments clearly exist regardless of whether humans are present to perceive them, as confirmed by Shelley's many attempts throughout the poem to depict Mont Blanc's inaccessible peak. If we cannot say what precise form Mont Blanc takes outside the correlationist circle, we can at least deduce its contingency – its full freedom to be or not be, change or remain constant, without reason or constraint. Such is the positive knowledge that Meillassoux wrests from correlationism, and such is the only sure lesson of "Mont Blanc."

Finally, no chapter on Shelley's ontological views would be complete without some consideration of his most ambitious poem, the four-act lyrical drama *Prometheus Unbound* (1820). Written in bursts over the course of a year and a half spent in various Italian locales, the poem is an imaginative rewriting of a lost original by the Greek tragedian Aeschylus. However, whereas Aeschylus' play is thought to have staged a reconciliation between Jupiter and Prometheus, Shelley's far more radical plot sees the former utterly defeated, for as he explains in the play's preface, neither philosophically nor politically would it have sufficed to "reconcil[e] the Champion with the Oppressor of mankind."[53] The poem is also far less concerned with the agon between Prometheus and his captor than with its overcoming, an unusual dramatic movement that has traditionally been read in either mytho-poetic or psychological terms. According to Abrams, for example, "In *Prometheus Unbound* Shelley renders the universal history of man in the dramatic form of visualizable agents and their actions," whereas for Bloom, Shelley's poem is a psychological drama in which "Jupiter is thesis, Prometheus is antithesis, and Demogorgon [the "agent of apocalypse, who overthrows Jupiter"] the transcending agent of synthesis, the dark force turning the cycle over."[54] What these divergent interpretations each assume is that Prometheus represents both humankind and the moral center of Shelley's poetic universe. In all such anthropocentric readings, the critical focus inevitably falls on Prometheus' endurance in the face of suffering, his revocation of his original curse on Jupiter, and his eventual emancipation. Subsequent deconstructive and New Historical interpretations have broadened our understanding of the text's stakes, but tend to remain fundamentally allegorical. Rajan, for example, astutely recognizes that following the "provisional" conclusion of "Mont Blanc," *Prometheus Unbound* represents a concerted attempt "to press beyond the ambiguities of skepticism to the finality of a holistic vision of the universe"; her deconstructive framework, however, inevitably leads her away from the ontological content of Shelley's vision and toward the supposedly self-negating reflexivity of its linguistic articulations.[55] New Historical inquiries have set Shelley's revolutionary vision not only in relation to the gradual and top-down views of reform promoted by his early intellectual mentor (and father-in-law) William Godwin, but also in the context of eighteenth-century geological theories.[56]

The more radical ramifications of Meillassoux's speculative materialism provide us with tools to push further toward understanding the ontology limned by *Prometheus Unbound*'s vision of planetary reform and renewal. We can do so, moreover, by drawing parallels to several of Meillassoux's most challenging concepts, which follow from *After Finitude*'s fundamental insights regarding correlationism in much the same way that *Prometheus Unbound* moves beyond "Mont Blanc." For Meillassoux, after all, radicalizing strong correlationism renders several definite conclusions about "the great outdoors." First, as discussed above, it allows for the deduction of the principle of factuality – the only necessity is contingency – which in turn justifies the law of non-contradiction, since if there can be no necessary entities, then something cannot simultaneously be itself and not-itself (because if it ceased to exist it would thereby exist again, rendering it ontologically necessary, and therefore impossible; see, e.g., *After Finitude*, 67). These may seem like slim reeds on which to balance thought's ability to think the unthinkable, but they turn out to allow Meillassoux to make some remarkable claims about the nature of time. If contingency is the only necessity, then it is also the only thing that is eternal. This holds true, importantly, for processes as well as entities, such that not only things but also the so-called laws of nature themselves are contingent rather than fixed or absolute. Time, properly understood, is entirely chaotic – a chaos that is not bound to appear as such, however, since it follows no absolute law whatsoever. (This is what distinguishes Meillassoux's ontology from those process-oriented philosophers, from Heraclitus to Deleuze, for whom flux is a necessary constant.)[57] Meillassoux calls this "hyper-Chaos": "a Time that is inconceivable for physics, since it is capable of destroying without cause or reason, every physical law, just as it is inconceivable for metaphysics, since it is capable of destroying every determinate entity, even a god, even God" (*After Finitude*, 64).

The destruction of a god, of course, is precisely what transpires in *Prometheus Unbound*. Such an event seems entirely impossible at the drama's opening as Prometheus hangs nailed to a rock wall in the Caucasus mountains. He is apparently doomed for eternity by Jupiter's decree. as his opening speech (directed at his absent captor) makes clear:

> Three thousand years of sleep-unsheltered hours
> And moments – aye divided by keen pangs
> Till they seemed years, torture and solitude,
> Scorn and despair, – these are mine empire: –
> More glorious far than that which thou surveyst
> From thine unenvied throne, O Mighty God! (1.12–17)

Initially, then, Prometheus' debased position – and, by extension, the oppression of all humanity, which suffers under Jupiter's tyranny – seems permanent. Most critics who read *Prometheus Unbound* subsequently focus on Shelley's protagonist's renunciation of hatred and his attempts to recall (in the senses of both "remember" and "take back") the curse he previously uttered on his enemy. Yet even before mentioning this purpose, Prometheus draws our attention to a more universal if less moralistic force of change:

> And yet to me welcome is Day and Night,
> Whether one breaks the hoar frost of the morn,
> Or starry, dim, and slow, the other climbs
> The leaden-coloured East: for then they lead
> Their wingless, crawling Hours, one among whom . . .
> Shall drag thee, cruel King, to kiss the blood
> From these pale feet . . . (1.44–8. 50–1)

Following classical mythology, the Hours of which Prometheus speaks are personified in the lyrical drama, as is the force of chaos, Demogorgon, who ultimately drags Jupiter off his throne and down to the underworld. These poetic devices, however, should not distract us from the way they anticipate Meillassoux's notion of hyper-Chaos. For although Shelley presents Jupiter's defeat as a moral victory, Demogorgon's own understanding of his role in this drama is amoral at best; when Prometheus' beloved, Asia, descends to Demogorgon's cave and attempts to convince him that Jupiter must be overthrown, Demogorgon is unconcerned by reports of Jupiter's tyrannical behavior. When Asia asks "Who is the master of the slave?," Demogorgon famously responds that "the deep truth is imageless" before showing her a vision of "the immortal Hours/ of whom thou didst demand. – One waits for thee" (2.4.115–16, 140–1). Such responses accord well with Meillassoux's logical but absolutely unreasonable hyper-Chaos which, as Robert Jackson explains, "doesn't provide us with an orderly foundation or even an ethical standard. Since it is autonomous and indifferent anything can happen, without reason, without law, and without purpose."[58]

Granted, there are significant elements of *Prometheus Unbound* that do not mesh well with Meillassoux's vision of hyper-Chaos: the prophecy that Jupiter will be overthrown, for example, and perhaps more importantly a metaphysical absolute even Demogorgon must recognize, which is that "Fate, Time, Occasion, Chance, and Change . . . To these/ All things are subject but eternal Love" (2.4.119–20). Nevertheless, the prophetic element of Shelley's plot contains a striking dynamic of contingency, heard in the echoing voice near the start of Act 2 who tells Asia that "In the world unknown/

Sleeps a voice unspoken;/ By thy step alone/ Can its rest be broken/ Child of Ocean!" (2.1.190–4). Critics usually identify this force as "potentiality," understood in the traditional sense of "latency" or "probability."[59] For his part, Meillassoux distinguishes between potentiality and what he calls *virtuality*, which occupies a far more important place in his ontology. To differentiate these two concepts, Meillassoux returns to what he calls "Hume's problem": the difficulty of proving that causality exists anywhere other than in the human mind. Hume's famous example from his *Enquiry Concerning Human Understanding* (1748) involves billiard balls: although we assume that when one ball strikes another the second ball will behave in a predictable fashion, we can neither know this for certain (since the past is no certain predictor of the future) nor know precisely what takes place between the two balls when they do touch. Rather than treat this as an epistemological problem, however, Meillassoux asserts that we can treat it ontologically by rephrasing Hume's question more or less as follows: what makes us think the laws of nature that seem to dictate the billiard balls' interaction are constant and eternal? The answer, says Meillassoux, is that we have remained content with probabilistic reasoning; since we have never seen the laws of nature change, we assume that they must remain constant. But is this assumption warranted? To prove that it is not, Meillassoux draws on modern mathematical resources unavailable to Hume. Whereas his mentor Badiou utilizes Cantorian set theory as the backbone of his ontology (as discussed in Chapter 3), for Meillassoux it is Cantor's discovery of multiple infinities that is of primary importance. Put simply, Cantor demonstrated not only that there are different kinds of infinite sets, some of which are larger than others, but also that mathematical infinity cannot be exhausted, since every set belongs to a "power set" that includes it as one of its subsets.[60] Set theory, in other words, proves that there is always a larger infinity available. The impossibility of reaching a totalized count enables Meillassoux to demonstrate that whereas probability (potentiality) can be calculated when a finite set of variables is available, the infinity of possible universes which over the course of hyper-chaotic time could come into existence renders all such calculations null. Nor is it any argument against hyper-Chaos to point to the apparent stability of natural laws throughout known history, since the non-totalizability of possible cases of what is means change can always occur without warning or precedent.

Applying set theory to possible worlds is not without controversy, as Paul Livingston points out;[61] nevertheless, it allows Meillassoux to defend his position that "the necessity of contingency" applies to natural laws as well as to material entities. Once the limits of probabilistic reason have been exposed, we enter a realm in which "time can bring forth any non-contradictory set of possibilities ... [including] new laws which were not 'potentially' contained in some fixed set of possibles. . ."[62] This, then, is Meillassoux's virtuality: an entirely immanent realm in which anything can (but doesn't have to) happen, and in which laws as well as entities can remain constant for extremely long periods but may also change suddenly and without reason.

Importantly, this doctrine of "advent *ex nihilo*" forms the core of the opening excerpt of the English translation of Meillassoux's still-unpublished masterwork, *The Divine Inexistence* (which began as his 1997 doctoral thesis). Here, Meillassoux puts forth what may be his most controversial concept: a "virtual God," who does not exist now but whose coming-into-being sometime in the future must remain open. Both the theist and the atheist, says Meillassoux, are confined by probabilistic reasoning: the former sees apparently constant universal laws and entities, and reasons that some entity must have brought them into existence; the latter sees a world history of nearly unmitigated, mostly unjust death and destruction and concludes that no God or gods could be in charge of such misery. Relieved of such constraints by the eternality of hyper-Chaos, however – in which "becoming is irreducible to an actualization of possible cases" – the speculative materialist can generate a new possibility.[63] God has never existed, and need not have existed, in order for matter, life, and thought – what Meillassoux calls the three orders or "Worlds" of material being – to come into existence.[64] Yet the possibility of a God-to-come also cannot be ruled out, thanks to the lack "of an eternally fixed reservoir of possibilities," which in turn allows for "becoming in excess of all deterministic or aleatoric constancy, since it could never be totalized in a divine law of laws."[65] The hypothesis of a virtual God, finally, allows Meillassoux to extrapolate an ethics from his ontology. If all existence is immanent, yet the possibilities of its becoming are in no way contained in or constrained by its past or current manifestations, then we may still hope for what Meillassoux calls "a world of Justice," with full justice for the dead and "immanent immortality" for the living. This new world would not be located in a different realm, but would be an extension of the only life we know, i.e. this life. In such a world, God may finally come into existence – but even this will only be meaningful, says Meillassoux, if we learn to act *now* in such a way that when God appears, it will be as though we had hoped for Him: "The authentic link of humans with God is thought as a link with the inexistent God of whom humans are the possible ancestor."[66] This link, which Meillassoux makes very clear is *not* "a Promethean identification of humans with God" but rather "the trace in humans of the madness of the world without God: capable of everything and thus capable of God," is the sole candidate for Meillassoux's concept of the divine.[67]

Not surprisingly, the foregoing deductions and conclusions continue to generate objections and arguments, and it remains unclear whether Meillassoux will ever publish *The Divine Inexistence* in full, or abandon it as a perennial work-in-progress.[68] Nevertheless, the ontology of the virtual and the ethics of immanent immortality that it provides are echoed in the vision of radical earthly rejuvenation that Shelley creates in the later acts of *Prometheus Unbound*. Shelley's approach to a non-metaphysical concept of the infinite is rendered not just via the total unstageability of his drama, but also in its linguistic patterns, specifically Shelley's consistent use of unusual negative constructions (examples noted by Timothy Webb include "*unmeant* hypocrisy," "*sleep-unsheltered* hours," "*unending* flight," "torture *unreprieved*," "*unreclaiming* tears," "the *untransmitted* torch of hope").[69] At the most general level, we may connect these negated adjectives and adverbs with the infinite itself, which Badiou notes is innately negative, since it literally designates "that which is not finite."[70] More concretely, the play is suffused with imagery that resembles the contours of Meillassoux's virtual, fourth world – the world of justice. Granted, unlike Meillassoux's concept of worlds or "orders," which can appear *ex nihilo* from what preceded them, the world of Justice brought about after Prometheus' unbinding is explicitly prophesied. Yet this is still very much in the spirit of Meillassoux's ontology, for as a faun in Act 2 explains, some creatures already enjoy

Sing[ing] those wise and lovely songs
Of fate and chance and God, and Chaos old,
And love, and the chained Titan's woful [*sic*] doom
And how he shall be loosed, and make the Earth

One brotherhood – delightful strains which cheer
Our solitary twilights, and which charm
To silence the unenvying nightingales. (2.2.91–7)

With another unusual negative adjective concluding this passage, Shelley's faun describes not only how hyper-Chaos ("fate and chance") can bring forth anything other than the non-contradictory, but also how the aspiration for justice ("brotherhood") must be maintained in this world such that when the fourth world comes to pass, it will have been actively desired.

Once Demogorgon dethrones Jupiter and Prometheus is freed, all the personified spirits along with Asia and her sisters give voice to their joy. The effects on humanity are felt immediately, as exemplified by an instantaneous abolition of the global slave trade. The Ocean tells Apollo:

Henceforth the fields of Heaven-reflecting sea
Which are my realm, will heave, unstain'd with blood
Beneath the uplifting winds . . .
Tracking their path no more by blood and groans
And desolation, and the mingled voice
Of slavery and command – (3.2.18–20, 29–31)

Now "unstain'd" with the blood of slaves, the ocean will become a medium for free travel and the free intercourse of humans – a result very much in harmony with Shelley's belief, declared in his *Defence of Poetry*, that "The abolition of personal slavery is the basis of the highest political hope that it can enter into the mind of man to conceive."[71] Later, the Spirit of the Hour who witnessed Jupiter's fall confirms that these alterations have affected all people, not just (former) slaves and their (former) traders:

The loathsome mask has fallen, the man remains
Sceptreless, free, uncircumscribed – but man:
Equal, unclassed, tribeless and nationless,
Exempt from awe, worship, degree, – the King
Over himself; just, gentle, wise – but man:
Passionless? no – yet free from guilt or pain . . . (3.4.193–8)

There could be few better descriptions, I think, of Meillassoux's general contention that any advent of a world of justice "contains *the sole* conceivable radical novelty following the human: the recommencement of the human in just form ... as those who think *hope* by refusing the injustice done to their fellow humans, whether they are still alive or not."[72]

The quotation above suggests an aspect of Meillassoux's system that is worth noting, even just briefly, because it seems to go against the grain of most other SR work. Although Meillassoux is very interested in returning philosophy to a contemplation of "the great outdoors," his project is decidedly not anti-anthropocentric. On the contrary, Meillassoux explicitly privileges the human, especially the human capacity for thought, above all other entities and forces. It is the power of human thought, after all, that both forms the correlationist circle and learns to speculate beyond it, such that "humans have access to the eternal truth of the world" in a way other living creatures do not.[73] Moreover, it is thought that forms the third world or order in Meillassoux's system, from which – and *only* from which – the fourth world of Justice may appear. Human thought thus represents for Meillassoux the highest achievement the universe can bring forth, and although Meillassoux clarifies that his concept of "the human" is philosophical rather than purely biological – "By 'humans,' of course, we mean rational beings capable of grasping the absolute truth of contingency, and not simply the bipedal species in which such a reality now happens to be encountered" – it is clear that the virtual God can only emerge from the perfection of humanity brought about by the fourth world's advent. Similarly, when the Chorus of Spirits wishes to articulate how it will renovate the world in the wake of Prometheus' unbinding, Shelley is clear that all changes will take their cue from humanity's now-perfected model: "We will take our plan/ From the new world of man/ And our work shall be called the Promethean" (4.156–8). As the Spirit of the Hour attests, however, the alterations that subsequently occur take place at the level not just of the human but also of all material entities and the physical laws they obey:

There was a change ... the impalpable thin air
And the all-circling sunlight were transformed
As if the sense of love dissolved in them
Had folded itself round the sphered world.
My vision then grew clear and I could see
Into the mysteries of the Universe. (3.4.100–5)

Recalling Wordsworth's "see[ing] into the life of things," the Spirit describes how sight has been altered not merely at the personal level but in the atmosphere itself, which is transformed in the wake of Prometheus' unbinding without any explanation – that is, in the same spirit that Meillassoux argues natural laws can (but don't have to) change over the course of hyper-chaotic time. Indeed, in *Prometheus Unbound* even the effects of time are subject to alteration, as Act 4 opens with the burial of Death itself:

> Strew, oh strew
> Hair, not yew!
> Wet the dusty pall with tears, not dew!
> Be the faded flowers
> Of Death's bare bowers
> Spread on the corpse of the King of Hours! (4.15–20)

This is an effectively literal realization of what Meillassoux says must be the primary condition brought by a world of justice: the demonstration "that *this life* possesses in itself the dimension of immortality ... *such that I am only capable of expecting the renewal without end of what is here in this world*."[74] To avoid the metaphysical pitfalls of conventional theism, it is this world, not another, which must be capable of bringing the dead back to life, thus granting them justice.[75]

Despite these striking points of contact between Meillassoux's speculative materialism and Shelley's grand vision of worldly renewal in *Prometheus Unbound*, there appears also to be a significant point of divergence. For all his quasi-mystical abstraction, Meillassoux is staunchly anti-metaphysical, denying the existence of any necessary entity or process except pure contingency itself. Shelley, by contrast, clearly believes in the metaphysical value of at least one force that transcends what exists and is, by his account, entirely necessary: love. As quoted above, early in the play Demogorgon asserts that love is the only entity to exist above and beyond the vagaries of "Fate, Time, Occasion, Chance, and Change"; in his final speech, which concludes Act 4, he likewise describes how

> Love from its awful throne of patient power
> In the wise heart, from the last giddy hour
> Of dread endurance, from the slippery, steep,

And narrow verge of crag-like Agony, springs
And folds over the world its healing wings. (4.557–61)

The words "awful throne" recall similar phrases Shelley uses in
"Mont Blanc" to limn the inscrutable origins of the river Arve,
the sublimely obscure seat of power that the poem tries repeatedly
to comprehend. At the finale of *Prometheus Unbound*, however,
Love's power is portrayed as both graspable and benevolent,
"spring[ing]" from the pinnacle of Agony like a giant bird gather-
ing the world in its healing, winged embrace. Is there any way to
reconcile this with Meillassoux's vision? We might begin to do so,
I think, by returning to Pyle's observation that, for Shelley, love is
itself manifested primarily as beauty: "the aesthetic" in Shelley's
poetry is never mere "sensuous beauty," but "the comings and
goings of the spirit of beauty" which "generates the binding force
of love" that holds the key to humanity's and the planet's joint
renewals.[76] Significantly, although love does not explicitly appear
in Meillassoux's philosophy, beauty plays an unambiguous role:
it represents the anticipation of the order of justice in this world,
in those moments when we recognize or feel a sense of fleeting
harmony between something in this world and "our desire for
perfection" only realizable in the fourth world. Moreover, if we
fail to recognize beauty in the here and now, says Meillassoux,
the world of justice's arrival will be barren: "beauty will result
from the fact that just people in the third World have actually
hoped for this [fourth] World, thereby enabling the possibility that
it could arise *as if this hope were the source of it*."[77] Just as the
new, renovated world that appears in the final act of *Prometheus
Unbound* is a world of justice and beauty not despite but *because*
it encodes the memory of previous injustices – from Prometheus'
imprisonment to African slavery to an imperfect atmosphere –
that are now corrected, so too Meillassoux's world of justice will
only be meaningful insofar as we wished for and worked toward
it without being able to force its arrival. (Its advent, of course,
must remain without reason and *ex nihilo*.) Thus Shelley's love
and Meillassoux's beauty may be reconciled after all; and thus
Shelley, an atheist who believes in metaphysical principles derived
from human potential, might very well agree with Meillassoux,
an atheist who believes in the possibility of a God-to-come, when
the latter concludes *The Divine Inexistence* by throwing his substantial intellectual weight behind "the philosophical link and

immanent form of hope – *believing in God because he does not exist.*"[78]

Notes

1. The original Latin reads "Quod clara at perspicua demonstratione careat pro vero habere mens omnio nequit humana." My thanks to Chris Washington for this translation.
2. Percy Bysshe Shelley, *The Necessity of Atheism* (Amherst, NY: Prometheus Books, 1993), 31. Subsequent citations are given parenthetically in the text. This text is the version published in 1813 as a note to Shelley's early epic poem, *Queen Mab*.
3. Shelley wrote this part of the pamphlet in French, perhaps in homage to Voltaire (one of his heroes); I have used the standard but uncredited translation.
4. Lee Braver, *A Thing of This World: A History of Continental Anti-Realism* (Evanston: Northwestern University Press, 2007), 57.
5. Shelley, *A Defence of Poetry*, in *Shelley's Poetry and Prose*, ed. Donald H. Reiman and Neil Fraistat (New York: Norton, 2002), 514. Unless otherwise noted, subsequent citations of Shelley's work are from this edition and are given parenthetically in the text. For more on Shelley's repeated use of the Allegory of the Cave, see e.g. Stuart Peterfreund, *Shelley among Others: The Play of the Intertext and the Idea of Language* (Baltimore: Johns Hopkins University Press, 2001), 83, 145–6.
6. For example, Shelley's first major long poem, *Queen Mab* (1811), begins with a soul rising from a sleeping body, prompting the poem's narrator to observe "how different! One aspires to Heaven/ Pants for its sempiternal heritage,/ . . . The other . . . like an useless and worn-out machine,/ Rots, perishes, and passes" (I.148–9, 152, 155–6).
7. See Paul de Man, "Shelley Disfigured," in *The Rhetoric of Romanticism* (New York: Columbia University Press, 1984), 116.
8. Ray Brassier, *Nihil Unbound: Enlightenment and Extinction* (Basingstoke: Palgrave Macmillan, 2007), xi.
9. Peter Gratton, *Speculative Realism: Problems and Prospects* (New York and London: Bloomsbury, 2014), 143. Gratton's book provides a highly readable account of both core SR thinkers and a number of writers traveling at least partially in its orbit; my approach differs both in my selection of "orbital" SR thinkers, and in my interest in linking SR to a similar set of concerns articulated by the British Romantics.

10. Humphry House, "The Poetry of Adolescence," in *Shelley: A Collection of Critical Essays*, ed. George M. Ridenour (Englewood Cliffs, NJ: Prentice-Hall, 1965), 48.

11. See Richard Holmes, *Shelley: The Pursuit* (London and New York: Penguin, 1987), 7–9.

12. Leone Vivante, "Shelley and the Creative Principle," in *Shelley: A Collection of Critical Essays*, ed. George M. Ridenour (Englewood Cliffs, NJ: Prentice-Hall, 1965), 31.

13. E.g., in his *Defence of Poetry*, as analyzed in Timothy Morton, "An Object-Oriented Defense of Poetry," *New Literary History* 43.2 (2012): 205–6.

14. Quoted in Jack Donovan, "The Storyteller," in *The Cambridge Companion to Shelley*, ed. Timothy Morton (New York: Cambridge University Press, 2006), 90.

15. Monika Lee, "'Nature's Silent Eloquence': Disembodied Organic Language in *Queen Mab*," *Nineteenth-Century Literature* 48.2 (1993): 171.

16. For a stimulating account of eighteenth-century advances in microscopic technology and knowledge, see Barbara Maria Stafford, *Body Criticism: Imaging the Unseen in Enlightenment Art and Medicine* (Cambridge, MA: MIT Press, 1991), esp. "Magnifying," 341–98. On *umwelts*, see Jakob von Uexküll, *A Foray into the Worlds of Animals and Humans*, trans. Joseph. D. O'Neill (Minneapolis: University of Minnesota Press, 2010).

17. William Blake, "Auguries of Innocence," in *The Selected Poems of William Blake* (Ware: Wordsworth Editions, 1994), 135, l. 1.

18. Brassier, *Nihil Unbound*, xi. Subsequent citations are given parenthetically in the text.

19. Richard Harter Fogle, "The Abstractness of Shelley," in *Shelley: A Collection of Critical Essays*, ed. George M. Ridenour (Englewood Cliffs, NJ: Prentice-Hall, 1965), 22; Forest Pyle, *Art's Undoing: In the Wake of a Radical Aestheticism* (New York: Fordham University Press, 2014), 59.

20. For a fuller but accessible account of Churchland's theories of mind, see Paul M. Churchland, *The Engine of Reason, the Seat of the Soul: A Philosophical Journey into the Brain* (Cambridge, MA: MIT Press, 1995).

21. Maxwell Bennett and Peter Hacker, "The Conceptual Presuppositions of Cognitive Neuroscience: A Reply to Critics," in Maxwell Bennett, Daniel Dennett, Peter Hacker, and John Searle, *Neuroscience and Philosophy: Brain, Mind, and Language*, intro. and conclusion by

Daniel Robinson (New York: Columbia University Press, 2007), 162.

22. Harold Bloom, "The Unpastured Sea: An Introduction to Shelley," in *Romanticism and Consciousness: Essays in Criticism*, ed. Harold Bloom (New York: Norton, 1970), 378.

23. Jerrold Hogle, "Language and Form," in *The Cambridge Companion to Shelley*, ed. Timothy Morton (New York: Cambridge University Press, 2006), 152–3.

24. For a helpful summary of Laruelle's infamously opaque "non-philosophy," especially in conversation with SR, see Steven Shaviro, *The Universe of Things: On Speculative Realism* (Minneapolis: University of Minnesota Press, 2014), 128–31.

25. See the introduction to the poem by Reiman and Fraistat in *Shelley's Poetry and Prose*, 93.

26. Pyle, *Art's Undoing*, 32.

27. Ibid., 32–5.

28. Ray Brassier, "I am a nihilist because I still believe in truth," interview with Marcin Rychter, *Kronos* (March 4, 2011), http://www.kronos.org.pl/index.php?23151,896 (accessed June 22, 2015). This interview also contains helpful statements by Brassier distinguishing his positions from those of Nietzsche (who conflated "meaning" with "intelligibility," according to Brassier) and the existentialists (who believed in what Brassier identifies as an essentially folk-psychological view of the mind).

29. Ibid: "Science harbours metaphysical presuppositions whether it wants to or not. Far better for it to be aware of them so that it is able to tell which of its metaphysical assumptions are empirically fertile, and which are obstructive and redundant. The only credible metaphysic is one that is sensitive to the philosophical implications of the natural sciences, as exemplified by the way in which physics has reconfigured our intuitive notions of space, time, and causality; or biology has forced us to revise (if not abandon) our intuitive understanding of species and essence."

30. Ray Brassier, "Postscript: Speculative Autopsy," in Peter Wolfendale, *Object-Oriented Philosophy: The Noumenon's New Clothes* (Falmouth: Urbanomic, 2014), 413.

31. Quoted in Holmes, *Shelley: The Pursuit*, 339.

32. Ibid., 339.

33. Harold Bloom, *The Visionary Company: A Reading of English Romantic Poetry*, rev. ed. (Ithaca: Cornell University Press, 1971), 294.

34. Coleridge, "Hymn to Sun-rise, in the Vale of Chamouni," in *Poetical Works*, ed. Ernest Hartley Coleridge (Oxford: Oxford University Press, 1969), 377, l. 5.

35. Ibid., ll. 40–3.

36. Earl Wasserman, "Mont Blanc," in *Shelley: A Collection of Critical Essays*, ed. George M. Ridenour (Englewood Cliffs, NJ: Prentice-Hall, 1965), 72, 76.

37. Morton, "An Object-Oriented Defense of Poetry," 217.

38. Quentin Meillassoux, *After Finitude: An Essay on the Necessity of Contingency*, trans. Ray Brassier (London and New York: Continuum, 2008), 1–2. Subsequent citations are given parenthetically in the text.

39. For a critique of the distinction between primary and secondary qualities that is nonetheless sympathetic to Meillassoux's anti-correlationist goals, see Shaviro, *Universe of Things*, 113–17. In sum, Shaviro finds Meillassoux guilty of what Whitehead would call "the bifurcation of nature," in which "sensory experience[s]" are falsely separated from the "physical actualities that generate" them (114).

40. Quentin Meillassoux, *Time Without Becoming*, ed. Anna Longo (Mimesis International, 2014), 9. This volume comprises the text of a talk given by Meillassoux at Middlesex University, London, on May 8, 2008, followed by an exegetical essay by Longo.

41. Especially given the turn toward ecocriticism, literary critics have become quite interested in these sorts of questions. For examples that take up similar questions, albeit from non-SR perspectives, see Noah Heringman, *Romantic Rocks, Aesthetic Geology* (Ithaca: Cornell University Press, 2004); Christopher Hitt, "Shelley's Unwriting of Mont Blanc," *Texas Studies in Language and Literature* 47 (2005): 139–66; Nigel Leask, "Mont Blanc's Mysterious Voice: Shelley and Huttonian Earth Science," in *The Third Culture: Literature and Science*, ed. Elinor S. Shaffer (Berlin: de Gruyter, 1998), 182–203.

42. As Chris Washington observes, this formulation of the correlationist question is akin to the classic riddle "If a tree falls in a forest but no one is around to hear it, does it make a sound?" See Washington, "Speculative Realism and Romanticism," *Literature Compass* 12.9 (2015): 448–60. My thanks to the author for sharing the pre-publication manuscript with me.

43. See Meillassoux, *After Finitude*, 36–8; Meillassoux, *Time Without Becoming*, 20–3. For clarity's sake, I have drawn on the latter text's terminology here.

44. Graham Harman, *Quentin Meillassoux: Philosophy in the Making*, 2nd ed. (Edinburgh: Edinburgh University Press, 2015), 6.

45. When this manuscript was in its final stages of preparation, another interpretation of "Mont Blanc" was published that mobilizes Meillassoux's concepts: see Anne C. McCarthy, "The Aesthetics of Contingency in the Shelleyan 'Universe of Things,' or 'Mont Blanc,' without Mont Blanc," *Studies in Romanticism* 54.3 (2015): 355–75. As her title suggests, McCarthy thinks critics have over-estimated the importance of the mountain itself in Shelley's ontology, and encourages us to focus on the ravine of Arve as Shelley's "figure for the relationship between mind and world" (356).

46. Shaviro, *Universe of Things*, 58–9, 114.

47. Ibid., 116. Chris Washington also finds "Mont Blanc" congenial to an OOP-informed reading, although he is more interested in questions of temporality than aesthetics; see Washington, "Speculative Materialism and Romanticism."

48. Greg Ellermann, "Speculative Romanticism," *SubStance* 44.1 (2015): 166–7. For Frances Ferguson's interpretation to which Ellermann refers, see "Shelley's *Mont Blanc*: What the Mountain Said," in *Romanticism and Language*, ed. Arden Reed (London: Methuen, 1984), 202–14.

49. Ellermann, "Speculative Romanticism," 168–9. See also Quentin Meillassoux, "Iteration, Reiteration, Repetition: A Speculative Analysis of the Meaningless Sign," trans. Robin Mackay, https://cdn.shopify.com/s/files/1/0069/6232/files/Meillassoux_Workshop_Berlin.pdf (accessed December 23, 2015).

50. Transcript of panelists' responses to "Presentation by Graham Harman," *Collapse* 3 (2007): 393, "Speculative Realism" conference special issue, ed. Robin Mackay.

51. William Keach, "[*Mont Blanc*]," in *Shelley's Poetry and Prose*, ed. Reiman and Fraistat, 670.

52. Ibid., 674. Not coincidentally, given his predilection for a realist ontology built on the supposed objectivity of mathematized primary qualities, Meillassoux has also produced a word-count-oriented book of philosophical literary criticism; see *The Number and the Siren: A Decipherment of Mallarmé's* Coup de Dés, trans. Robin Mackay (London: Urbanomic, 2012).

53. Shelley, Preface to *Prometheus Unbound*, in *Shelley's Poetry and Prose*, ed. Reiman and Fraistat, 206.

54. M. H. Abrams, *Natural Supernaturalism: Tradition and Revolution*

in Romantic Literature (New York: Norton, 1971), 300; Bloom, *Visionary Company*, 310.

55. Tillotama Rajan, *Dark Interpreter: The Discourse of Romanticism* (Ithaca: Cornell University Press, 1980), 88–9.

56. See, e.g., Cian Duffy, *Shelley and the Revolutionary Sublime* (Cambridge: Cambridge University Press, 2005); Michelle Geric, "Shelley's 'cancelled cycles': Huttonian Geomorphology and Catastrophe in *Prometheus Unbound* (1820)," *Romanticism* 19.1 (2013): 31–43.

57. See Meillassoux, *Time Without Becoming*, 25–6.

58. Robert Jackson, "Hyper-Chaos," in *The Meillassoux Dictionary*, ed. Peter Gratton and Paul J. Ennis (Edinburgh: Edinburgh University Press, 2015), 94.

59. See, e.g., D. J. Hughes, "Potentiality in *Prometheus Unbound*," *Studies in Romanticism* 2 (1963): 107–26.

60. See Quentin Meillassoux, "Potentiality and Virtuality," *Collapse* 2 (2007), 66–7; Paul Livingston, "Cantor, Georg," in *The Meillassoux Dictionary*, ed. Peter Gratton and Paul J. Ennis (Edinburgh: Edinburgh University Press, 2015), 37–8; see also, e.g., Ian Stewart, *Taming the Infinite: The Story of Mathematics from the First Numbers to Chaos Theory* (London: Quercus, 2008), 316–22. A succinct explanation also appears in Alain Badiou, *Number and Numbers*, trans. Robin Mackay (Cambridge and Malden, MA: Polity, 2008), 74.

61. See Livingston, "Cantor," 39–40.

62. Meillassoux, "Potentiality and Virtuality," 72.

63. Quentin Meillassoux, "Appendix: Excerpts from *L'inexistence Divine*," trans. Graham Harman, in Harman, *Meillassoux: Philosophy in the Making*, 227. Hereafter cited as *Divine Inexistence*.

64. Meillassoux, *Divine Inexistence*, 236. Cf. Thomas Nagel's much-maligned recent book, *Mind and Cosmos: Why the Materialist Neo-Darwinian Conception of Nature is Almost Certainly False* (Oxford: Oxford University Press, 2012), which argues for the insufficiency of existing scientific frameworks to explain the creation and evolution of life, especially conscious life, from "dead matter." But for a study that productively complicates Nagel's common-sense view of what constitutes "dead matter," see Eugene Thacker, *After Life* (Chicago: University of Chicago Press, 2010).

65. Meillassoux, *Divine Inexistence*, 228.

66. Ibid., 281.

67. Ibid., 281, 283.

68. See, e.g., Paul Livingston, "Realism and the Infinite," *Speculations*

4 (2013): 105–6; see also Adam Kotsko, "Quentin Meillassoux and the Crackpot Sublime," *The New Inquiry* (May 9, 2012), http://thenewinquiry.com/essays/quentin-meillassoux-and-the-crackpot-sublime (accessed July 29, 2015), which despite its title contains a judicious examination of Meillassoux's ideas in relation to more traditional Christian theology. For the most complete account of Meillassoux's theological ideas published so far, see Christopher Watkin's chapter on him in his *Difficult Atheism: Post-Theological Thinking in Alain Badiou, Jean-Luc Nancy, and Quentin Meillassoux* (Edinburgh: Edinburgh University Press, 2011). Watkin finds Meillassoux's "post-theological integration" (133) compelling but (not surprisingly) incomplete.

69. Timothy Webb, "The Unascended Heaven: Negatives in *Prometheus Unbound*," in *Shelley's Poetry and Prose*, ed. Reiman and Freistat, 694–711.

70. Alain Badiou, *Le fini et l'infini* (Montrouge: Bayard, 2010), 9; my translation.

71. Shelley, *Defence of Poetry*, 525.

72. Meillassoux, *Divine Inexistence*, 241.

73. Ibid., 239.

74. Ibid., 237.

75. For a more detailed account of this element of the fourth world, see Quentin Meillassoux, "Spectral Dilemma," *Collapse* 4 (2008): 261–75. Here, Meillassoux develops a new name to describe his "original regime of thought, in rupture with both theology and atheism: a *divinology*" (275).

76. Pyle, *Art's Undoing*, 32–5.

77. Meillassoux, *Divine Inexistence*, 269.

78. Ibid., 287.

5

Keats, Vital Materialism, and Flat Ontology

John Keats was hardly the best-known British Romantic poet during his lifetime; that honor probably belongs either to Wordsworth, who became Poet Laureate in 1843, or Byron, whose private life was anything but. Yet Keats's life and death have been subject to at least as much myth-making as those of his peers. Duncan Wu has recently debunked the three most persistent myths: Keats "was never the deprived yokel he is reputed to have been"; he was not gay, despite Oscar Wilde's later adoration; and he was *not* killed by the words of unkind reviewers (a rumor that both Byron and Shelley promulgated for their own ends).[1] As with much myth-making, however, there is a kernel of truth to each of these: although Keats's family was upwardly mobile, his father's position as head hostler at the large tavern owned by his maternal grandfather was not considered especially genteel, nor was Keats's training as an apothecary and surgeon; although his heterosexuality is clear from his letters and engagement to Fanny Brawne, his poetry was frequently denounced for its supposedly feminine qualities; and he was certainly the target of several nasty reviews.[2] If an aura of exceptionality continues to surround Keats, this may be because few poets of any generation have produced as much world-class poetry as Keats did at such a young age. (He died at 25 of tuberculosis – the same disease that had previously killed his mother and brother.) That he was ambitious to leave his mark on English literature is well known; that he was able to do so, notwithstanding the self-effacing nature of his chosen epitaph – "Here lies one whose name was writ in water" – remains remarkable. For many readers, especially outside academia, Keats remains the British Romantic poet *par excellence*.

In its general contours, then, the reception history of Keats's poems can stand for that of the Romantic poets as a whole: from widely reviled on their first appearances, to widely celebrated. What distinguishes Keats's case, however, is the specific nature of the early critiques to which he and his work were exposed. Although many of the Romantics were criticized in their day for tending toward pantheism or animism (or, in Byron's case, even Satanism), none was as regularly villainized as Keats for his "crimes" against good taste. Even the other Romantic poets disparaged his work: Wordsworth complained of Keats's "pretty Paganism," Byron accused him of "always frigging his imagination," and Shelley probably did him no favors when he memorialized Keats posthumously in *Adonais* (1821) as being "a portion of the loveliness/ Which once he made more lovely."[3] What all of these descriptions recognize, however, is the undisguised pleasure frequently articulated and consistently offered by Keats's poetry; it is the "sheer physicality of Keats's enjoyment of poetry," both his own and others', that seems to have impressed – and frequently bothered – his fellow Romantics.[4] Keats himself was unapologetic; his letters as well as his poems are full of self-consciously admiring descriptions of things that he found beautiful. Accordingly, although the conservative, Romantic-era critic John Gibson Lockhart was arguably wrong to characterize Keats as a working-class pretender, his infamous jibe – "It is a better and a wiser thing to be a starved apothecary than a starved poet; so back to the shop Mr John, back to 'plasters, pills, and ointment boxes,' &c." – is not entirely misguided, since its final list of medical items, despite being offered disdainfully, echoes many of Keats's own catalogues of objects. Indeed, for Keats the pleasures offered by the material world, and then by that world translated into words, seem to have been very closely related. In a letter to his friend John Hamilton Reynolds from March 1818, for example, Keats lightheartedly depicts the Devonshire landscape to which he had recently moved by referring to the sublime views frequently described in Ann Radcliffe's late-eighteenth-century Gothic novels: "I am going among Scenery whence I intend to tip you the Damosel Radcliffe – I'll cavern you, and grotto you, and waterfall you, and wood you, and water you, and immense-rock you, and tremendous sound you, and solitude you."[5]

Later in this chapter I will look much more closely at several of Keats's many poetic invocations of material things – his "seductive lists," as one critic nicely puts it.[6] First, however, I want to establish a theoretical connection that may already be obvious:

many Speculative Realist texts also contain copious lists of things. Ian Bogost has identified lists or litanies of things as an integral part of SR's philosophical project, not just a stylistic tic: "The off-pitch sound of lists to the literary ear only emphasizes their real purpose: disjunction instead of flow. Lists remind us that no matter how fluidly a system may operate, its members nevertheless remain utterly isolated, mutual aliens."[7] Bogost is thinking primarily of Harman's object-oriented philosophy, which as we saw in Chapter 1 consistently emphasizes the autonomy of objects. The two SR-affiliated theorists with whom this chapter is concerned, however, tend to use lists differently, since each of them is primarily interested in the connections and unexpected affiliations between things rather than in their essential alienation from each other. Each is deeply invested, too, in unpacking the potential ethical ramifications of recognizing the essential connectedness of things. For Jane Bennett, a political scientist whose work is more closely associated with the New Materialism movement than with SR *per se*, these interests and investments manifest themselves primarily in her commitment to thinking about how a greater appreciation of the agency of non-human actants can have ethical effects. For Levi Bryant, a philosopher with a deep knowledge of Deleuze, the turn to non-humans has led him to develop, first, an object-oriented ontology that is similar but far from identical to Harman's object-oriented philosophy, and more recently a machine-oriented ontology that Bryant calls "onto-cartography." As these descriptions suggest, despite their similar goals and overlapping Deleuzian origins, Bennett's and Bryant's philosophical projects diverge in some significant directions. Yet though it may seem odd to claim that two such different approaches to a non-anthropocentric ontology could be found within the work of the same poet, Keats's own well-known concept of "negative capability" – "when man is capable of being in uncertainties, Mysteries, doubts, without any irritable reaching after fact or reason"[8] – is ample warrant for reading multiplicity into his famously evocative poems. After considering Bennett's ideas of "enchantment" and "vibrant matter" alongside some of Keats's narrative poetry, then, I turn to Bryant's "flat ontology" and machinic couplings to shed new light on some of Keats's best-known odes. Each of these concepts and approaches offers ways of thinking and feeling not only beyond the human but also potentially beyond life and death itself – prospects that would have been attractive to a poet who complained, even before the end of his too-short life, that he was already living a "posthumous existence."[9]

One of the most fascinating aspects of studying Keats's oeuvre is observing the speed with which he matured as a poet and a thinker. Scarcely five years separate his earliest known compositions of 1814 and the so-called "Spring Odes" of 1819, in which "we reach, if only for a brief while, a high plateau where in mastery of phrase [Keats] has few equals in English poetry," as Walter Jackson Bate put it over half a century ago.[10] Without questioning the superior quality of the later work, however, it is no longer necessary to subscribe to Bate's view that Keats's earlier efforts suffered from a "luxurious abandonment to the conventionally 'poetic' objects and images that intrigued a youthful romantic poet."[11] On the contrary, it is precisely this "abandonment" to the attractions and agencies of objects that gives Keats's early poems their unique power to move and inspire readers. To adapt a wonderful witticism from Morton, if "relations are from Shelley, [then] objects are from Keats."[12]

The dedicatory sonnet of Keats's first published collection, *Poems* (1817), acknowledges the debt Keats felt he owed to his friend and mentor, the radical poet and publisher Leigh Hunt. Addressed directly to Hunt – a polarizing figure whose enemies would soon set their sights on Keats[13] – the opening poem establishes Keats's fascination with objects both natural and artificial. Although history's golden age is long over, the octave seeks to recall an idyllic past:

> Glory and loveliness have pass'd away;
> For if we wander out in early morn,
> No wreathed incense do we see upborne
> Into the east, to meet the smiling day:
> No crowd of nymphs soft voic'd and young, and gay,
> In woven baskets bringing ears of corn,
> Roses, and pinks, and violets, to adorn
> The shrine of Flora in her early May.[14]

Keats's first line presents the current age's lack of "glory and loveliness" as a fact – one that the rest of the poem, and by extension all of Keats's future poetic output, will implicitly or explicitly seek to remedy. The subsequent clauses present what is arguably Keats's first poetic litany, albeit in negative terms: *no* incense rises in the east any longer, *no* "crowd of nymphs" arrives bearing corn and flowers to celebrate Spring's arrival. But by recalling and describing these phenomena, the poet is able to grant them renewed existence, at least in the minds of readers:

> But there are left delights as high as these,
> And I shall ever bless my destiny,
> That in a time, when under pleasant trees
> Pan is no longer sought, I feel a free,
> A leafy luxury, seeing I could please
> With these poor offerings, a man like thee. (ll. 9–14)

Although Pan – the Greek god of the wild – is no longer worshipped, Keats follows in the footsteps of the octave's vanished nymphs by continuing to bring offerings of his own, namely his poems, which he hopes Hunt (and by extension readers in general) will enjoy. Keats's evocative description of what he feels on this occasion is a "leafy luxury": a sense of taking relaxed, spontaneous pleasure in his ability to bring pleasure to others via the words and images of his poems.

Another way to describe what Keats identifies in this sonnet as the constituent condition of his historical moment, however, would be to draw on Bennett's critical narrative in her book *The Enchantment of Modern Life* (2001). As noted in previous chapters, we live in a modern world that is self-consciously disenchanted. Although the details of this "story"[15] differ depending on which version is being told (Bennett focuses on the philosophies of Max Weber, Hans Blumenberg, and Simon Critchley), the basic parameters remain the same: since the Enlightenment, the world has been increasingly denuded of its wonder and mystery through a combination of technological progress and rational calculation. The effects have been clear and, in Bennett's opinion, more deleterious than generally recognized: disenchantment promotes our increasing alienation from the world, which in turn leads to joylessness, cynicism, and a lack of generosity toward others. (As Keats puts it, "glory and loveliness have pass'd away.") The countermeasure that Bennett proposes is deceptively simple: we must re-attach ourselves to the world, affectively speaking, by seeking out and cultivating moments when we are "struck and shaken by the extraordinary that lives amid the familiar and the everyday" (*Enchantment*, 4).[16] Such moments – catalysts for the rapt, attentive, open state of mind she calls "enchantment" – create an "affective force," according to Bennett, that in turn "might be deployed to propel ethical generosity" (3). Not unlike Wordsworth's belief that love of nature will lead to love of our fellow human beings, Bennett believes that learning to cultivate "a more radical permeability" to the world around us will enlarge what she calls our "moral imaginary" (29).

The immediate connection between Bennett's work in *The Enchantment of Modern Life* and most other SR-related approaches is that such moments come about primarily via paying attention to the agency of non-human things. In a litany that looks backward to Keats as well as forward to those of SR practitioners, for example, Bennett names "nonhuman animals, the wind, rocks, trees, plants, tools, [and] machines" as potential sites of enchantment (29); elsewhere, she devotes sections to phenomena as diverse as nanotechnology and khaki pants for their enchanting potential.[17] So the basic thrust of her program – that we should learn to pay greater attention to the agency of the non-human world that surrounds and even penetrates us at all times – resonates with the general anti-anthropocentrism of most SR approaches. More specifically, to my mind, Bennett's program has much in common with Latour's: both theorists propose that we spend less time critiquing the world around us and more time learning to re-describe it in ways that promote our common attachments to it. By contrast, her work would seem to have the least in common with that of Brassier, who (as we saw in Chapter 4) wants us to complete the Enlightenment project of disenchanting the world in order to recognize properly its innate meaninglessness. Yet Bennett is clear that her vision of the world invokes no teleology, much less an "intelligent design" or divine purpose; as she puts it, "A world capable of enchanting need not be designed, or predisposed toward human happiness, or expressive of intrinsic purpose or meaning" (11). Instead, Bennett self-consciously presents her vision of a world filled with pockets of potential enchantment as a "weak ontology," "necessarily speculative and contestable ... more than subjective but less than objective" (161). If this is a "weird realism" like Harman's and Morton's object-oriented philosophy – and what could be more weird than her reading of the Gap's "dancing khakis" advertisements as "in a tradition of works of art that explore the phenomenon of . . . dead things coming alive, of objects revealing a secret capacity for self-propulsion" (112)? – then it is simultaneously less decisive than OOP as an account of how objects exist and interact, and more overtly geared toward producing affects and then ethical orientations in human actants. In this latter sense, Bennett's vision may have most in common with Badiou's explicitly political program, inasmuch as each provides an ontological account of reality specifically designed to encourage new modes of being and acting. Whereas Badiou's system is built on an objective mathematical core, however, Bennett's is much more phenomenological. If in her words "Enchantment is a feeling of being connected in an affirmative way to existence," then the "sense of fullness" that it momentarily engenders "encourages the finite human animal, in turn, to give away some of its own time and effort on behalf of other creatures" – but by Bennett's own admission, there is "no guarantee that this will happen" (156). Enchantment is a mode, not an operation.

Turning now to consider enchantment's role in Keats's poetry, we can easily find examples from the same 1817 collection which began with the dedicatory poem to Hunt discussed above. "On First Looking into Chapman's Homer," one of its best-known sonnets, recounts Keats's response to reading George Chapman's Elizabethan-era translation of the Greek epics. With its rough-hewn couplets, Chapman's translation – lent to Keats by none other than Hunt – had become less popular than Alexander Pope's more recent and smoother version, but for Keats it was an authentic revelation. In his sonnet's first quatrain, Keats figures himself as a wanderer and adventurer, not unlike Odysseus:

> Much have I travell'd in the realms of gold,
> And many goodly states and countries seen;
> Round many western islands have I been
> Which bards in fealty to Apollo hold. (ll. 1–4)

Having already read much Golden Age literature in translation if not always in the original – a point that his critics would later exploit as evidence of his less-than-elite education – Keats presents himself as an experienced (mental) traveler. Yet after encountering Chapman's translation of what the second quatrain calls "deep-brow'd Homer" (l. 6), Keats subsequently tries out several extended similes to articulate his feelings:

Then felt I like some watcher of the skies
When a new planet swims into his ken;
Or like stout Cortez when with eagle eyes
He star'd at the Pacific – and all his men
Look'd at each other with a wild surmise –
Silent, upon a peak in Darien. (ll. 7–12)

Despite the historical inaccuracy (it was Vasco de Balboa who saw the Pacific Ocean from atop a mountain in Panama; when the error was pointed out to him in manuscript by a friend, Keats chose not to correct it),[18] what is most striking here is the depth of the sense of wonder being described; indeed, Keats's image of the European explorers looking at each other "silent[ly]" and "with a wild surmise" closely resembles Bennett's specification that an enchanted state is frequently characterized by "the temporary suspension of chronological time and bodily movement" (*Enchantment*, 5). Such suspension is what allows us to become unusually sensitive to the surprising, overlooked qualities and agencies of the things around us. Subsequently, says Bennett, we are ushered into a "mood of fullness, plenitude, or liveliness" (5) which, with practice and purpose, can lead to greater ethical generosity.

Keats's sonnet ends well before such results are realized. But even without a record of what follows this scene of momentary transfixion, there is something potentially problematic about the poem's use of European colonizers as figures for wonderment; as Keats would have known from his source materials, Cortés's expedition led directly to the destruction of the Aztec Empire.[19] Less ominous is the "watcher of the skies" who discovers a new planet through a telescope; here, Keats is likely thinking of the recent discovery of Uranus by William Herschel.[20] In both cases, however, there is a noticeable lacuna in the place where, in Bennett's system, ethical action would spring from the affect generated by enchantment. Certainly, there is a "subintentional disposition in favor of life" (*Enchantment*, 158) that is palpable in "On First Looking into Chapman's Homer," and is brought to the surface in many of Keats's other poems, as we will see. If Keats neglects to confirm a direct link between wondrous feelings and ethical action, however, then this may be because, unlike Bennett, he shows little interest in attaching explicitly useful consequences to aesthetic responses. In the same letter where he mentions his idea of "negative capability" as a poet's greatest asset, for example, he declares that "with a great poet the sense of Beauty overcomes every other consideration, or rather obliterates all consideration."[21] Such a statement of "pure" artistic intent distinguishes Keats's poetics not only from Bennett's "enchanted materialism" but also from Wordsworth, whose program in "Tintern Abbey" and elsewhere draws direct connections between learning to appreciate "all the mighty world/ Of eye and ear" and cultivating one's "moral being."[22] Reading Chapman's Homer may make Keats feel equally alive to the world's possibilities, but it delivers no definite moral or ethical imperative.

The first main poem of Keats's 1817 volume, "I stood tiptoe upon a little hill," exemplifies his commitment to a purposeless aesthetic vision. Set in a luxuriously detailed pastoral landscape, the poem's descriptions are finely articulated but devoid of further meaning, at least for humans. Although there is some talk of a "natural sermon" being given by a nearby stream (l. 71), Keats makes no attempt to translate the water's "hurrying freshnesses" into a lesson of any kind (l. 70). The poem's many litanies of closely observed natural phenomena seem designed to induce a state of becalmed enchantment in readers – at one point, the poem's speaker describes gazing at the moon until his "soul is lost in pleasant smotherings" (l. 132); a few lines later, he reports a feeling of being "uplifted from the world" (l. 139). Neither of these enchanted moments, however, leads to ethical acts in any conventional sense. Instead, what Keats repeatedly suggests is that appreciating moments of beauty and wonder leads primarily to the desire to write more poetry. The previously mentioned feeling of being "uplifted from the world," for example, is followed by Keats's origin story of the classical myth of Psyche and Eros:

So felt he, who first told, how Psyche went
On the smooth wind to realms of wonderment;
What Psyche felt, and Love, when their full lips
First touch'd; (ll. 141–4)

Likewise, Keats attributes the myth of Narcissus to a similarly material experience:

What first inspired a bard of old to sing
Narcissus pining o'er the untainted spring?

In some delicious ramble, he had found
A little space, with boughs all woven round;
And in the midst of all, a clearer pool, [. . .]
And on the bank a lonely flower he spied . . . (ll. 163–7, 171)

The experience of wonderment, for Keats, leads most directly *not* to Bennett's hoped-for ethical actions, but rather to the creation of narratives that attempt to imbue those experiences with meaning and communicate them to others. This lack of interest in the edifying or even socializing dynamics of wondrous experience is what Keats's early critics were objecting to when they called his poetry masturbatory; it is also what the literary critic Marjorie Levinson indicates, at least in part, when she states that "Keats produces a writing which is aggressively *literary*" almost to the point of parody.[23] This is neither to suggest, as used to be common, that Keats's poetry is devoid of politics or political interests, nor that it can be fully explained by its socio-political contexts (as New Historical critics in the 1980s and 1990s sometimes seemed in danger of arguing).[24] Rather, for Keats, political or ethical acts cannot be divorced from acts of reading and writing themselves: beauty begets poetry, which begets more beauty, and so on. If there is an ethics here, then it stresses the need for constant interpretation and rearticulation of (the experience of) reality before all else.[25]

Bennett is not naïve about the potential ambiguity of her concept of enchantment. She knows that ethical action does not follow necessarily or automatically from wondrous encounters, and that any such "dispositions" must be nurtured through a paradoxical mix of spontaneity and practice. Likewise, she is clear that interpretation is a necessary element of any decision to act, especially one influenced by emotion: "A metaphysical imaginary is always engaged in political interpretations, and this imaginary works indirectly at the level of affect. To render it explicit is to make it more available as a rhetorical strategy" (*Enchantment*, 161). But Keats seems skeptical even of this degree of linear cause and effect; if enchantment is a positive force, it is because it indexes the world's beauty and the subject's capacity for wonder and appreciation. This is displayed most clearly in the 1817 volume in its longest poem, the somewhat unfortunately titled "Sleep and Poetry." Keats begins with another litany of pleasure-giving natural objects, held together by the human power of observation and the formal power of parallel structure and rhetorical questions:

What is more gentle than a wind in summer?
What is more soothing than the pretty hummer
That stays one moment in an open flower,
And buzzes cheerily from bower to bower?
What is more tranquil than a musk-rose blowing
In a green island, far from all men's knowing?
More healthful than the leafiness of dales?
More secret than a nest of nightingales?
More serene than Cordelia's countenance?
More full of visions than a high romance? (ll. 1–10)

The answer, given immediately afterward, is "Sleep": "Soft closer of our eyes!/ Low murmurer of tender lullabies!" (ll. 11–12). But as befits a text that outlines Keats's self-understanding of his authorial development and ambitions – it has been called Keats's "Tintern Abbey"[26] – it turns out that there is a source of pleasure even greater than sleep: "Poesy" (l. 47). If sleep offers greater imaginative rewards than the experiences of "the great outdoors" with which the poem begins, then poetry is greater again because it affords opportunities to convert the affect of those experiences into something more concrete and communicable. Under the influence of the desire to write poetry,

       . . . a bowery nook
Will be elysium – an eternal book
Whence I may copy a lovely saying
About the leaves, and flowers – about the playing
Of nymphs in woods, and fountains; and the shade
Keeping a silence round a sleeping maid;
And many a verse from so strange influence
That we must ever wonder how, and whence
It came. (ll. 63–70)

Keats's imaginary repertoire may be implicitly political, at least inasmuch as his critics repeatedly questioned his presumption, as a supposedly "Cockney" poet, to lay claim to classical influences like those in the above passage. But this kind of enchantment, although certainly less passive than sleep, is not necessarily directed to any end beyond its translation into writing. Even when Keats wishes specifically to find "an enchanted grot" (l. 76), he does so not to cultivate Bennett's disposition toward ethical generosity, but rather so that he may "Write on my tablets all that was permitted,/ All that was for our human senses fitted" (ll. 79–80). Sentiments like these appear to anticipate a phenomenological (rather than a Speculative) outlook, one in which human sense perception is hailed as the only proper medium for knowledge of the world at large. As such, for my purposes they are most important as indices of Keats's determination to use the sensuous experience of being enchanted by the world as the catalyst to produce more poetry. And while it is possible to discover a politics in Keats's insistent aestheticization of experience,[27] it is equally possible to take Keats at his word in "Sleep and Poetry" that his desire to write is primarily driven by creative ambition: "O for ten years, that I may overwhelm/ Myself in poetry; so I may do the deed/ That my own soul has to itself decreed" (ll. 96–8).

Where enchantment plays a significant role in Keats's poetry, furthermore, it does so not only as a catalyst for authorial and by extension readerly inspiration (as Robert Mitchell has shown, seeing in Keats's work a fascination with "the poetics of trance"),[28] but also as a potentially dangerous state. In this vein, the "enchanted grot" of "Sleep and Poetry" anticipates the better-known "elfin grot" to which the Knight-at-Arms is "lured" in Keats's disquieting ballad, "La Belle Dame Sans Merci" (1820). I put "lured" in quotation marks because, despite Nicholas Roe's authoritative description of it as a "tale of erotic fixation and entrapment,"[29] there is in fact some debate regarding precisely what happens and who is responsible for the poem's unhappy outcome. Regardless of whether we understand the poem as an imitation of chivalric misadventure or whether we agree (as I am inclined to) with Barbara Johnson, who argues that "By the end of the poem, it becomes impossible to know whether one has read a story of a knight enthralled by a witch or of a woman seduced and abandoned by a male hysteric," the activities in question undeniably take place in an atmosphere of enchantment that obscures and frightens rather than clarifies or enlightens.[30] As soon as the knight meets the "beautiful . . . faery's child" while out riding, for example, he explains that "I set her on my pacing steed,/ And nothing else saw all day long" (ll. 14, 17–18) – a description bearing an unmistakable resemblance to Bennett's characterization of enchantment as being "transfixed, spellbound" (Enchantment, 5). One question critics have not generally asked about this poem, however, concerns the ambiguous role of the many objects named within it. Whatever the nature of the relationship between the knight and the mysterious, possibly non-human lady, their "courtship" is mediated by a series of objects whose presences seem to exercise an inscrutable power over one or both of them. The knight reports that

> I made a garland for her head,
> And bracelets too, and fragrant zone;
> She look'd at me as she did love,
> And made sweet moan. (ll. 21–4)

In return,

> She found me roots of relish sweet,
> And honey wild, and manna dew;
> And sure in language strange she said,
> I love thee true. (ll. 25–8)

As Johnson indicates, the ambiguities of "*as* she did love" (my italics) and "language strange" make it impossible for readers to decide whether the sexual relationship that follows is truly consensual. Likewise, when the knight tells of his eventual nightmare, in which the cadaverous ghosts of former kings and warriors warn him that "La belle Dame sans merci/ Hath thee in thrall!" (ll. 43–4), we should not only be uncertain about the legitimacy of his sense of victimization, but also wary of the fine line between enchantment and enthrallment. It is not clear from Bennett's account how one avoids the latter state, with its sickly fascination and enforced passivity, while nonetheless remaining open to the former. This is a problem Bennett acknowledges only occasionally, for example when she describes "the exciting and slightly unnerving power that personal computers" – which have only become smaller, more mobile, and more ubiquitous since the 2001 publication of her book – "can wield over their owners, as when one finds it difficult to pull oneself away from the screen after playing around on the Internet too long" (*Enchantment*, 171). Regardless of how we interpret the Knight's interaction with the belle dame, he is clearly unnerved by her continued power over him long after she has disappeared. Accordingly, whether he is enchanted, enthralled, or just physically ill, Keats's knight inhabits a landscape suffused with the sense of "fundamental loss" that Bennett's affirmation of the possibility of enchantment is designed to counter. This is reflected in the desolate landscape descriptions that frame the poem, where the "sedge is wither'd from the lake/ And no birds sing" (ll. 3–4, 47–8). The desiccated, despoiled state of the natural world in "La Belle Dame" is the objective correlative of the Knight's own diminished affect, drained away by his darkly enchanting encounter. In other words, the state of enchantment that Bennett wants us to cultivate and deploy in the name of ethical generosity is, for Keats, an ambivalent state that should be entered into warily if at all, since it can just as easily lead to morbid self-absorption.

At least one more element of "La Belle Dame sans Merci" warrants attention: the role of objects. In the stanzas quoted above, we see not only the effects of a kind of enchanted state, but also how this state is enhanced and extended by objects exchanged between the Knight and the lady. He gives her a garland, bracelets, and a belt ("fragrant zone") made from picked flowers; she feeds him "roots of relish sweet," wild honey, and "manna dew." Instead of clarifying or cementing the nature of the relationship between them, however, these exchanges deepen the mystery of who is taking advantage of whom. There is an implication, for example, that the food the knight has eaten was drugged or enchanted – "And there she lulled me to sleep" (l. 33) – but this is only after the Knight admits that "there I shut her wild, wild eyes/ With kisses four" (l. 32). Moreover, in an alternate version of the poem published by Hunt, "she lulled me to sleep" is replaced by "And there we slumbered on the moss," a shared condition of rest that suggests no foul play whatsoever. Similarly, it is impossible to tell precisely what the Knight intends when he fabricates the garland, bracelet, and belt for his would-be Lady. Are they gifts, chivalric tokens of loyalty, or payment for future services of a sexual nature? Even if we could know the Knight's intentions, moreover, we could not know how they are received by the lady herself.

In their stubborn opacity and irreducibility to human agendas, the objects in "La Belle Dame sans Merci" are excellent examples of what Bennett has recently called "thing-power." This term comes from her most recent book, *Vibrant Matter: A Political Ecology of Things* (2010), which moves beyond enchantment to develop more fully a related concept, "vital materialism." By turning toward thingly agency, Bennett is following the "second" direction of enchantment, away from "the humans who *feel* enchanted" and "toward the agency of the things that *produce* (helpful, harmful) effects in human and other bodies."[31] Put another way, where *Enchantment* retains a basic anthropocentrism due to its investment in the production and manipulation of human affect, *Vibrant Matter* explicitly switches to focus on the *things* that catalyze those affects, arguing that they too enjoy a kind of affective life. As Bennett explains, "My aim . . . is to theorize a vitality intrinsic to materiality as such, and to detach materiality from the figures of passive, mechanistic, or divinely infused substance" (*Vibrant*, xiii). Accordingly, *Vibrant Matter* interweaves readings of theories of affect (including those of Spinoza, Bergson, and Deleuze) with case studies that examine the "nonhuman forces operating outside and inside the human body" (xiv), including trash, electricity, food, and stem cells. As in *The Enchantment of Modern Life*, a strong ethical impetus drives Bennett's work, but rather than focus on things primarily to investigate how they can expand the sphere of human generosity, Bennett is now clear that she intends to encourage readers to "Give up the futile attempt to disentangle the human from the nonhuman. Seek instead to engage more civilly, strategically, and subtly with the nonhumans in the assemblages in which you, too, participate" (116).

As her vocabulary here suggests, *Vibrant Matter* is indebted to DeLanda (assemblages) and Latour (the hybridity of human and non-human), although it eschews their systematicity for a more syncretic, wide-ranging approach. In a chapter on "edible matter," for instance, Bennett considers food as "conative bodies" that work in and through other bodies, including "a person's 'own' body" (39; the quotation marks around "own" draw attention to the artificiality of that possessive marker when the body is understood as an assemblage of actants). She uses a wide range of examples, including our changing understanding of the effects of lipids on human nervous systems, the dietary theories of Nietzsche and Thoreau, and finally the "slow food" movement. Her purpose, made explicit at the chapter's end, is to re-vision food, not as a passive or inert substance that we simply consume, but rather "as itself an actant in an agentic assemblage that includes among its members my metabolism, cognition, and moral sensibility" (51).

But what happens when food becomes part of a dark enchantment – or, to put this in Bennett's terms, when it becomes part of an assemblage that works to compromise "cognition" and "moral sensibility"? This is the scenario that Keats explores in *The Eve of St. Agnes* (1820), a lush romance in Spenserian stanzas.

Probably Keats's most popular narrative poem, *Eve* tells of how the intrepid Porphyro woos his love, Madeline, eventually stealing her away from her hostile family's castle. As in "La Belle Dame sans Merci," however, the poem's framing elements and extravagant details complicate any simple interpretation of its action. The ominous setting – a medieval castle on St. Agnes' Eve, traditionally believed by Catholics to be a night when virgin girls may dream of their future husbands – is established through the kind of Gothic descriptions Keats was familiar with from reading Radcliffe:

> At length burst in the argent revelry,
> With plume, tiara, and all rich array,
> Numerous as shadows haunting fierily
> The brain, new stuff'd, in youth, with triumphs gay
> Of old romance. (5.1–4)

The owner of the youthful brain "stuff'd" with "old romance" is of course Madeline herself, who has heard the folk tales of St. Agnes' Eve from "old dames full many times" (5.9) and is eager to experience its visions. Consequently, she is already in a half-enchanted state well before excusing herself from the evening's festivities:

> She danc'd along with vague, regardless eyes,
> Anxious her lips, her breathing quick and short:
> The hallow'd hour was near at hand: . . .
> Hoodwink'd with faery fancy; all amort,
> Save to St. Agnes and her lambs unshorn,
> And all the bliss to be before to-morrow morn. (8.1–3, 7–9)

Between her unseeing eyes and her eagerness to retire to her bedroom, Madeline is clearly already at least partially given over to a trance-like state, albeit one that dulls her external senses rather than sharpens them, as Bennett might have hoped. Keats's consonants, alternately breathy and fricative – "hallow'd hour," "faery fancy" – complement the description of Madeline's breathing as "quick and short," itself a symptom of arousal. As Jack Stillinger observes in a classic article, the most telling word here is "hoodwinked," which suggests not only Keats's skepticism regarding the Catholic superstitions surrounding St. Agnes' Eve but also the duplicitous nature of Porphyro's subsequent exploitation of them to seduce Madeline.

Although Porphyro later refers to himself as "A famish'd pilgrim – saved by miracle" (38.6), Stillinger convincingly argues that we must understand this description ironically, "unless Keats has forgotten, or hopes the reader has forgotten, all the action leading to the consummation."[32] Traditionally, the early "action" that has drawn the most critical attention is Porphyro's decision to hide in Madeline's closet and observe her undress and prepare for sleep. But Bennett's focus on the vibrancy of edible matter licenses us to pay equal attention to Keats's careful, sensual delineation of the food Porphyro lays out to entertain Madeline when she awakens:

> And still she slept an azure-lidded sleep,
> In blanched linen, smooth, and lavender'd,
> While he from forth the closet brought a heap
> Of candied apple, quince, and plum, and gourd;
> With jellies soother than the creamy curd,
> And lucent syrops, tinct with cinnamon;
> Manna and dates, in argosy transferr'd
> From Fez, and spiced dainties, every one,
> From silken Samarcand to cedar'd Lebanon. (30.1–9)

In his pre-OOP writing on this poem, Morton notes that these "curds" and "syrops," far from being the "children's foods" that many critics have taken them for, were in fact "menu items in sophisticated medieval and early modern food, and Keats' use of them is sophisticated" as well.[33] Certainly, Keats's litany of delicacies does more than merely supplement Porphyro's seduction of Madeline, which is both confirmed and obscured by an evocative euphemism: "Into her dream he melted" (36.5). Instead, says Morton, the rhetorical pattern established by Keats's mouth-watering descriptions both limns "the routes of the early modern spice trade" and repeatedly turns nouns into adjectives: "azure-lidded," "lavendered" sheets, "candied" apple, "silken Samarcand," "cedar'd Lebanon."[34] The effect is to confuse –"Keats courts disorientation" in much of his poetry, Emily Rohrbach observes[35] – while still retaining some distinction between foreground and background, "substance and accidence," or (in OOP's vocabulary) real and sensual qualities, such that readers share Madeline's half-unconscious sensory overload as the scene unfolds. And when she awakens – in a beautifully ironic touch, she is (a)roused by Porphyro's rendition of "La Belle Dame sans Merci" – she cannot tell whether she is still dreaming, and Porphyro takes advantage of her enchanted state to "melt" into her "dream" (36.5). Their intercourse lacks anything even approaching today's understanding of consent, to put it mildly, and from a poetic standpoint it is also the ultimate confusion of appearance and reality. Such confusion is subsequently prolonged and generalized by the shifting verb tenses of the poem's final stanzas; from "She hurried at his words" (40.1) to "They glide, like phantoms, into the wide hall" (41.1) to "And they are gone: aye, ages long ago/ These lovers fled away into the storm" (42.1–2), we are led from the past into the present and then back into the distant past, where we are reminded the entire poem has taken place. As readers, we too are awoken somewhat rudely from the shadowy reverie of *The Eve of St. Agnes*.

What, then, becomes of the feast that Porphyro lays out for Madeline? Famously, it is never eaten; notwithstanding Porphyro's self-description as a famished pilgrim, the lovers escape the castle without consuming a single delicacy. In Bennett's view, paying attention to the agency of food can help decenter the human from our accounts of how things happen and what matters, encouraging us "not only to shift one's ideas about what counts as an actor but also to focus one's attention away from individuals and onto actants in assemblages" (*Vibrant*, 42). As *The Eve of St. Agnes* demonstrates, food need not even be digested in order to play an active role in such assemblages. In fact, the smorgasbord of seductive foods that Porphyro arranges seems most "lively, affective, and signaling," to use Bennett's terms (117), by remaining uneaten, at least by humans. (Presumably, if left in place, it will eventually be consumed by rodents, insects, bacteria, and other non-human denizens of the castle.) But if the role that food plays in Madeline's seduction remains ambiguous, its role in the reader's seduction is clear: like all the other "vibrant matters" in Keats's poem, the puddings and creams of Porphryo's banquet call to us all the more vibrantly for remaining undigested and, as a result, largely unassimilated to purely human devices and desires.

Keats did not stop writing long poems after *The Eve of St. Agnes*; always attracted to classical themes, he would pen several volumes of an original epic, *Hyperion* (1820), as well as an alternative version, *The Fall of Hyperion*, that likewise remained unfinished at his death. Most critics agree, however, that Keats's lasting poetic reputation was secured by the series of odes he wrote during the spring of 1819. Although they stop short of a straightforward sequence, these poems – I will focus on a trio of the best known: "Ode to a Nightingale," "Ode on a Grecian Urn," and "To Autumn" – are connected by their profound engagement with themes of mortality, beauty, and love, as well as by their sophisticated rhyme schemes and image clusters. Helen Vendler describes Keats's odes as "inexpressibly complex articulations of language in architectural form," in which images recur and transform to become "a network of combinatorial powers engaged in a constantly shifting set of relations."[36] Following Morton's witty observation regarding Keats's affinity for objects, however, I want to focus on the thing-centered nature of these poems, more specifically Keats's use of the formal opportunities offered by the ode to conduct rigorous albeit poetical examinations of their central objects. In so doing, these poems produce a certain political point of view even though their content is not explicitly political; as Jacques Rancière has recently put it, the "weave" of Keats's poetry "determines . . . neither the relationship of the poet *to* politics, nor the presence of politics in the poem," but rather "the very politics *of* the poetry" itself.[37] To accomplish this unpacking of the politics of Keats's odes, I draw on Levi Bryant's writings on objects and (more recently) "machines." Bryant's onticology and onto-cartography bring together elements of Deleuzian and object-oriented matrices in the service of an ontology that is immanent, realist, and speculative; the synthetic yet original nature of his ideas makes him an ideal "final" SR thinker to discuss in this book. Furthermore, Bryant's forthrightness regarding the political implications of his accounts of reality makes his work particularly well suited for making visible the formally enmeshed politics of Keats's odes in the manner Rancière advocates.

More than most of the other poems I've discussed in *Romantic Realities*, Keats's Spring Odes have accumulated a body of criticism and commentary disproportionate to the relative brevity of the individual poems themselves, none of which exceeds eight stanzas. They are also encrusted with layers of Romantic mythology, including the idea that they encode Keats's foreknowledge of his own death (of which there is little evidence in his letters), and that he wrote them spontaneously (against which there is ample manuscript evidence that Keats revised them thoroughly). Given these poems' hyper-canonicity, then, I will assume a certain degree of familiarity with them, reminding readers of their broad outlines but moving quickly to more theoretical levels of analysis.

The opening clause of "Ode to a Nightingale," "My heart aches" (l. 1), not only immediately establishes the intensely personal tone for which the Romantics in general and Keats in particular are well known, but also captures the reader's attention with what Bloom calls its "hammer beats of three heavily accented syllables."[38] The poem's narrative arc is deceptively simple: Keats or the poem's speaker (for brevity's sake I will assume they are one and the same, although critics do not entirely agree on this) hears the song of an unseen nightingale and is led into a series of reveries in which he fantasizes about escaping from his everyday life, first into the forest with the bird and later via suicide. At the end of the sixth stanza, Keats realizes that killing himself would mean never hearing the nightingale's song again, and resigns himself to living as the bird flies out of earshot and away. The poem's famous final question suggests that the entire experience has transpired under the influence of another trance-like, enchanted state: "Fled is that music: – Do I wake or sleep?" (l. 80). For a mid-twentieth-century critic like Richard Fogle, "Nightingale" is a "perfect rondure" capped by a "slow withdrawal, symbolized by the retreat of the bird itself so that objective description and subjective emotion are fused."[39] More recent critics, not surprisingly, have found the poem more ambiguous; after observing that a "movement back to the real world" informs both "Nightingale" and "Ode on a Grecian Urn," for example, Rajan asserts that their celebration of specific objects as "emblems of an art that knows no dissonance" inevitably throws into relief the insufficiency of Keats's own poetry as a vehicle of their expression.[40] Likewise, albeit in a more historicist vein, Maureen McLane notes that "Nightingale" participates in a long tradition of "explor[ing] birdsong as a lesser yet kindred *poiesis* – an *ahistorical* song, a *non-artificial* song, an unindividuated *species* song – as opposed to the historical, mortal, artifactual, individual work of human making," but sees the cost of such an opposition as the exposure of the poem's own artificiality, "a phantasized triumph-of-life over death and mutability."[41]

Valuable as they are, these readings share a working assumption that Keats's nightingale is best understood as a symbol – an assumption warranted not only by the language of the poem itself but also by its centrality to much modern Romantic criticism.[42] The primary drawback to this approach, however, is that it immediately robs the bird of agency within the poem, draining it of autonomy to draw attention to the poet's acts of linguistic creation and manipulation. But the ode itself makes no such move. Instead, it arguably works to preserve the bird's relative self-sufficiency; as Paul Sheats notes, "The nightingale . . . is notable for what it is not: the Philomela of poetic tradition, or indeed any humanizing personification beyond that briefly suggested by 'Dryad' [in line 7]."[43] An instructive contrast here is Shelley's "To a Skylark," which announces its subject's immateriality in its opening lines, "Hail to thee, blithe spirit!/ Bird that never wert," and devotes four later stanzas to unspooling similes comparing the bird to various characters, animals, and plants.[44] The resolute materiality of Keats's nightingale, by contrast, demands or at least allows for a different kind of approach, one that sees its significance not in what it means or stands for but in how it operates.

Bryant's onticology provides the tools for precisely this kind of analysis. A major springboard for Bryant's onticology (or "object-oriented ontology"; he uses both terms synonymously) appears in his earlier work on Deleuze; near the conclusion of that book, a critical overview of Deleuzian metaphysics, Bryant observes of Deleuze's transcendental empiricism that it "does not assume in advance what subjects and objects *ought* to be in the sense of formal essences, but instead sees them as productions out of a field of immanence where immanence is immanent to nothing save itself."[45] This same position is implicit, I think, in the subtitle of the introductory chapter of Bryant's *The Democracy of Objects* (2011), which lays out the thrust of his onticological project: "Towards a Finally Subjectless Object." Like Deleuze's philosophy of immanence, as well as much OOP and ANT, Bryant's onticology is devoted to breaking down the traditional subject–object dichotomy that Western philosophy has inherited most directly from Descartes. For Bryant, however, this distinction is not only erroneous but actively harmful: "Insofar as the form of distinction implicit in the culturalist mode of distinction . . . relegates nonhuman objects to the unmarked space of the distinction, all sorts of factors become invisible that are pertinent to why collectives involving humans take the form they do."[46] Like his fellow Speculative Realists, Bryant sees the first step toward making these factors – "the material unconscious" of our existences, as he has recently put it[47] – visible again is to break the correlationist circle. But instead of proceeding like Meillassoux and turning correlationism against itself (as discussed in Chapter 4), Bryant draws on philosopher of science Roy Bhaskar's theories in his seminal book, *A Realist Theory of Science* (1975). Here, Bhaskar argues that although the knowledge produced by scientific inquiry is clearly conditioned by history and society, the things about which that knowledge is being produced are not: "the specific gravity of mercury, the process of electrolysis, the mechanism of light propagation. None of these 'objects of knowledge' depend[s] upon human activity."[48] As Bryant explains, this is the central albeit implicit tenet of all scientific experimentation, for "if objects were dependent on mind, perception, or culture, then there would be nothing to discover in the closed systems produced in the experimental setting" (*Democracy*, 50). The fact that science is possible, and that the "generative mechanisms" or objects observed in closed scientific experiments are also frequently active or at least detectable in the "open systems" of the world at large (where they may be present even when prevented from generating the events of which they are capable), strongly suggests that "the transcendental conditions under which experimental activity is intelligible are *ontological* in character" (47). They really exist in the world, not just in "the mind that regards the world" (51). Nevertheless, Bhaskar's ontology – which Bryant adapts by expanding his framework so that the category of "real beings" includes not just "natural" objects but also human-made products, material as well as imaginary – is not a naïve realism that assumes the world is precisely as we perceive or observe it. What this kind of realism – as well as the anti-realist argument that observers unknowingly construct the world around them – forgets, Bryant points out, is that "the observer *is* an *object*" (63). Bryant's adaptation of Bhaskar's ontology thus breaks the correlationist circle and puts humans back into our proper ontological place in the universe, as one among many entities in a "democracy of objects," the nature of which we have only begun to explore.

But what, precisely, does it mean to be an object in Bryant's system? Drawing on Locke's critique of the Aristotelian concept of substance, Bryant upholds the traditional distinction between an object's (enduring) substance and its (transitory) qualities, but asserts that the former is not merely "the object *stripped* of all its qualities or, as Locke puts it, a bare substratum" (89). Instead, Bryant thinks of an object's substance in quasi-Deleuzian terms, as its "virtual proper being." Like DeLanda (whose Deleuzian ontology was discussed in Chapter 2), Bryant proposes that we conceive an object's substance not in terms of its permanent qualities but in terms of its powers: "the capacities of an object or what it can *do*" (89). But since many of these capacities are never realized, at least not simultaneously, the object's being remains virtual; as Bryant explains, "The powers of an object are never something that is *directly* manifested in the world. . . . The domain of power possessed by an object is always *greater* than any local manifestation or actualization of an object" (89). In Bryant's onticology, an object's qualities are neither more nor less than "acts" (90), or active emanations of the object's virtual proper being manifested at a particular moment. Here, Bryant draws on the distinction between geometry and topology: where the former deals with exact measurements, the latter is the domain of spatial relations like contiguity and inside/outside. Analogously, an object's virtual proper being must be understood topologically as an internal organization that remains invariant despite changing external conditions; its qualities, by contrast, can be thought of geometrically inasmuch as they are subject to local variations in their actualization (see 91–2). This process of actualization – the movement from the possibilities of an object's virtual proper being to the realities of its qualities – is a profoundly "*creative*" one that requires "*work*" for it to occur (118): the work of entering into relations with other objects. The shared characteristics of all objects, and the networks of relations into which they all enter to greater or lesser degrees, form the basis of the worldview that Bryant calls "flat ontology": "Flat ontology is not the thesis that all objects contribute equally, but that all objects equally exist. In its ontological egalitarianism, what flat ontology thus refuses is the erasure of any object as the mere construction of another object" (290).

Although the foregoing account of Bryant's onticology is incomplete, I think we can now turn to Keats's "Ode to a Nightingale" and see what is revealed when it is viewed accordingly. As already suggested, the general trend in recent criticism has been to highlight the abyss of difference that separates Keats (as both the poet and the poem's narrator) from his subject, the nightingale whose recurring song means that it "wast not born for death, Immortal bird!/ No hungry generations tread thee down" (ll. 61–2). Bryant's onticology, however, allows us to "flatten" this difference between poet and bird, bringing them into focus as objects with different virtual proper beings, of course, but whose interactions positively activate each other's qualities. Such a view does not automatically return to the celebratory readings of earlier critics, but neither does it join the pessimism of many deconstructive and New Historicist interpretations. Certainly, Keats is well aware of his human limitations, especially *vis-à-vis* the bird's perceived freedom to fly where it wants and to sing "in full throated ease" (l. 10). Insofar as the bird's song causes Keats to feel envious of it, however, onticology reminds us that it is only *in response to* the nightingale's song that Keats is prompted to write the poem about their relationship; within the poem's own terms, in other words, Keats's very ability to write poetry would remain unactualized without the bird's melodic stimulation. And although Keats's virtual proper being is more limited than the bird's – he cannot literally fly into the woods, nor can he "sing" his poetry as spontaneously as the bird produces its vocalizations – the qualities that Keats can produce or evince once he has entered into an imaginative relation with the bird are practically unlimited; expressions of weariness, nostalgia, elation, sorrow, and resignation are all precipitated by his encounter.

Furthermore, although these are the best-known elements of the poem, they are not the only ones worth considering. In his classic essay on "the Greater Romantic lyric," Abrams establishes the Romantic paradigm whereby a material event – in this case, the bird's song – becomes the springboard for a series of increasingly transcendent meditations by the poet. Not surprisingly, given the traditionally anthropocentric view of the Romantics, Abrams assumes this relationship is unidirectional; in his view, "Romantic writers, though nature poets, were humanists above all, for they dealt with the non-human only insofar as it is the occasion for the activity which defines man: thought, the process of intellection."[49] But if we do not automatically privilege human thought over other types of actions of which different objects are capable, then we can uncover another set of dynamics in the poem. More specifically, Bryant's concept of objects as having simultaneously a proper being that always remains at least partially virtual, and a set of shifting qualities best understood as local manifestations of that being, allows us to see the nightingale, like the poem's speaker, as an object endowed with a high degree of "autonomy, independence, and self-determination" – the main characteristics of most objects under normal conditions, according to Bryant

(*Democracy*, 196). In this light, the actual nightingale's absence throughout most of Keats's ode indicates, not its relative lack of importance, but rather its "virtual" independence from the narrator's various constructions of it. Its invisibility to the speaker, who can only picture it "in the forest dim" (l. 20), renders it more, not less, autonomous, independent, and self-determining than has usually been appreciated. Even its song is explicitly present only in the first, sixth, and final stanzas of the poem; we never learn what the bird is "actually" doing during the stanzas when Keats, lost in the train of thought that Abrams's classic paradigm captures so well, pays no attention to it. But nowhere does the poem itself presuppose, as most critics have, that the bird is important only insofar as it has meaning *for* Keats. On the contrary, with the help of Bryant's onticology, we can see clearly that the qualities it manifests in relation to the speaker – its song and powers of flight – are implicitly presented as local manifestations of the bird's virtual proper being. The rest of the bird's being – what it eats, its mating habits, its health and disposition – goes undescribed and remains unknown to the speaker-poet. In this way, the nightingale exists on an equal ontological footing with Keats. (Its imaginative incarnation as figured by the poem can also be said equally to exist, but for reasons of space I will stick to its "real" incarnation within the poem's "world.")[50] After all, try as Keats might, he famously cannot fully identify with the bird. His alienation becomes acute in the penultimate stanza, when the bird's song is placed in a historical context in excess of any individual lifetime, regardless of species: "The voice I hear this passing night was heard/ In ancient days by emperor and clown" (ll. 63–4). But precisely by refusing to overlook the differences between man and bird, the poem asserts the truth of Bryant's flat ontology: the emotional and creative relations that Keats enters into with the bird do not reduce either party's virtual autonomies, but essentially confirm them. To reduce Keats's nightingale to its effects on the poet-speaker – indeed, even to use the proprietary construction "Keats's nightingale" – is to ignore the way Keats's ode allows (in Brian Massumi's evocative phrase) both "the animal and the human, each in its own right, as well as one in relation to the other, [to] participate in this expressive becoming. . ."[51]

Of course, paying attention to animals does not guarantee a non-anthropocentric approach; as Cary Wolfe warns, "Just because we direct our attention to the study of nonhuman animals

... does not mean that we are not continuing to be humanist –
and therefore, by definition, anthropocentric."[52] Along these lines,
however, we should also note that reading Keats as other than a
humanist does not require us to discard, ignore, or downplay his
exquisitely human observations, sentiments, and mortal thoughts.
Instead, it allows us to contemplate the room his poetry makes
for non-humans to assume their proper places *alongside* humans
in what Bryant calls the "interactive networks ... that play an
affording and constraining role with respect to the local manifestations of objects" (*Democracy*, 205). Bryant observes here that
his concept of "interactive networks" is similar to the ecological
"mesh" described by Morton, but clarifies that his version encompasses not just so-called natural phenomena but also "regimes of
attraction [that] can include physical, biological, semiotic, social,
and technological components" (206). Bryant's understanding of
"the democracy of objects" is thus potentially even more useful
than Morton's "meshwork" when we seek to describe networks
of relations that include non-living, even artificial things – which is
what Keats attempts to do in "Ode on a Grecian Urn."

Even more than "Ode to a Nightingale," this Spring Ode has
attracted so much criticism over the decades that it has become
something of a litmus test for critical assumptions and methodological orientations. Perhaps most famously, it forms the titular
basis for Cleanth Brooks's classic New Critical study, *The Well
Wrought Urn: Studies in the Structure of Poetry* (1947). In this
landmark of close reading, Brooks analyzes "Ode on a Grecian
Urn" as a bravura exercise in artistic self-reflection, arguing that
"the poem itself is obviously intended to be a parable on the
nature of poetry, and of art in general."[53] Brooks characteristically
seeks to resolve the poem's tensions, especially between the urn's
perceived timelessness and the speaker's explicit mortality. More
recent critics, by contrast, frequently opt to exacerbate them,
with Vendler in particular claiming that "Ode on a Grecian Urn"
encodes "a classic case of the dilemma which the psychologists of
perception ... call the dilemma of figure and ground": "figure"
here is the "reality" of the images on the urn – which Keats
famously spends much of the poem describing – and "ground"
is the material reality of the urn itself, which "marks the breaking of the spell."[54] Vendler nevertheless agrees with Brooks that
the poem's famous concluding lines, in which the urn directly
explains that "Beauty is truth, truth beauty, – that is all/ Ye know

on earth, and all ye need to know" (ll. 49–50), productively sus-
pends the preceding stanzas' oppositions. Deconstructive critics,
not surprisingly, also read the poem closely, but see rupture and
open-endedness rather than closure; in her reading of the ode's
oscillations between "surface and depth, with the figured curtain
of art and what lies beneath it," Rajan argues that it ultimately
"avoids some of its deeper recognitions and shelters its vision of
the urn in a fictitiousness that excludes [its] real function," which
was quite possibly funerary.[55] Barbara Johnson turns this into a
general principle of all human cognition of things, arguing that
"the work of art depends on the missing thing, but that thing is
not perceived directly . . . Keats's 'Ode on a Grecian Urn' is made
up of apostrophes to the inanimate object, not of answers to the
questions the speaker asks, or any knowledge that the object might
convey."[56]

This is an accurate description of the poem from a literary
perspective, to be sure. But Bryant's onticology (and, I will argue
in a moment, his even more recent onto-cartography) allows us to
deploy a different kind of knowledge, one that (as we saw above)
replaces the traditional subject–object dichotomy – in which only
the former has knowledge of the latter – with a democracy of
objects in which all entities have partial knowledge of whatever
they act upon, with, or through. Near the end of *Democracy
of Objects*, Bryant reminds us that "objects are constitutively
withdrawn from other objects" in two simultaneous but distinct
ways:

> on the one hand, objects are withdrawn in the sense that they are
> always in excess of any of their local manifestations. Objects always
> have a virtual domain that is never exhausted by any of their local
> manifestations. On the other hand, objects are withdrawn in the sense
> that they are never directly perturbed or "irritated" by other objects,
> but rather always translate perturbations into information according
> to their own endo-structure, organization, or distinctions. (262)

My reading of "Ode to a Nightingale" focused on the first of
these types of withdrawal, to consider how the bird's consistent obscuration from the speaker-poet's sight signals its virtual
proper bring in excess of any of its local manifestations. A similar
case could probably be made for "Ode to a Grecian Urn," in
which Keats's many questions directed to the urn – beginning with

"What leaf-fringed legend haunts about thy shape/ Of deities or mortals, or of both/ In Tempe or the dales of Arcady?" (ll. 5–7) – consistently fail not only to elicit answers but also to exhaust the urn's potential significance. But the urn, unlike the nightingale, is a product of human artifice, albeit one whose makers and original functions have been lost to "Silence and slow Time" (l. 2). From the perspective of Bryant's flat ontology, in which (to paraphrase Bogost) all objects equally exist even if they do not exist equally, it is all the more pressing that we liberate the urn from its perceived obligation to contain or emit meanings *for us*. Keats's choice of a Grecian urn as the object of his attentions, after all, is not arbitrary; the ancientness of the urn is precisely what has liberated it from its original functionality and rendered it available for Keats's meditations.[57]

Let us move, then, to the second of Bryant's categories of withdrawal, to see how Keats's ode allows both urn and speaker to "translate" each other in ways that render them simultaneously strange and familiar. The relation established between Keats and the urn over the poem's course is famously labile. It begins on a note of admiration, similar to the "happiness" Keats experiences when identifying with the nightingale at the start of that poem, as he praises the urn for being a "Sylvan historian, who canst thus express/ A flowery tale more sweetly than our rhyme" (ll. 3–4). As the ode progresses, though, it becomes increasingly clear that the urn's flowery tales may not do justice to the full range of human experience; in particular, the "breathing human passion" at the end of the third stanza, which "leaves a heart high-sorrowful and cloy'd,/ A burning forehead, and a parching tongue" (ll. 28–30), is juxtaposed with the perfect but frozen passions displayed by figures on the urn's front. (As feminist critics have pointed out, the perspective of the poem here is notably, albeit silently, masculinist; Keats spares no thought for the probable terror of the female being chased, or the sexual violence that would be visited on her were she caught.) The reverse side of the urn, as readers well know, makes the "cold pastoral" explicit (l. 45); here, Keats focuses on the village left permanently abandoned by the villagers who have gone out to perform a sacrifice, leaving their town eternally "silent" and "desolate" (ll. 39, 40). Accordingly, although Keats's letters contain similar sentiments, the urn's famous parting words – "Beauty is truth, truth beauty" (l. 49) – should not be taken at face value.[58] In addition to concluding that the urn is cold, for example, Keats by this time has also accused it of "teas[ing] us out of thought" (l. 44) with its seemingly timeless artifice. The urn may present itself as a "friend to man" (l. 48), and Keats himself may even be inclined to see it that way – but this does not mean its perspective is necessarily generalizable.

For earlier critics like Wasserman, the disconnect between the urn's final statement and the needs of human readers was not surprising, because "the ode is not an abstract statement or an excursion into philosophy. It is a poem about things."[59] Wasserman, of course, assumes a subject/object dichotomy that Bryant's ontiocology rejects. Once we are no longer bound by that distinction, however, the ode's status as "a poem about things" becomes more complicated. When both urn and poet-speaker are viewed together as objects or "things," that is, the poem becomes less an account of a person trying to see how much he can learn or imagine about a thing, and more an experiment in how far each entity can be seen to motivate or activate qualities in the other that were previously not manifest. Keats, after all, must "speak" for the urn, as its silence in the opening stanza makes clear; in doing so, he gives voice to its figures and "attitude[s]" (l. 41) in ways that the urn on its own cannot. For its part, the urn activates Keats's own poetic voice, facilitating his observations on (among other themes) the ideal versus the real and the historical versus the timeless. In this light, Keats's late accusation that the urn "dost tease us out of thought" takes on additional interest. Is to be rendered "out of thought" to be drained of cognition, or released from it? Either way, the urn makes Keats even more thing-like – that is, literally "out of thought" – than he was at the poem's start, while Keats in turn provides the figures on the urn with a number of "thoughts" that are, of course, literally impossible for them to harbor. Accordingly, although the lifespans of urn and human remain vastly different from each other – the former will persist long after "old age shall this generation waste" (l. 46) – their respective existences are brought closer together by the poem's final stanza, such that their ontological differences at least temporarily recede, and the "entangled" nature of their existences is foregrounded.[60] "Ode on a Grecian Urn" thus demonstrates presciently the truth of Bryant's "flat ontology": all things equally exist, even if all things do not exist equally.

Keats takes the democracy of objects one step farther in his last Spring Ode, "To Autumn," which concretizes its titular abstract subject in surprisingly sensual ways. Fittingly, Bryant too has moved past his initial foray into onticology in his most recent book, *Onto-Cartography: An Ontology of Machines and Media* (2014). Putting these two texts together allows us to appreciate in new ways the unusual achievements of Keats's final ode. "To Autumn" has long been considered the culmination of Keats's poetic accomplishments in shorter verse, not only because it caps the sequence of Spring Odes but also because (in Walter Jackson Bate's words) "each generation has found it one of the most nearly perfect poems in English."[61] For Bate, like other mid-twentieth-century New Critics, the poem is most remarkable for how it achieves "so many different kinds of resolution" in merely thirty-three lines: movement and stasis, perfection and imperfection, life and death are held in eternal suspense. As Geoffrey Hartman notes, unlike the previous Odes, in "To Autumn" there is no "turn" away from "imaginative fancy"; instead, "The poem starts on enchanted ground and never leaves it."[62] Combined with its lack of a first-person speaker, this means the poem "has no epiphany or decisive turn or any absence/presence dialectic . . . the ode remains resolutely meditative."[63] Significantly, Hartman's deconstruction here coincides almost perfectly with Bate's New Criticism: both approaches find in "To Autumn" an almost zen-like peace that accompanies the erasure of the poet's subjectivity. From its opening address – "Season of mists and mellow fruitfulness,/ Close bosom-friend of the maturing sun" (ll. 1–2) – to its rejection of pathos ("Where are the songs of Spring? Aye, where are they?/ Think not of them, thou hast thy music too" [ll. 23–4]), the poem quietly establishes what Bloom calls its "serene triumph" over the crises of the previous Odes.[64] But what, precisely, is the secret of "To Autumn"'s success?

One way to answer this question is to see how the poem evades what Forest Pyle identifies as the most enduring dualism of Keatsian criticism: "The opposition between strength and weakness has from the very beginning framed our understanding and evaluation of Keats; and it is an opposition that has governed every effort to fashion a narrative of the poet's career."[65] Without a first-person speaker, however, "To Autumn" immediately slips through this trap: it is quite literally subjectless in this sense, and therefore perfectly machinic in the sense that Bryant argues we should learn to think of all entities. As he puts it in the introduction to *Onto-Cartography*, what follows begins with the premise that worlds are composed of units or individual entities existing at a variety of levels of scale, and that are themselves composed of other entities. I call these entities "machines" to emphasize the manner in which entities dynamically operate on inputs producing outputs.[66]

Why "machines" and not "objects," the term Bryant favored in his previous book? As explained later in *Onto-Cartography*, "object" still implies "subject" as its supposed opposite, no matter how thoroughly the distinctions between them are debunked (37). Even more importantly, the switch to machines avoids thinking of entities as "possessing qualities" (37), a characterization that too readily invites a return of essentialism. Thinking of entities as machines, by contrast, means that "our first thought is not of its properties or qualities, as much as its *operations*. . . . The first question to ask of any machine is not 'what are its properties?', but rather 'what does it do?'" (38–9). Conceptualizing entities as machines, in other words, not only escapes the subject–object dualism implied even in the use of the latter term, but also replaces qualitative characterizations with a range of operations. This allows Bryant to retain his concept of "virtual proper being," introduced in *Democracy of Objects*, but to redeploy it to denote the operations of which any given machine is theoretically capable. This does not mean, of course, that all powers can or even will operate during the machine's existence; rather, "powers are characterized by *independence* from their manifestations" (41). Thus a machine has "powers" or "capacities" as its virtual proper being, whereas its "local manifestation" refers to "the exercise [or operation] of a power" in a given situation. Whether, when, and to what extent a machine's operations commence depend in large part on the types of inputs it receives, generates, or claims for itself; such inputs need not always come from outside the machine, moreover, but – like a person's thoughts or like radioactive decay, two of Bryant's many examples (42) – they can come from within. The manifestations of such operations can take several forms: "qualitative" (meaning that they transform some quality of the machine that produced them), "agentive" (meaning that they transform the activity or behavior of the machine), or "material" (meaning that they generate an output distinct from the machine) (43–4). Regardless, they all have something in common, as Bryant clarifies that "Manifestations are not manifestations to or for someone."

Once they manifest themselves locally, they exist regardless of whether they are used by another machine, acknowledged, or even perceived.

With this basic outline of the foundations of Bryant's onto-cartography in mind, we can now generate a new answer regarding why "To Autumn" registers with readers as "one of the most perfect poems in English." This answer, in fact, is relatively simple: the poem "thinks" autumn, not really as a season (despite its first line), much less as a state of mind (for as previous critics have noted, there is no "mind" or active subjectivity in this ode), but rather as a machine for creating poetic effects. Autumn, in Keats's subtly powerful representation, is a machine that operates on inputs – the dropping temperatures, the changing quality of light – to create a variety of seasonally appropriate outputs. Thus by the middle of the first stanza autumn is described as

> Conspiring with [the sun] how to load and bless
> With fruit the vines that round the thatch-eves run;
> To bend with apples the moss'd cottage-trees,
> And fill all fruit with ripeness to the core. (ll. 3–6)

If we were to replace "conspiring" with "operating," the machinic processes being described would be obvious. Indeed, what the above passage describes is neither more nor less than the operations of photosynthesis, which Bryant says exemplifies machinic ontology: "operations that take place in response to inputs from outside the [plant] machine such as water, sunlight, and various soil nutrients" (*Onto-Cartography*, 42). Of course, one machine's outputs can become another machine's inputs, assuming the latter is able to operate on them; such are the "flowers" that are "set budding" by the late seasonal sun "for the bees,/ Until they think warm days will never cease,/ For Summer has o'er-brimm'd their clammy cells" (ll. 8–11). Here, Keats's use of the preposition "for" should be understood strictly as a poetic convention, since as an output of the machinic processes of botanical growth, flowers would grow regardless of whether the bees perceive or interact with them.[67] That the bees involuntarily help pollinate the flowers as they gather nectar means that Keats has seized on a perfect example of what Bryant calls "exo-relations" between machines (see *Onto-Cartography*, 76). Moreover, when one machine provides a flow (of inputs) for another machine, "that machine functions as a *medium* for another machine" (47). "To Autumn"'s opening stanza beautifully renders this, as the autumnal season becomes a series of machines, each of which functions not only in its own right but also as a medium for another machine's operations.

This onto-cartographic reading of "To Autumn" might appear to run into trouble in the poem's second stanza, which shifts to address the season directly:

> Who hath not seen thee oft amid thy store?
> Sometimes whoever seeks abroad may find
> Thee sitting careless on a granary floor,
> Thy hair soft-lifted by the winnowing wind;
> Or on a half-reap'd furrow sound asleep,
> Drows'd with the fume of poppies . . . (ll. 12–17)

Despite an absence of direct nomenclature, the poem here clearly personifies autumn as a living, human figure who languidly performs the season's operations of harvesting, gleaning, and pressing apples for cider (at the stanza's end). Far from abandoning the opening stanza's machinic ontological vision, however, this stanza establishes Keats's recognition that another class of machines exists beyond the corporeal. Just as for Harman an object does not need to be "real" in order for its qualities to be discovered, for Bryant a machine need not be wholly material in order for its operations to be actualized: "Recipes, scores of music, numbers equations, scientific and philosophical theories, cultural identities, novels, and so on, are all examples of incorporeal machines" (*Onto-Cartography*, 26). Each of these examples, of course, requires a corporeal element or body in order to manifest itself. Bryant's point is not that incorporeal machines have no corporeal body, however, but rather that their incorporeality resides "in the capacity of these machines to be multiply instantiated, iterated, or copied while retaining their identity" (26). The second stanza's personification of autumn thus does not break with the machinic ethos of the first stanza, but instead extends it in the form of a poetic instantiation of the incorporeal machine of the season itself: an anthropomorphized figure, yes, but one that makes visible and local the otherwise incorporeal operations of the spirit of autumn itself. For although the operations performed by autumn are varied – harvesting, winnowing, gleaning, pressing – and in reality require a number of machines working in various configurations, the poetic trope of personification allows them all to be brought together and embodied in a single figure. Autumn is a machine that takes the inputs of the time of year, operates on them, and produces a series of outputs that the poem faithfully, beautifully records. Of course there is still authorial agency involved, since Keats chooses which processes to depict and which to leave out, as well as what language to use to represent them. He does so with such subtlety and intelligence, however, that we are as satisfied by the poem's evocative selection as the "o'er-brimm'd" bees depicted in the first stanza's conclusion (l. 11).

After the poem's disembodied speaker reassures autumn that there is no need to mourn the passing of spring because "thou hast thy music too" (l. 23), the remainder of the third and final stanza becomes a catalogue of autumnal outputs and effects:

> While barred clouds bloom the soft-dying day,
> And touch the stubble-plains with rosy hue;
> Then in a wailful choir the small gnats mourn
> Among the river sallows, borne aloft
> Or sinking as the light wind lives or dies;
> And full grown lambs loud bleat from hilly bourn;
> Hedge-crickets sing; and now with treble soft
> The red-breast whistles from a garden-croft;
> And gathering swallows twitter in the skies. (25–33)

Vendler's interpretation of these lines – "In the last moment of the ode, both loss and its compensatory projections . . . are forgotten in an annihilation of subjectivity and a pure immersion in the actual" – is entirely convincing, as far as it goes. We take nothing important from it, then, to shift its register from the humanistic to the machinic, such that what Vendler interprets as "an annihilation of subjectivity" becomes simply a full realization of the non-anthropocentric vision of existence that the poem offers from its opening lines onward. Now, autumn's operations produce outputs in all three of Bryant's categories. Qualitatively, autumn gives way to winter as, for example, birds that can no longer find sustenance in the harvested fields must take to the skies; agentively, autumn alters its own internal organization as the fields of grain are slowly harvested and processed; materially, autumn produces both the harvest's fruits *and* the feelings of contentment, melancholy, and resignation evoked by the poem's shifting registers.

Onto-cartography provides a way to describe Keats's last Spring Ode in terms that identify its achievement via the perspicuity of its ontological vision. But it also allows us to go a step farther by recognizing that "To Autumn" doesn't just depict autumn as a machine; additionally, the poem *itself* is a machine – a word-assemblage that, when coupled with a reader, produces effects in the form of changes in the reader's mental and emotional states. This is not unique to Keats's poem; as Bryant observes,

> We must not forget that works of art are machines. What seems unique to a great work of art is that it is strangely oblivious to the world into which it falls ... in the sense that it is capable of producing effects of a very different nature as a result of the inputs that pass through it in different historical and cultural contexts. ... A great work of art is an infinitely, or at least indefinitely, productive machine. (*Onto-Cartography*, 52)

Contemporary literary critics might wonder about Bryant's implicit distinction, drawn via the slippage between "works of art" in the first sentence quoted above and "*great* work[s] of art" (italics added) to which the rest of the passage refers; as scholars like John Guillory and Jane Tompkins have convincingly argued, literary canonicity is so historically and culturally overdetermined that judgments of the inherent "greatness" of a given text always need to be to treated with suspicion.[68] Yet Bryant's extension of his onto-cartographic method into the realm of art and literature is laudable in its attempt to account for the apparent semiotic inexhaustibility of "great" literature while retaining the openness to cultural factors that most literary critics now consider mandatory. To quote from *Onto-cartography* one more time:

> A great work of art is plastic in the sense that it is *pluripotent*. It is a machine that is capable of resonating in a variety of ways given the historical and cultural milieus that it encounters. ... With pluripotent works such as this, we get a reciprocal determination. They both act on their historical and cultural milieu and are acted upon by their historical and cultural milieu. The milieu actualizes the work in a particular way, leading it to be interpreted in a certain way. But the work also organizes the historical and cultural milieu in a particular

way leading us to attend to certain cultural phenomena as significant while ignoring others. (52)

Astutely, this account tracks closely with several of contemporary literary theory's basic frameworks. Bringing together elements of reader-response theory (different readers will input different interpretive flows into the text-machine and therefore receive different outputs from it), Marxian theory ("Always historicize"),[69] and post-structuralism's death of the author, Bryant recodes them all from an onto-cartographic perspective. Recognizing literary texts as themselves machines might strike some literary critics as reductive. From the standpoint of a flat ontology, however, such a move merely reminds us that, like all objects/machines, the literary object/machine is both autonomous – it does not finally exist *for* us – and always part of assemblages that both influence and are influenced by it.

If Keats's "To Autumn" makes a particularly appropriate poem for me to conclude with, then this is not only because its workings exemplify several of Bryant's central concepts, but also because it embodies the more general anti-anthropocentrism and anti-correlationism at the heart of so much SR and SR-related work – and, as I have tried to show throughout this book, at the heart of much canonical Romantic poetry, too. At the same time, introducing a machinic or, more broadly, an SR dimension to the study of British Romantic poetry does not mean having to abandon or repudiate our other modes of analysis, including those of a more explicitly or pointedly political nature. Bryant himself has been at the forefront of addressing concerns that SR-related approaches – with the obvious exception of Badiou's evental philosophy – threaten to elide or invalidate the gains made by other, more explicitly critical kinds of theory. In fact, says Bryant, we do not need to choose between critical theory (CT) and SR; we can employ both, allowing them to inform and even modify each other depending on the circumstances. Bryant has even proposed a division of theoretical labor that he calls (nodding to Lacan's "borromean knot" of the Imaginary, the Symbolic, and the Real orders of reality) "Borromean Critical Theory," in which

The domain of the Symbolic would retain the claims of traditional CT and would constitute what we might call "semiopolitics" or the critical unmasking and debunking of discourses and narratives legitimizing various power relations and identities . . . The domain of the Imaginary would be the domain of human and alien phenomenology . . . Finally, the domain of the Real would be the exploration of those properties that really do belong to things and the efficacy things organize on other things.[70]

Such a division would, of course, present real problems for the practitioner, not least because the Lacanian Real that Bryant identifies as the proper domain of SR is also usually understood to be "impossible," traumatic, and inaccessible to rational idea- tion or representation.[71] Understood as the realm of "the material unconscious," however, Bryant's transcoding becomes immedi- ately relevant: we can no longer afford to ignore the material Real of our existences, and SR gives us the tools to apprehend that Real in substantively productive ways. Moreover, by demonstrat- ing that SR is compatible with other, more explicitly political approaches to questions of interpretation, Bryant confirms what has been the basic operating assumption of this book: that SR provides an essential tool for humanities scholars looking to add to our toolbox of interpretive – or, with Latour's cautions in mind, descriptive – methodologies.

The constructivist assumptions that underpinned most forms of literary criticism and theory in the second half of the twentieth century need not be abandoned; ideology critique can and should remain an essential task of the humanities. Nevertheless, since all "unjust social assemblages" are maintained and facilitated at some level by material formations as well as by ideological dis- courses, we should endorse Bryant's strong sense – shared, to a greater or lesser degree, by the other SR thinkers considered in this study[72] – that we need to develop better methods of analyzing "the role that things themselves play in organizing power" at the most fundamental levels.[73] Speculative Realism. as I have tried to show throughout this book, provides some of the most promising avenues for developing these methods and pursuing these analyses. Moreover, to the extent that I have succeeded in showing that the canonical British Romantic poets were already trying out a variety of SR-style ideas and insights in the decades surrounding Kant's uptake across Europe, their poetry continues to resonate with our most pressing philosophical and ethico-political challenges today.

Notes

1. Duncan Wu, *Thirty Great Myths About the Romantics* (Malden, MA, and Oxford: Wiley Blackwell, 2015), 190.
2. Ibid., 185–211.
3. Shelley, *Adonais*, in *Shelley's Poetry and Prose*, ed. Donald H. Reiman and Neil Fraistat (New York: Norton, 2002), 423, ll. 379–80.
4. Nicholas Roe, *John Keats: A New Life* (New Haven, CT: Yale University Press, 2012), xix.
5. Keats, letter to J. H. Reynolds, March 14, 1818, in *Selected Letters*, ed. Robert Gittings and John Mee (Oxford: Oxford University Press, 2002), 71.
6. Antonia Till, Introduction to *The Works of John Keats* (Ware: Wordsworth Editions, 1994), xiv.
7. Ian Bogost, *Alien Phenomenology, or What It's Like to be a Thing* (Minneapolis: University of Minnesota Press, 2012), 40. Bogost has coined the term "Latour Litany" for such lists of seemingly unrelated things, and his website features a "Latour Litanizer" that allows users to generate their own; see http://bogost.com/writing/blog/latour_litanizer/ (accessed August 30, 2015).
8. Keats, letter to George and Tom Keats, December 21 or 27, 1817, in *Selected Letters*, ed. Gittings and Mee, 41.
9. Quoted in Roe, *Keats: A New Life*, xx.
10. Walter Jackson Bate, "Keats' Style: Evolution toward Qualities of Permanent Value," in *English Romantic Poets: Modern Essays in Criticism*, ed. M. H. Abrams (New York: Oxford University Press, 1960), 341.
11. Ibid., 342. See also Bate's *From Classic to Romantic: Premises of Taste in Eighteenth-Century England* (New York: Harper and Brothers, 1946).
12. Timothy Morton, "An Object-Oriented Defense of Poetry," *New Literary History* 43.2 (2012): 217.
13. For a very readable account of Hunt's relations not only with Keats but also with Shelley and Byron, see Daisy Hay, *Young Romantics: The Shelleys, Byron, and Other Tangled Lives* (New York: Farrar, Straus, and Giroux, 2010).
14. John Keats, "Dedication: To Leigh Hunt, Esq.," in *The Works of John Keats* (Ware: Wordsworth Editions, 1994), ll. 1–8. Unless otherwise noted, subsequent citations of Keats's poems are given parenthetically in the text from this edition.

15. Jane Bennett, *The Enchantment of Modern Life: Attachments, Crossing, and Ethics* (Princeton: Princeton University Press, 2001), 56. Subsequent citations are given parenthetically in the text.

16. For a similarly motivated but differently framed argument for our re-immersion in the world, see Michel Onfray, *A Hedonist Manifesto: The Power to Exist*, intro. and trans. Joseph McClellan (New York: Columbia University Press, 2015).

17. For a recent, full-length inquiry into the "wonder" of nanotechnology, see Colin Milburn, *Mondo Nano: Fun and Games in the World of Digital Matter* (Durham, NC: Duke University Press, 2015).

18. The conventional view is that Keats left this error uncorrected to preserve the meter of his poetic line; for an ingenious argument that the decision also makes thematic sense, see Charles Rzepka, "'Cortez: Or Balboa, or Somebody like That': Form, Fact, and Forgetting in Keats' 'Chapman's Homer' Sonnet," *Keats–Shelley Journal* 51 (2002): 35–75.

19. Specifically, Keats read William Robertson's multi-volume *History of America* (1777, 1796), which describes the cruelties of Spanish conquistadors in detail.

20. Roe, *Keats: A New Life*, 109.

21. Keats, *Selected Letters*, ed. Gittings and Mee, 42.

22. Wordsworth, "Tintern Abbey," ll. 106–7, 112.

23. Marjorie Levinson, *Keats's Life of Allegory: The Origins of a Style* (Oxford: Basil Blackwell, 1988), 5.

24. For a more thorough consideration of the "historical considerations" of Keats's poetry, see Emily Rohrbach, *Modernity's Mist: British Romanticism and the Poetics of Anticipation* (New York: Fordham University Press, 2015), 60.

25. Cf. Emily Rohrbach and Emily Sun, "Reading Keats, Thinking Politics: An Introduction," special issue of *Studies in Romanticism* 50.2 (2011): 229–37, especially their observation that Keats "construes the world as a place of learning through the activity of reading" (233).

26. See, e.g., Harold Bloom, *The Visionary Company: A Reading of English Romantic Poetry*, rev. ed. (Ithaca: Cornell University Press, 1971), 363.

27. See, e.g., Noel Jackson's argument that Keats's explicitly sensuous writing "reflects an understanding of the literary commodity as an internally divided form": *Science and Sensation in Romantic Poetry* (Cambridge: Cambridge University Press, 2008), 170. The best-known contemporary theorist of the political value of the aesthetic

is probably Jacques Rancière; see, e.g., *The Politics of Aesthetics*, ed. and trans. Gabriel Rockhill (London and New York: Bloomsbury, 2004).

28. See Robert Mitchell, *Experimental Life: Vitalism in Romantic Science and Literature* (Baltimore: Johns Hopkins University Press, 2013), 154–6; here he focuses on "Ode to a Grecian Urn," which I discuss below from a different angle, but trance and enchantment are clearly similar, although the former tends to be self-induced and therefore voluntaristic.

29. Roe, *Keats: A New Life*, 314.

30. Barbara Johnson, *A World of Difference* (Baltimore: Johns Hopkins University Press, 1987), 37. For a helpful overview of trends in interpretation of "La Belle Dame," see Gary Farnell, "The Enigma of *La Belle Dame sans Merci*," *Romanticism* 17.2 (2011): 195–208, esp. 195–8.

31. Jane Bennett, *Vibrant Matter: A Political Ecology of Things* (Durham, NC: Duke University Press, 2010), xii. Subsequent citations are given parenthetically in the text.

32. Jack Stillinger, "The Hoodwinking of Madeline: Skepticism in *The Eve of St. Agnes*," in *Keats: A Collection of Critical Essays*, ed. Walter Jackson Bate (Englewood Cliffs, NJ: Prentice-Hall, 1964), 71–90.

33. Timothy Morton, *The Poetics of Spice: Romantic Consumerism and the Exotic* (Cambridge: Cambridge University Press, 2000), 150.

34. Morton, *Poetics of Spice*, 159.

35. Rohrbach, *Modernity's Mist*, 58.

36. Helen Vendler, *The Odes of John Keats* (Cambridge, MA: Belknap Press of Harvard University Press, 1983), 10.

37. Jacques Rancière, "The Politics of the Spider," *Studies in Romanticism* 50.2 (2011): 240.

38. Bloom, *Visionary Company*, 407.

39. Richard H. Fogle, "A Note on *Ode to a Nightingale*," in *English Romantic Poets: Modern Essays in Criticism*, ed. M. H. Abrams (New York: Oxford University Press, 1960), 383.

40. Tillotama Rajan, *Dark Interpreter: The Discourse of Romanticism* (Ithaca: Cornell University Press, 1980), 164.

41. Maureen N. McLane, *Balladeering, Minstrelsy, and the Making of British Romantic Poetry* (Cambridge: Cambridge University Press, 2008), 267.

42. See, e.g., Paul de Man's offhand reference to "the symbol of the nightingale" in "Image and Emblem in Yeats," in *The Rhetoric of*

Romanticism (New York: Columbia University Press, 1984), 174. Perhaps more than any other single volume, the essays in this collection influenced a generation of critics to focus nearly exclusively on Romantic poetry as a linguistic construct.

43. Paul D. Sheats, "Keats and the Ode," in *The Cambridge Companion to John Keats*, ed. Susan J. Wolfson (Cambridge: Cambridge University Press, 2001), 90.

44. Shelley, "To a Skylark," in *Shelley's Poetry and Prose*, ed. Donald H. Reiman and Neil Fraistat (New York: Norton, 2002), 304, ll. 1–2.

45. Levi Bryant, *Difference and Givenness: Deleuze's Transcendental Empiricism and the Ontology of Immanence* (Evanston: Northwestern University Press, 2008), 265.

46. Levi Bryant, *The Democracy of Objects* (Ann Arbor: Open Humanities Press, 2011), 23. Subsequent citations are given parenthetically in the text.

47. Levi Bryant, "The Material Unconscious," blog post on *Larval Subjects*, August 12, 2015, https://larvalsubjects.wordpress. com/2015/08/12/the-material-unconscious (accessed October 9, 2015). Bryant's blog has long been one of the most substantial, influential SR sites on the web.

48. Roy Bhaskar, *A Realist Theory of Science* (London and New York: Verso, 2008), 21.

49. M. H. Abrams, "Structure and Style in the Greater Romantic Lyric," in *Romanticism and Consciousness: Essays in Criticism*, ed. Harold Bloom (New York: Norton, 1970), 202.

50. See Andrew Bennett and Nicholas Royle's fundamental thesis that "A literary work . . . is a work of imagination. It takes us into another world, whether this is construed as another version of *this* world or as somewhere *out of this world*, beyond the world, unearthly." See *This Thing Called Literature: Reading, Thinking, Writing* (London and New York: Routledge, 2015), 8.

51. Brian Massumi, "The Supernormal Animal," in *The Nonhuman Turn*, ed. Richard Grusin (Minneapolis: University of Minnesota Press, 2015), 2.

52. Cary Wolfe, *What is Posthumanism?* (Minneapolis: University of Minnesota Press, 2010), 99.

53. Cleanth Brooks, "Keats's Sylvan Historian: History without Footnotes," in *The Well Wrought Urn: Studies in the Structure of Poetry* (New York: Harcourt, Brace, and World, 1947), 153.

54. Vendler, *Odes of Keats*, 127.

55. Rajan, *Dark Interpreter*, 133. For a brief (and critical) account of the supposition that the poem's urn was used to hold the ashes of dead people, see Klaus Hofmann, "Keats's Ode to a Grecian Urn," *Studies in Romanticism* 45 (2006): 252 n. 5.

56. Barbara Johnson, *Persons and Things* (Cambridge, MA: Harvard University Press, 2008), 65.

57. See, e.g., Nick Groom's observation that "These historical remains were for Keats necessarily only partially legible – objects for contemplation and interpretation; sometimes, like the Gothic relics of Britain, present, sometimes remembered": "Romantic Poetry and Antiquity," in *The Cambridge Companion to British Romantic Poetry*, ed. James Chandler and Maureen N. McLane (Cambridge: Cambridge University Press, 2008), 47.

58. In a November 1817 letter to his friend Benjamin Bailey, for example, Keats writes that "What the imagination seizes as Beauty must be truth"; at the end of 1818, he wrote to his brother and sister-in-law that "I never can feel certain of any truth but from a clear perception of its Beauty" (Keats, *Selected Letters*, ed. Gittings and Mee, 36, 175). In the first instance, however, he is speaking of the power of the imagination to *create* its own truths, and the second is qualified by a self-deprecating admission that he is too ignorant to speak authoritatively on any issues unrelated to "taste." Both quotations are cited in Stephen Hebron, "An Introduction to 'Ode on a Grecian Urn': Time, Mortality, and Beauty," *The British Library: Discovering Literature: The Romantics and Victorians*, http://www.bl.uk/romantics-and-victorians/articles/an-introduction-to-ode-on-a-grecian-urn-time-mortality-and-beauty (accessed October 21, 2015).

59. Earl Wasserman, *The Finer Tone: Keats' Major Poems* (Baltimore: Johns Hopkins University Press, 1953), 14.

60. See the work of Ian Hodder, another recent interlocutor of SR, especially *Entangled: An Archaeology of the Relationships between Humans and Things* (Malden, MA, and Oxford: Wiley-Blackwell, 2012).

61. Walter Jackson Bate, "The Ode *To Autumn*," in *Keats: A Collection of Critical Essays*, ed. Walter Jackson Bate (Englewood Cliffs, NJ: Prentice-Hall, 1964), 156.

62. Geoffrey H. Hartman, "Poem and Ideology: A Study of Keats's 'To Autumn'," in *Romantic Poetry: Recent Revisionary Criticism*, ed. Karl Kroeber and Gene W. Ruoff (New Brunswick, NJ: Rutgers University Press, 1993), 424.

63. Hartman, "Poem and Ideology," 424–5.
64. Bloom, *Visionary Company*, 433.
65. Forest Pyle, *Art's Undoing: In the Wake of a Radical Aestheticism* (New York: Fordham University Press, 2014), 72.
66. Levi Bryant, *Onto-Cartography: An Ontology of Machines and Media* (Edinburgh: Edinburgh University Press, 2014), 6. Subsequent citations are given parenthetically in the text.
67. I make no claims here to offer a substantial account of the role of vegetation in Romantic-era literature; on this subject, see, e.g., Theresa M. Kelley, *Clandestine Marriage: Botany and Romantic Culture* (Baltimore: Johns Hopkins University Press, 2012).
68. See, e.g., John Guillory, *Cultural Capital: The Problem of Literary Canon Formation* (Chicago: University of Chicago Press, 1993); Jane Tompkins, *Sensational Designs: The Cultural Work of American Fiction, 1790–1860* (Oxford: Oxford University Press, 1986).
69. This is the opening phrase and overriding directive of Fredric Jameson's watershed text of Marxian literary criticism, *The Political Unconscious: Literature as a Socially Symbolic Act* (Ithaca: Cornell University Press, 1983), 1.
70. Levi Bryant, "Politics and Speculative Realism," *Speculations* 4 (2013): 20–1. For other articulations of this argument, see also Bryant's short essay "Towards a Realist Pan-Constructivism," in *Dark Trajectories: Politics of the Outside*, ed. Joshua Johnson (Hong Kong: [NAME] Publications, 2013), 122–34, and the last chapters of both *Democracy of Objects* and *Onto-Cartography*.
71. See, e.g., Alenka Zupančič's description of the Lacanian Real as what "always inscribes itself in a given continuity as a rupture, a break, or an interruption": *Ethics of the Real: Kant and Lacan* (New York and London: Verso, 2011), 235.
72. Harman's new book on the socio-political ramifications of OOP, *Immaterialism: Objects and Social Theory* (Cambridge: Polity, 2016), was not available at the time of writing, but looks highly promising in this regard.
73. Bryant, "Politics and Speculative Realism," 19.

Conclusion

An ever-present danger when using contemporary concepts to illuminate historical literary texts is presentism: allowing today's concerns, assumptions, and interpretive frameworks overly to color how we see and understand the past. There are ways to defend this, of course, starting with Joan Copjec's observation that "no historical moment can be [entirely] comprehended in its own terms."[1] But as I hope this book has effectively demonstrated, the pairing of Speculative Realism and British Romanticism requires no such justification.

Let us briefly review the reasons why this is so. The common proposition of all SR and SR-related work is that the correlationist circle must be broken open or otherwise overcome; likewise, the common position of the Romantic poets I have discussed in the foregoing chapters is that it is not only possible but also desirable for us to direct our thinking toward Meillassoux's "great outdoors," taken both literally as the "natural world" and more broadly as what exists *tout court*. The Speculative Realists jointly seek to break thought out of its Kantian prison and free us to speculate once more on reality itself; since they were writing at a moment when Kantianism was not yet hegemonic, the Romantic poets already enjoyed such freedom, albeit to varying degrees. Admittedly, SR's commitment to immanentism does not have a precise parallel for the Romantics, not all of whom shared Shelley's atheism, and some of whom (Wordsworth and Coleridge in particular) became more conventionally religious as they grew older. Nevertheless, the Romantics anticipate SR's interest in accounting for material phenomena in material terms; furthermore, I have argued that the spectrum of ontological positions articulated in their poetry and prose corresponds to a surprising degree with the variety of approaches offered by the Speculative Realists themselves. We have seen this via my coupling of Wordsworth's poetry with the object-oriented philosophy of Harman and Morton; Coleridge with the neo-Schellingianism of Grant, and DeLanda's process philosophy; Byron with Latour's network theories and the evental philosophy of Badiou; Shelley with Brassier's nihilism and Meillassoux's speculative materialism; and Keats with the vital materialism of Bennett, and Bryant's onticology/onto-cartography.

I have focused throughout this book on conceptual and content-driven comparisons between the Speculative Realists and a selection of canonical British Romantic poets, but there is also a shared intent between these two groups of writers separated by almost two centuries. For both, the work of thinking about the nature of reality is vital and important not merely to advance knowledge for its own sake, but also because how we understand the world has profound consequences for how we act in and on it. Wordsworth and Shelley articulate this conviction especially clearly. The former, in his Preface to *Lyrical Ballads*, is clear that his poems are meant not just to entertain and instruct (the classic definition of literature's double calling), but to help enlarge his readers' sympathies; the latter goes even farther in his *Defence of Poetry*, asserting in ardent paragraphs that poetry

> awakens and enlarges the mind itself by rendering it the receptacle of a thousand unapprehended combinations of thought. Poetry lifts the veil from the hidden beauty of the world, and makes familiar objects be as if they were not familiar . . . The great instrument of moral good is the imagination; and poetry administers to the effect by acting upon the cause.[2]

Like Meillassoux, whose conviction that we must free ourselves from correlationism is fueled by his opposition to irrationalism and fundamentalism, and like Bryant when he reminds us that a flawed ontology lends support to a flawed epistemology, Shelley and Wordsworth see their poetic work as laying the foundation for the common creation of a better world.

Of course, although the Romantics anticipate many SR concerns and concepts, they necessarily do so imperfectly and unintentionally. I chose the above lines from Shelley because they reflect most closely those elements in his thought that anticipate SR-themed concerns, for example, but readers familiar with the *Defence* may have noticed that I left out its anthropocentric middle section, in which Shelley describes the moral imagination as the power by which "the pains and pleasures of [our] *species* must become [our] own" (my italics). I draw attention to this omission as a reminder of the limits of the affiliation between SR and Romanticism. The greatest overall difference between the Romantic poets I have surveyed – and, arguably, many of their peers too – and the proponents of SR and SR-related philosophies is probably that the latter's anti-anthropocentrism is not typically shared by the former, whose common investment in the power of the human imagination is usually too great to allow humanity to be displaced too far from the center of their accounts of reality. The exceptions to this trend in SR circles are Meillassoux and Badiou, who each place a great deal of importance on the significance of human thought, since for Meillassoux only humans are capable of reasoning beyond the correlationist circle, and for Badiou only humans are capable of producing and becoming subjects to new truths.

In general, though, SR takes a strong stand against anthropocentrism – and herein lies its greatest potential to shape actively the reality it also seeks to re-describe. Even here, however, there are significant differences between its practitioners. The most brutal dismissal of humanity's significance comes from Brassier, whose nihilism dictates that consciousness is reduced to mere biological function, and human cognition to a mere vanity project. Grant's neo-Schellingian position – because consciousness comes from nature, it is therefore not cut off from reality in any absolute sense – is somewhat more redemptive, setting itself against the "manufactory arrogance" of all idealisms rather than the presumptions of cognition *in toto*.[3] The anti-anthropocentrism of the other theorists is more positive still; speaking generally, DeLanda's process-oriented philosophy, Latour's frameworks of networks and modes, Bennett's vital materialism, Harman's and Morton's OOP, and Bryant's onticology and onto-cartography all share a desire to put humans back into contact and context with the world at large, especially its material components whose agency we so frequently ignore or misapprehend. Moreover, this is where the ethics of SR manifests itself most clearly. As I discussed in previous chapters, for example, an ethical imperative is strongly present in Bryant's flat ontology, as well as in Morton's insistence that we recognize ourselves as merely part of the "meshwork" of things, thereby rejecting the hierarchical dualism of subject/object that has for so long legitimized our reckless exploitation of supposedly "dead" matter and "lower" life forms. Add to this Harman's insistence that no object or entity ever fully discloses itself, such that we must drop our arrogant pretensions to know anything fully, and the ethical dynamic of the SR paradigm shift is clear.

If new ways of understanding the world and our place in it seem more pressing than ever, then SR's interventions into contemporary philosophy and theory could not be more timely. In *Guerilla Metaphysics*, his follow-up to *Tool-Being*, Harman makes the case for philosophy's return to objects by arguing, in part, that "the fact that there is no proper of meaning does not entail that there is no proper of being."[4] Of course, epistemological questions are not going anywhere; despite Latour's claim that critique has run out of steam, critical interpretation can and must remain a key weapon in every (post-)humanist's arsenal. But the fate of the planet and the fate of our species – human beings – are more tightly bound up than ever before. (The planet will survive our extinction, but probably not vice versa.) In this sense, ontology and epistemology are thoroughly imbricated, and we must (re-)learn to attend to both.[5] Accordingly, striving to get our ontological accounts right can only help us improve our epistemological critiques. The Speculative Realists I have discussed in this book know this; the Romantic poets whose works I have analyzed via SR's insights knew it too. Now those of us across the so-called humanities are beginning to recognize it as well. The problem is no longer that the world is too much with us, as Wordsworth put it; rather, we have not been with the world enough, or at least not in the right ways. We need to return to the world that matters, before it is too late. The Speculative Realists and the British Romantics, taken separately but especially together, can help us do that.

Notes

1. Joan Copjec, "Introduction," in *Supposing the Subject*, ed. Joan Copjec (London and New York: Verso, 1994), ix.
2. Shelley, *A Defence of Poetry*, in *Shelley's Poetry and Prose*, ed. Donald H. Reiman and Neil Fraistat (New York: Norton, 2002), 517.
3. Iain Hamilton Grant, *Philosophies of Nature after Schelling* (London and New York: Continuum, 2006), 172.
4. Graham Harman, *Guerilla Metaphysics: Phenomenology and the Carpentry of Things* (Chicago and LaSalle: Open Court Press, 2005), 115.

5. On the confluence of theory and global warming, see e.g. the titles in Open Humanities Press's series *Critical Climate Change*, ed. Tom Cohen and Claire Colebrook.

Index

Abrams, M. H., 6, 7, 26, 29, 62, 65, 67, 81, 171, 211–12
actor-network-theory (ANT), 9, 106–7, 109, 127, 129, 208
Adorno, Theodor, 150, 157
Aeschylus, 170
aesthetics, 40, 169, 180, 195–6
Arnold, Matthew, 15

Badiou, Alain, 4, 9, 100–1, 110–13, 164, 194, 223, 232, 233
Bakhtin, Mikhail, 135
Bate, Walter Jackson, 191, 217
Benjamin, Walter, 151
Bennett, Jane, 10, 190, 192–5, 197–205, 232, 233
Bergson, Henri, 78, 167
Berkeley, George, 4, 64
Bhaskhar, Roy, 209
Blake, William, 6, 10, 150
Bloom, Harold, 6, 72, 155, 162, 171, 207, 217
Bogost, Ian, 190, 215, 225n7
Bostetter, E. O., 87
Brassier, Ray, 3, 7, 9, 145, 150–3, 157–60, 164, 183n28–9, 193, 232, 233
Braver, Lee, 65, 92n15, 144
Brooks, Cleanth, 213
Bryant, Levi, 5, 7, 9, 190, 206, 208–24, 232, 234
Buell, Lawrence, 38
Byron, Lord (George Gordon), 9, 91, 99–110, 113–37, 188, 189, 232
  Childe Harold's Pilgrimage, 101, 102–10, 113, 126, 135
  Don Juan, 101, 126–36
  The Giaour, 113–20, 125
  Manfred, 119, 120–6, 137

Cantor, Georg, 174
Cavell, Stanley, 87
Churchland, Paul, 152, 182n20
Class, Monika, 67, 92n17
Coleridge, Samuel Taylor, 9, 15, 51, 60–8, 71–7, 79, 81–91, 99, 147, 156
  Biographia Literaria, 60–2, 71, 82
  Christabel, 90–1
  "Constancy to an Ideal Object," 91
  "The Eolian Harp"/ "Effusion XXXV," 28, 63, 65–7, 71–5, 76–7, 147
  "Frost at Midnight," 75–6
  "Hymn before Sun-rise," 161
  "Kubla Khan," 76–7, 81–6, 114
  "The Rime of the Ancient Mariner," 76–7, 86–91
  "This Lime-Tree Bower My Prison," 28, 75, 76
Coleridge, Sara (Fricker), 62, 65–6, 71, 73–5
Copjec, Joan, 231
correlationism, 2, 37, 164–5, 166–7, 232
Critchley, Simon, 192
Cullen, William, 18

Darwin, Erasmus, 18, 100
de Man, Paul, 145, 227n42
deconstruction, 2, 7, 23, 27, 62, 145, 171, 211, 217
DeLanda, Manuel, 9, 23, 63, 78–85, 148, 164, 209, 232, 233
Deleuze, Gilles, 9, 23, 78–81, 148, 167, 190, 208, 209
Democritus, 23
Descartes, Réné, 163, 208

Eliot, T. S., 34, 99
Ellermann, Greg, 5, 168–9
Empedocles, 23
England, Amelia, 87, 88, 98n98

Fay, Elizabeth, 6
Ferguson, Frances, 29, 31, 41
Fichte, Johann, 68–9, 72
Fogle, Richard, 151, 207
Foucault, Michel, 23
Frye, Northrop, 6

Gauss, C. F., 79
Gill, Stephen, 15
Godwin, William, 10, 15, 65, 171
Grant, Iain Hamilton, 3, 9, 63, 67–8,
    70–1, 78, 164, 232, 233
Gratton, Peter, 145, 181n9
Guattari, Félix, 79
Guillory, John, 222

Halmi, Nicholas, 57n77, 58n79,
    130
Hamilton, Paul, 63, 144, 146
Harman, Graham, 3, 5, 6, 7, 9, 16, 23–5,
    28, 30, 32, 35, 47–50, 111, 121,
    159, 168, 190, 193, 220, 232, 233,
    234
Hartley, David, 17–20, 32, 61, 64
Hartman, Geoffrey, 50–1, 217
Hazlitt, William, 66
Hegel, G. W. F., 22, 68, 81, 100
Heidegger, Martin, 3, 6, 16, 24
Hirsch, E. D., 44
Hogle, Jerrold, 156
Holmes, Richard, 146
House, Humphry, 146
Hume, David, 4, 18–20, 32, 40, 43, 64,
    103–4, 174
Hunt, Leigh, 191, 192, 194
Husserl, Edmund, 25, 167
hyperobjects, 46–9

Jackson, Emily B., 99
Jackson, Noel, 18, 226n27
Jackson, Robert, 173
Jacobus, Mary, 31, 44
Johnson, Barbara, 199–200, 214
Johnston, Adrian, 78

Kant, Immanuel, 1, 3, 5, 9, 22, 32, 40, 51,
    60–1, 63–4, 67–70, 144, 157, 164,
    166, 224, 231
Keach, William, 169–70
Keats, John, 10, 188–92, 194–208,
    210–17, 219–23, 232
    The Eve of St. Agnes, 202–5
    Hyperion, 205
    "I stood tiptoe upon a little hill,"
        196–7

"La Belle Dame Sans Merci," 199–201,
    203
"Ode on a Grecian Urn," 213–16
"Ode to a Nightingale," 206, 207–8,
    210–13, 214
"On First Looking into Chapman's
    Homer," 194–5
"Sleep and Poetry," 197–9
"Sonnet to Leigh Hunt," 191–2
"To Autumn," 216–17, 219–23
Koehler, Margaret, 32
Kotsko, Adam, 187n68
Kramnick, Jonathan, 20

Lacan, Jacques, 68, 118, 223–4
Laruelle, François, 157, 159
Latour, Bruno, 4, 9, 23, 100–1, 104–10,
    127–37, 164, 193, 224, 232, 233
Leask, Nigel, 60
Lee, Monika, 147
Levinas, Emmanuel, 16, 167
Levinson, Marjorie, 197
Livingson, Ira, 12n3
Livingston, Paul, 173
Locke, John, 17, 20–2, 163, 209
Lockhart, J. G., 189
Lovejoy, A. O., 7

McCarthy, Anne, 185n45
McGann, Jerome, 6, 26, 62, 82–3, 86,
    103, 114, 115, 120, 124
McKusick, James, 85
McLane, Maureen, 207
Makdisi, Saree, 49
Massumi, Brian, 212
Meillassoux, Quentin, 2–3, 4–5, 6, 23–4,
    26, 33, 110, 145–6, 163–81, 208,
    231, 232, 233
Mellor, Anne, 6, 55n54
Merleau-Ponty, Maurice, 35
Michaels, Walter Benn, 44
Mill, J. S., 15
Mitchell, Robert, 52n15, 88, 98n99, 199,
    227n28
Mole, Tom, 110
Moore, Thomas, 110, 116
Morton, Timothy, 5, 8, 9, 16, 34, 38–40,
    45–8, 87, 148, 159, 163, 164, 169,
    191, 193, 213, 232, 233

Nagel, Thomas, 186n64
Napoleon, 108, 114, 146
New Criticism, 2, 213, 217
New Historicism, 2, 7, 27, 29, 62, 171,
    197

Newton, Isaac, 15
Nietzsche, Friedrich, 4, 37, 56n62, 114,
    120, 121, 202
Noys, Benjamin, 142n70

object-oriented philosophy (OOP), 3, 16,
    24–5, 34–5, 37–41, 43, 45–6, 50,
    208

Perry, Seamus, 63
Pfau, Thomas, 74, 93n15
Plato, 111, 144, 151, 153
Polidori, John, 120
Pope, Alexander, 194
Potkay, Adam, 15–16
Pottle, Frederick, 16–17
Protevi, John, 89, 98n101
Pyle, Forest, 151, 158, 159, 180, 217

Radcliffe, Ann, 10, 189, 203
Rajan, Tillotama, 31, 62, 75, 171, 207
Rancière, Jacques, 206
Redfield, Marc, 6, 44
Reid, Thomas, 64
Reimann, Bernhard, 79
Richardson, Alan, 82
Roe, Nicholas, 199
Rohrbach, Emily, 204
Ruskin, John, 34

Sartre, Jean-Paul, 122
Saussure, Ferdinand de, 4
Schelling, Friedrich, 3, 9, 51, 63–4, 68–76,
    77–8, 153
Schlegel, Friedrich, 114
Sellars, Wilfrid, 152
Shakespeare, William, 147
Shaviro, Steven, 95n61, 168–9, 183n24,
    184n39
Sheats, Paul, 208
Shelley, Mary, 120
Shelley, Percy, 5, 6, 9–10, 91, 143–62,
    165–81, 188, 189, 231–3
    Alastor, 151, 155–7
    A Defence of Poetry, 5, 144, 146–7,
        159, 160, 177, 232–3
    "Hymn to Intellectual Beauty," 157–60
    "Mont Blanc," 161–3, 165–6, 167–70
    The Necessity of Atheism, 143–4
    "Ode to Heaven," 149–50
    On Life, 144–5, 162
    "Ozymandias," 155
    Prometheus Unbound, 149, 150, 169,
        170–80
    Queen Mab, 147–51, 153–4

"To a Skylark," 208
"To Wordsworth," 155
The Triumph of Life, 151
Simpson, David, 60–1
Smith, Adam, 103
Southey, Robert, 25, 127
Spinoza, Baruch, 144
Stillinger, Jack, 203–4

Thacker, Eugene, 186n64
Thoreau, David Henry, 202
Tompkins, Jane, 222

Uexküll, Jakob von, 148

Vendler, Helen, 206, 213, 221
Vivante, Leone, 146

Washington, Chris, 12n3, 181n1, 184n42,
    185n47
Wasserman, Earl, 6, 162, 216
Watkin, Christopher, 187n68
Webb, Timothy, 176
Wellek, René, 83
Whitehead, Alfred North, 23, 78
Wilde, Oscar, 188
Wittgenstein, Ludwig, 4
Wolfe, Cary, 212–13
Wordsworth, Dorothy, 16, 31, 41, 77
Wordsworth, William, 5, 6, 15–21, 24,
    25–38, 40–50, 60–1, 63, 75–7, 99,
    155, 179, 188, 189, 193, 196, 231,
    232, 234
    "The Brothers," 35
    "Expostulation and Reply," 28
    "Lines left upon a seat in Yew-Tree,"
        27
    "Lines written a few miles above
        Tintern Abbey," 27, 29–32, 38, 46,
        51
    "Lines written at a small distance from
        my house," 27
    "Lines written in early spring," 27–8
    "Lucy" poems, 40–6
    "Nutting," 32–4
    "Preface" to Lyrical Ballads, 6, 15–21,
        51, 196, 198, 232
    The Prelude, 8, 29, 46–51
    "The Tables Turned," 28
    "There Was a Boy," 34
    "The Thorn," 34
    "The World is Too Much with Us,"
        36–7

Žižek, Slavoj, 4, 35, 68